INTERPRETING PERSONALITY TESTS

A Clinical Manual for the MMPI-2, MCMI-III, CPI-R, and 16PF

ROBERT J. CRAIG

JOHN WILEY & SONS, INC.

New York • Chichester • Weinheim • Brisbane • Singapore • Toronto

To Jim Butcher, Ph.D.; Ted Millon, Ph.D.;
Harrison Gough, Ph.D.; and Raymond Cattell, Ph.D.,
for their creativity, innovation, and basic understanding
of personality psychology.

This publication is designed to provide accurate and authoritative information in regard to the subject matter covered. It is sold with the understanding that the publisher is not engaged in rendering professional services. If professional advice or other expert assistance is required, the services of a competent professional person should be sought.

Library of Congress Cataloging-in-Publication Data:

Craig, Robert J., 1941 –
    Interpreting personality tests: a clinical manual for the MMPI-2, MCMI-III, CPI-R, and 16PF/Robert J. Craig.
    p.   cm.
    Includes bibliographical references and index.
    ISBN 0-471-34818-X (hardcover : alk. paper)
    1. Personality tests. I. Title.
BF698.5.C73 1999
155.2´83—dc21   98-54152
                                                  CIP

Printed in the United States of America.

10 9 8 7 6 5 4 3 2 1

Contents

ABOUT THE AUTHOR

Robert J. Craig, Ph.D., ABPP, ABAP, is Professor of Psychology at the Illinois School of Professional Psychology, Chicago, and Director of the Drug Abuse Treatment Program at the Department of Veterans Affairs Chicago Health Care System, West Side Division. He is board certified in both clinical psychology and administrative psychology and is a Fellow in the American Psychological Association, the Society for Personality Assessment, and in the Academy of Clinical Psychology. He is Consulting Editor to the *Journal of Personality Assessment* and has published extensively in the areas of psychodiagnostics, personality assessment, and personality tests.

Introduction

As an intern in clinical psychology at a 5,000-bed state mental hospital, I discovered a book by Irving Weiner that presented test signs for schizophrenia. The book was detailed and clearly written and I found myself hoarding it at my desk and frequently consulting it when preparing test interpretations for my supervisor. I told my fellow interns about it and they, too, began to rely on this text for basic interpretation information when evaluating patients with severe mental illness, especially schizophrenia. I wondered why my teachers at the university had not acquainted us with this book and why it was not a part of our testing curriculum.

In the many years that have elapsed since those halcyon days, personality "cookbooks" have become standard tools for the practicing psychologist involved with personality assessment. Indeed, all major personality tests have such resources and all have developed computerized versions of these standardized interpretations.

Although use of such materials is extensive, it is important to understand the issues involved in resorting to the use of standard statements from interpretive manuals or computer-generated reports. Following is a brief overview of the history of personality cookbooks.

In the early 1940s and into the 1950s, there was a debate within clinical psychology on whether a statistical treatment of psychological test data leads to more accurate predictions than does a clinical psychologist's looking at that same data. Clinical psychologists and experimental clinical psychologists were actively researching this issue. Paul Meehl of the University of Minnesota published an influential book (Meehl, 1954) in which he conducted a literature review of this

1

research and found that the best any clinician could do in any study was to tie the statistical treatment of the data in terms of predictive accuracy. In most studies, an actuarial treatment of the data generally beat the individual predictor. In a classic article entitled "Wanted—A Good Cookbook," Meehl (1956) argued that once you had an empirically derived and validated interpretive statement for a test sign, then all the clinician had to do was to look up the interpretation for any particular sign. Meehl further argued that an entire test could be interpreted in this way and that the clinicians did not have to waste their time interpreting personality tests, because standardized interpretations could be contained in these personality cookbooks. Instead, psychologists could be spending their time in more valuable ways, such as doing psychotherapy or other forms of psychological intervention.

Meehl (with Starke R. Hathaway) developed and published the first personality cookbook, entitled *An Atlas for the Clinical Use of the MMPI* (Hathaway & Meehl, 1951). This book consisted of hundreds of Minnesota Multiphasic Personality Inventory (MMPI) profile code types and extensive actuarial data about the person who generated this code type, including not only extensive demographic information and personality description derived from the MMPI, but also such things as length of stay in the psychiatric ward, clinical diagnosis, course of treatments, response to psychotherapy, and outcome. The idea was that if your patient's MMPI profile matched (exactly) the one in the text, then your patient should have a similar psychological profile, demographics, and treatment response. The problem was that few MMPI codes exactly matched the ones in the atlas. Hence, clinicians found themselves relaxing some of the rules and applying test data to a profile code type that was closest in appearance to one in the atlas. Of course, this resulted in interpretive inaccuracies. The historical importance of the atlas was to demonstrate that such an approach to the treatment of psychological test data was feasible.

In the decades that followed, this interpretive practice quickly spread. Machines became available that could score psychological tests and personality research continued to develop an empirical base that made possible the compilation of objective statements for test signs. This approach was richest for the MMPI. For example, Malcolm

Gynther, working in a state mental hospital in Missouri, did a file search of defined MMPI code types; consulted patient medical records; and determined common diagnoses, symptoms, and personality descriptions associated with these code types. Gynther published these separately in journals, and later, his basic research was included in the publications of many MMPI interpretive manuals. Gilberstadt and Duker (1963), experimental clinical psychologists at the University of Minnesota, obtained an agreement with the Veterans Administration (VA) hospitals in that they would machine-score VA patient MMPIs in return for use of the MMPI data and patient information. They were subsequently able to provide the VA clinician with an actuarial interpretive profile that listed patients' symptoms and possible diagnoses. Their database was eventually published and made available to psychologists outside the VA hospital system. Marks, Seemen, and Haller (1975) took a strictly actuarial approach to MMPI interpretation. Their research found common MMPI code types, with rigidly defined rules for establishment of the MMPI profile type. They also were able to provide the clinician with myriad personal information about the person with this code type, along with Q-sort statements of personality description that were most like and most unlike the patient with this code type. Their work remains the most extensive actuarial treatment of psychological test data even today.

While this work was in progress, computerization became commonplace in the scientific community and some psychologists who had developed hard-copy interpretive cookbooks began to make these available through computer reports. The first-generation computer reports were rudimentary by today's standards. The first one to appear commercially was published through the Psychological Corporation and relied on MMPI data from the Mayo Clinic. The computer report consisted of one-page statements on the meaning of a scale's elevation. It neither addressed the basic code type nor took into account content interpretation. Others soon followed.

David Lachar, at the Lafayette Clinic in Detroit, published a frequently used MMPI cookbook and also made this same information available through computer-generated reports. The book really was Lachar's intrepretive library as to what would be reported by the computer for many types of validity scale configurations and MMPI scale elevations. The report, published by Western Psychological Services, also was prepared in a more narrative and readable style. As mentioned earlier, there was the Gilberstadt and Duker computer report for VA psychologists, and other prominent clinicians soon followed with their own versions of computer reports.

Ray Fowler, working with the Hoffman-LaRoche pharmaceutical firm, made available, at cost, an MMPI computer-generated personality interpretation that used more elegant language, sounded more like a psychological report, and interpreted test content scales. Alex Caldwell at the University of California, Los Angeles published a computer-generated psychological report from MMPI test data that looked like a report generated through personal consultation with Caldwell by the referring clinician. It also included sections on personality dynamics, etiology and recommended treatment. Jim Butcher at the University of Minnesota published, through National Computer Systems (NCS), a well-refined MMPI report that interpreted both validity, clinical and content scales (Butcher, 1987). His interpretation took into account the vast research findings on the MMPI scale interpretations and has a strong empirical base in the statement library. The increasing sophistication of these first-generation computer-derived personality reports is apparent. Second-generation MMPI computer reports are even more elegant and include those developed by national experts (Butcher at NCS, Roger Greene, Psychological Assessment Resources) and practicing clinicians (Giles Rainwater; Psychometric Software, Inc.; Lewak, Marks, & Nelson; Applied Innovations Inc.).

Although this history has focused on the MMPI, presently all major objective personality tests (e.g., the ones covered in this manual) all have personality interpretive cookbooks and computer-generated interpretive reports available for purchase.

It is now clearly possible to automate the entire process of psychological testing, including giving pretest instructions and information; scoring the test; transforming scores; combining data; and preparing reports containing raw scores, norms, profiles, statements answered in a critical direction, and narrative interpretive statements. This capability has not been without its critics. Matarazzo (1986) argued that cookbook approaches to personality test interpretation are essentially unvalidated and present canned interpretations that may not be applicable to an individual patient. He further argued that the interpretation of tests needs to take into account an individual's personal history and may have differential meaning based on the individual's unique characteristics and the context of the assessment.

There is general agreement that cookbook interpretations, whether formatted in text or via computer, need empirical validation. Presently, there is great variability as to the scientific base of many interpretive statements. Most of them are generated through a combination of research validation and expert clinical opinion. Most should be considered automated clinicians rather than true actuarial descriptions of personality.

So it is with the interpretive statements in this manual. Although the empirical literature was consulted, most statements should be considered those of expert clinical opinion that has appeared in the clinical literature. They should be confirmed through consultation with other sources of information, including clinical interviews. The MMPI and Minnesota Multiphasic Personality Inventory-2 (MMPI-2) have the most extensive research literature associated with this development and hence have the strongest empirical base for the interpretive statements. Even here, the statements should be considered as clinical hypotheses awaiting confirmation.

The clinician who uses this manual takes full responsibility for any actions taken as a result of its use. The American Psychological Association (APA) Code of Ethics stipulates that "psychologists retain appropriate responsibility for the appropriate application, interpretation, and use of assessment instruments, whether they score and interpret such tests themselves or use automated or other services" (APA, 1992).

It is hoped that this manual provides the clinician with a valuable source of interpretive information for the major objective personality tests currently in frequent use. As with any test, the context of the evaluation, cultural/ethnic/racial considerations, and changing empirical information need to be taken into account when making final interpretive decisions for any test sign(s).

References

APA. (1992). Ethical principles of psychologists and code of conduct. *American Psychologist, 47,* 1597–1611.

Butcher, J. (1987). *Computerized psychological assessment: A practitioner's guide.* New York: Basic Books.

Gilberstadt, H., & Duker, J. (1963). *A handbook of clinical and actuarial MMPI interpretations.* Philadelphia: W.B. Saunders.

Hathaway, S. R., & Meehl, P. E. (1951). *An atlas for the clinical use of the MMPI.* Minneapolis: University of Minnesota Press.

Marks, P. A., Seeman, W., & Haller, D. (1975). *The actuarial use of the MMPI with adolescents and adults.* Baltimore: Williams & Wilkins.

Matarazzo, J. D. (1986). Computerized clinical psychological test interpretations: Unvalidated plus all mean and no sigma. *American Psychologist, 41,* 14–24.

Meehl, P. E. (1954). *Clinical vs. statistical prediction.* Minneapolis: University of Minnesota Press.

Meehl, P. E. (1956). Wanted—a good cookbook. *American Psychologist, 11,* 263–272.

CHAPTER 1

Minnesota Multiphasic Personality Inventory–2 (MMPI-2)

History and Development of the Original Minnesota Multiphasic Personality Inventory

STARK R. HATHAWAY, a psychologist at the University of Minnesota, and J. Charnley McKinley, a neurosurgeon at the University of Minnesota Hospital, began working on a test that would become the Minnesota Multiphasic Personality Inventory (MMPI) in the late 1930s. They were interested in developing a screening tool that would detect the major psychopathologies extant at that period of time. They started with over 1,100 items and made a quantum leap in assessment methodology when they developed and used the method of empirical criterion keying, or the method of group discrimination. Here, items are selected if they statistically differentiated between the normals and the criterion groups. The first article on the test was published in 1940 and the test itself was published in 1943 (Hathaway & McKinley, 1943). It has become the most frequently used psychological test.

Original MMPI Norms

The original normative groups for the MMPI consisted of 724 visitors to the University of Minnesota Hospital. As a group, they were representative of gender and marital status for the state of Minnesota in the

1930s. That meant most came from rural areas and were between the ages of 16 and 55. All were white. Four additional groups were added: (1) 265 precollege high school seniors coming to the university for precollege guidance, (2) 265 skilled workers from various government work projects during the Great Depression, (3) 254 patients hospitalized for physical diseases at the University of Minnesota Hospital, and (4) 221 hospitalized psychiatric patients at the University of Minnesota Hospital.

Need for Restandardization

As early as 1969, there was a symposium on the issue of revising the MMPI. It became evident that societal changes had occurred so that endorsement patterns on some scales were likely to have changed. The possibility of racial biases in some scales had been debated. Some items were awkwardly worded and some were no longer useful. Some content was considered objectionable. There was a gender bias in some of the items. Also, many issues in contemporary psychiatry were not tapped by the MMPI item pool. However, people were reluctant to significantly alter or drastically change the most frequently used test in psychology. It was not until the 1980s that it was finally decided to restandardize the MMPI. It took a total of 7 years to revise this test.

Minnesota Multiphasic Personality Inventory–2 Norms

The MMPI was restandardized using 1980 census figures. The Minnesota Multiphasic Multiple Personality Inventory–2 (MMPI-2) included 2,600 subjects from six states plus active-duty military personnel and Native American adults on a federal reservation in Washington State. There were 1,138 men and 1,462 women; ages ranged from 18 to 84. Ethnicity for men was 11% black, 84% white, 3% Hispanic, and 2% other; for women, ethnicity was 13% black, 82% white,

3% Hispanic, and 2% other. Additional samples included 1,462 members of the armed services, 1,312 college students, 271 airline pilot applicants, 423 inpatient psychiatric patients, 502 chronic pain patients, and 1,172 inpatient substance abusers. New content scales were develop and some previous supplemental scales lost too many items in revision for retention and hence were eliminated.

Transformed Scores

The MMPI had used a linear T Score transformation where percentile ranks at T 70 should be at the 90th percentile. However, it had been known for some time that this was not true. Hence this flaw was corrected by creating a new transformed score called a Uniform T Score, in which all T Scores would have the same percentile rank for all scales (excluding 5 and 10). A T Score of 65 is at the 92nd percentile, and so on.

Interpretation of the MMPI-2 Scales

VALIDITY SCALE: NUMBER OF ITEMS LEFT UNANSWERED

The following are among the reasons a respondent might omit an item or items:

- The item is considered offensive or personal
- Reading difficulties
- Rebelliousness
- Carelessness
- Confusion
- Obsession or overideation resulting in indecisiveness
- Severe psychomotor retardation resulting in insufficient energy to complete the task

- A desire to look good, resulting in fear that an accurate response might make the person look bad
- Lack of trust in the examiner's motives for "asking" certain questions

Not answering items on the MMPI-2 has the effect of suppressing scale elevation because the items are not endorsed and hence not counted in the scoring. On the MMPI, a respondent would have to omit 70 items before profile invalidity would be highlighted on the profile sheet by a T Score of 70. This was considered too many items left unanswered, so by convention, an MMPI profile was considered invalid if more than 30 items had been omitted. This tradition has been carried over to the MMPI-2, though the actual scale is no longer reflected on the MMPI-2 profile sheet. *Do not interpret the MMPI-2 if more than 30 items have been left unanswered.* However, if these omissions occur after item number 370, then the Validity and Clinical Scales can be interpreted but the Content and Supplemental Scales should not be interpreted. Also, a large number of omissions may suggest that the patient in treatment might focus on small details or be unnecessarily evasive. It is suggested that the examiner go back and try to get the respondant to answer enough questions so that this issue does not invalidate a profile.

LIE (L) SCALE

The Lie (L) Scale is a rationally derived 15-item scale, all keyed in the "false" direction. Items pertain to admitting behaviors that most people have at one time or another engaged in or would engage in if given the chance. A raw score of 4 is the mean, with a T Score of 50. Moderate L Scale scores (raw scores 5 to 7) suggest a rigid moral value system and presentation of unusual virtue, with overconforming and conventional behavior. Higher scores suggest a preoccupation with high moral standards and fear of disapproval unless the person scrupulously adheres to rigid moral prescriptions. Raw scores greater than 7 should be considered pathological and are quite rare. These patients may be self-righteous, overly scrupulous, and uncompromising; their concern with morality dominates their life. They are not willing to admit even minor flaws in their character. These patients may also be naive, may have low psychological-mindedness, and are willing to try to put up a good front. High L Scale scores suggest pervasive lying on the test. The scale is relatively transparent and a sophisticated testee can see through this scale such that lying would not be detected. *Do not interpret the MMPI-2 if scores on L are T > 65.*

F SCALE

The F Scale was developed by selecting those items that were infrequently endorsed (by < 10% of the normative sample) and consists of items reflecting serious psychopathology. A raw score of 4 is the mean at a T Score of 50. High scores (T > 90) on F can be due to confusion/psychosis, poor reading/dyslexia, exaggeration, or random responding. If Variable Response Inconsistency (VRIN) and True Response Inconsistency scores (TRIN) are within acceptable ranges and the F score is very high, then that would rule out confusion or reading problems. *As a general rule, do not interpret the MMPI if F is T > 100.* However, if F > 100 and VRIN is in an acceptable range (T < 80), some inpatient psychiatric patients and recently incarcerated felons obtain F values in this range and the profile may be interpreted, although the symptoms reported are probably an exaggeration. In such settings, an F score > 110 is suggested as the cutoff for invalidity.

- An F score between 50 and 64 suggests the patient has endorsed a particular problem area, such as family problems or personal difficulties. An item analysis would be needed to determine the specific area of concern.
- An F score between 65 and 79 can reflect a person with deviant social beliefs, unconventional thinking, current stress, a situational problem (e.g., going through a contested divorce, being stalked), and such personality traits as acting-out ten-

dencies, emotional instability, dissatisfaction, opinionated-ness, changeability, and restlessness.

- An F score between 80 and 99 may suggest psychosis, a plea for help (slight exaggeration to get your attention), or conscious malingering. Low F scores are generally not significant (assuming the person is not denying problems). They may suggest a person who is dependable, free from stress, honest, and unpretentious.

BACKSIDE F [F(B)] SCALE

The profile reflecting exaggeration is markedly similar in shape to the profile suggesting random responding. It was reasoned that perhaps a patient starts out by answering honestly but the weight of the questions and other motivations wear down the person so that towards the end of the test a random response is generated. To detect this, the developers created the Backside F, or F(B), Scale, which is a scale of items infrequently endorsed by the restandardization sample but contained on the last half of the test. Because all of the items necessary to interpret the clinical scales are contained in the front half of the test booklet, if F is valid but F(B) suggests invalidity, the Validity and Clinical Scales can be interpreted, but caution is suggested in interpreting the Content and Supplementary Scales. If both F and F(B) suggest profile invalidity, do not interpret the test. A T Score > 80 is recommended as suggesting profile invalidity with F(B). However, there are no norms for this.

K SCALE

The K Scale was developed as a measure of defensiveness (at high scores) or openness (at low scores). High K scores suggest an unwillingness to report problems or personal weaknesses, denial of trouble, a faked good response set, or a healthy ego defense system. Moderate K scores may indicate independence, resourcefulness, enthusiasm, positive self-esteem, nonauthoritarian values, and the existence of good interpersonal relations. (**Note:** These must be confirmed by the CLINICAL scales.) In certain testing contexts, high scores are to be expected (e.g., personnel selection, custody proceedings). Low K Scores (T < 40) suggest lowered defenses, exaggeration as a plea for help, poor coping abilities, or a tendency to be self-critical, as well as a willingness to report emotional difficulties. Low scorers tend to be socially retiring, inhibited in interpersonal relations, and socially conforming (see Scale 10, page 32). They tend to be psychologically well adjusted, are able to deal effectively with daily problems, and are enthusiastic and resourceful.

TRUE RESPONSE INCONSISTENCY (TRIN)

The TRIN Scale consists of 23 pairs of items opposite in content. A point is added or subtracted to a score if the paired item is responded to inconsistently as true or false. A high TRIN suggests yes-saying and a low TRIN suggests false-saying. True Response Inconsistency scores < 6 and > 12 suggest inconsistent responding. *A TRIN score of T > 80 suggests profile invalidity.* However, this is a new scale for which there are no established norms.

VARIABLE RESPONSE INCONSISTENCY (VRIN)

The Variable Response Inconsistency Scale consists of 67 pairs of items with either similar or opposite content. Each time a person answers in an inconsistent direction, a point is added or subtracted from the total score. *A VRIN Score of T > 80 suggests inconsistent responding and the profile may be invalid.*

- A high F score with a high VRIN score suggests random responding, poor reading ability, or confusion.
- A high F score with a low VRIN score suggests exaggeration or psychotic states.

   Low scores suggest the respondent was able to read and comprehend the test items, was attentive in responding to the items, did not have difficulty in understanding the content, and was not confused.

DISSIMULATION INDEX (F – K)

The Dissimulation Index (F – K) is established by taking the raw score difference between F and K. If that scores is > 15 or < – 15, then the profile may be either faked good or faked bad; for example:

- F = 20 and K = 12; F – K = +8; profile is valid
- F = 24 and K = 6; F – K = +18; suggests a faked bad profile
- F = 4 and K = 20; F – K = – 16; suggests a faked good profile

Use this index in borderline cases in which profile validity cannot be determined by the traditional validity indicators.

SUPERLATIVE SELF-ASSESSMENT SCALE (S)

The Superlative Self-Assessment Scale, or Scale S, has five component subscales: S(1), Belief in Human Goodness; S(2), Serenity; S(3), Contentment with Life; S(4), Patience/Denial of Irritability and Anger; and S(5), Denial of Moral Flaws. Because the scale was developed to screen airline pilots, the scale may have its greatest utility in executive assessment.

INFREQUENCY-PSYCHOPATHOLOGY [F(P)] SCALE

The Infrequency-Psychopathology, or F(p), Scale was developed to detect infrequent item endorsements among both normals and psychiatric patients in settings that had high base rates for psychopathology. The scale has 27 items that were infrequently endorsed by both normals and psychiatric patients and should be used as an adjunct with F and F(B).

Interpretive Strategy

1. If F is elevated, then inspect VRIN. If VRIN is T > 80, the profile is random.
2. If VRIN is okay, inspect TRIN; if TRIN is T > 80, the profile is invalid.
3. If VRIN and TRIN are okay, use F(p). If F(p) is elevated, then F Scale score elevation is due to malingering or exaggerating. If F(p) is okay, then an elevated F Scale score is due to psychopathology.

WEINER'S SUBTLE AND OBVIOUS ITEMS (S/O)

Weiner argued that patients attempting to malinger or exaggerate psychopathology for secondary gain would endorse psychopathological items that were directly related to a disorder (the obvious [O] items) but would respond normally to those items indirectly related to the disorder (the subtle [S] items). He identified the obvious and subtle items for Scales 2, 3, 4, 6, and 9. If the patient produces an MMPI-2 profile where T scores are > 65 on all five S/O scales, the profile may be a faked bad response set.

Use of the S/O scales is controversial. Some argue that the subtle items are really a statistical artifact in that a certain number of random items will be endorsed on a scale on the basis of statistical probability alone. Analogue research demonstrates that when subjects are instructed to fake a profile, the obvious items move in the faked direction, whereas the subtle items remain unchanged. Finally, this research shows that obvious items predict the criterion better than do the subtle items. Some have concluded that the S/O distinction does not add any additional information that cannot be obtained by interpreting the basic validity scales.

Use of the S/O item approach seems more frequent in forensic settings than in clinical settings, and studies occasionally appear that attest to the utility of the S/O approach.

MEAN PROFILE ELEVATION

The Mean Profile Elevation Index employs the average T Score elevations on the clinical scales, excluding Scales 5 and 10.

- 45 to 55 = normal
- 56 to 65 = general psychiatric patients
- 66 to 80 = psychiatric patients with severe psychosis, serious reading problems, confusion, or a faked bad response set
- 76 to 80 = possible deception/malingering
- > 85 = crude attempt to simulate psychosis

PERCENT MARKED TRUE OR FALSE

If the patient marked more than 80% of the items as true or false, this suggests an uncooperative subject and means the test should not be interpreted.

GOLDBERG INDEX

Using the T Scores from Scales L + Pa + Sc (Pa is the Paranoia Scale; Sc is the Schizophrenia Scale), subtract that total from the T Scores on Scales Hy – Pt (Hy is the Hysteria Scale; Pt is the Psychasthenia Scale). If this number is greater than 45, it suggests a psychotic profile; if the number is less than 45, it suggests a neurotic or normal profile. This index works better in inpatient settings.

Interpreting MMPI-2 Code Types: One-Point Codes

One-point codes are MMPI-2 profiles in which only one clinical scale score is T > 65 and the other clinical scales scores are T < 65.

CLINICAL SCALES

Hypocondriasis (Hs; 1)

High scores on Hypochondriasis (Hs) Scale 1 suggest an exaggerated concern over and frequent reports of excessive bodily complaints such that these people live in constant fear related to their perception of poor health. They may present with vague somatic symptoms that do not correspond to known anatomical pathways. Epigastric complaints and reports of chronic pain and fatigue are also common. Their life seems organized around perceived physical problems. They believe this disorder to be so disabling that it dominates their life. Their personality style is characterized by whining, demanding, hostile, bitter, sour, cynical, and complaining behaviors, along with attention-demanding acts. They are pessimistic, dissatisfied, unhappy people who are seen by others as selfish and self-centered. They also may be passive-dependent or passive-aggressive and unconsciously dominate interpersonal relations through their many physical complaints. (Some practitioners believe this scale measures dependency needs that have been displaced with somatic complaints.) These people tend to express their hostility indirectly. A psychodynamic explanation of their behavior suggests that these patients are expressing their hostility by making others around them miserable with their constant complaints. Psychoanalysts see hypocondriasis as a pre-oedipal injury. These patients may control unacceptable impulses through somatization defenses. To reduce stress, these patients may engage in fantasy or wishful thinking or emotionally distance themselves from the stressful situation. Their overall functioning has been greatly reduced by these perceived symptoms.

This scale can be described as measuring pessimism at the high end and optimism at the low end.

T scores in the range of 55 to 64 suggest patients with a medical problem who have endorsed only those symptoms associated with their disease and hence have attained a slight blip on the MMPI-2 profile. The exception to this is disease with systemic complications, such as multiple sclerosis, systemic lupus erythematosus, or advanced human immunodeficiency virus.

Patients with elevations on Scale 1 often lack psychological insight or resist psychological explanations of their behavior. They prefer to doctor-shop, seeking physical explanations of their problems. They are difficult to engage in psychological treatment.

Women with low scores on Scale 1 are seen as less likely to worry about their health, complain of headaches, lack energy, or appear excessively tired. Low scores also suggest a general optimistic approach to life for both genders.

Diagnoses associated with elevations on Scale 1 include somatoform disorder, hypocondriasis, conversion disorder, or depressive disorder and chronic pain syndromes. Sometimes patients with true medical problems have such a poor time coping with the disease that their reactions to the disease can be as problematic as the disease itself. In such cases, they may also obtain elevations on Scale 1 and the diagnosis would be psychological factors affecting physical condition.

Depression (DEP; 2)

Elevated scores (T > 65 T = 80) on the Depression (DEP) Scale, or Scale 2, suggest these patient feel depressed, unhappy, dysphoric, and indecisive; lack self-confidence; and feel inadequate, worthless, and helpless. They tend to have low energy; may also feel tense, irritable, and insecure; and feel like failures. They are pessimistic about the future, withdraw from social contact, and feel useless. They appear withdrawn and dependent. However, manifestations of dependency may be part of their clinical depression. When the depression abates, they return to premorbid personality functioning and may no longer appear dependent and helpless. The depression may be agitated, if Scale 7 or 9 scores are elevated, or there may be psychomotor retardation, if psychomotor retardation Scale 9 or D(2) scores are low. When faced with a stressful situations, high-scoring men tend to withdraw, whereas high-scoring women tend to blame themselves for the stressful situation. Their underlying personality seems to be both anxious and fearful, but this could be a manifestation of their clinical depression. If the Scale 2 score is more toward the low end of this range, then it suggests that the patient may be withdrawn but may be able to mask depression publicly.

- When the Scale 2 score is T > 80, the patient may present with psychotic symptoms, including mood-congruent hallucinations and delusions. (Also check scores of Scales F, BIZ [Bizarre Mentation], 6, and 8 for elevations.) Scores at this level also indicate patient is reporting vegetative signs of depression (loss of appetite, sleep disorders, loss of energy, sexual malfunctioning, etc.) as well as suicidal ideation. The clinician is urged to conduct a more comprehensive suicide risk assessment.
- When T > 100, the patient has quit trying and is going through the motions. At this point, the clinician may underestimate the severity of the problem, but the patient is experiencing total resignation.
- T = 60 to 65: These patients are unhappy, moody, dissatisfied with life; lack self-confidence; and are pessimistic and despondent. However, they do not typically have a clinical depression, they tend to be conscientious and agreeable, they do not show evidence of anger, and they are highly responsible. A depressive personality disorder needs to be ruled out. In such cases, patients may have a depressive personality disorder but not clinical depression.
- In college counseling settings, elevations on Scale 2 may suggest emotional turmoil most likely resulting from relationship problems but not necessarily clinical depression (depending on the elevation). These individuals are described as shy, withdrawn, nonaggressive, and lacking in self-confidence. Peak Scale 2 scores in college populations usually reflect situational problems.
- A clinical elevation on Scale 2 is seen as a positive sign for treatment because it suggests psychic distress that is ego alien. Few people enjoy being depressed and most patients are motivated toward symptom relief. There are effective treatment plans for depression.

- Low scores on Scale 2 (T < 40) among men suggest they are less likely to report trouble sleeping, have fewer health concerns, are less likely to worry and fret over small details, are not indecisive, are not overly sensitive to rejection, and do not give up easily. They are more likely to be self-confident. They would be described as cheerful, easygoing, and optimistic. Low scores among women suggest they are likely to be more cheerful; less likely to have insomnia, health concerns, or worries; less likely to complain of headaches; and less likely to get nervous or jittery. They also tend to have higher needs for achievement, exhibition, autonomy, dominance, change, and heterosexuality on the Adjective Checklist and score lower on needs for deference, succorance (dependence), and abasement. For both genders, low scores also reflect a cheerful disposition.

Diagnoses associated with elevations of Scale 2 include major depression, dysthymia, adjustment disorder with depressed mood, or substance-induced mood disorder (refer to the MAC-R [MacAndrew Alcoholism Scale–Revised], AAS [Addiction Admission Scale], and the APS [Addiction Potential Scale]), depending on severity, duration, and nature of the etiology.

Note: Elevation on Scale 2 is quite common among many medical and psychiatric disorders. It represents psychic distress and is a good barometer of current mood.

Hysteria (Hy; 3)

Elevations on the Hy Scale, Scale 3, are characterized by histrionic personality traits. These patients tend to be seen as flighty, manipulative, seductive, flirtatious, interpersonally engaging, exhibitionistic (some, blatantly so), and uninhibited but also indifferent, self-centered, and demanding of attention and affection. Some are blatantly exhibitionistic. However, their relationships are superficial, despite an appearance of friendliness. They are likely to be moody and become momentarily upset but then are easily consoled. They appear gregarious, socially at ease, and very spontaneous. Their major defenses include denial and repression. They are prone to react semantically under stress. When not particularly stressed, these patients seem bland and may show a kind of *belle indifference*. Underneath, these patients have strong dependency needs and are likely to present with vague physical problems that may include headaches, pain, and weaknesses. Their physical problems or complaints, if psychologically based, have a tendency to spontaneously disappear. They lack insight into their motivations and appear psychologically immature and sometimes even naive and infantile. Denial of psychological bases of their problems becomes even more evident when scores on Scales K and 1 are also elevated along with that on Scale 3. These patients tend to give up when stressed. They are prone to marital problems.

Patients with elevations on Scale 3 tend to resist or deny psychological explanations of their behavior. Clinical lore suggests they are more susceptible to suggestion, direct advice, hypnosis, and concrete recommendations.

Moderate elevations on Scale 3 probably suggest people who are sensitive, emotional, friendly, optimistic, enthusiastic, pleasant, cheerful, and affectionate and who are likely to inhibit the expression of anger.

Men with low scores on Scale 3 are more likely to act shy and less likely to appear excessively tired.

Diagnoses associated with Scale 3 include histrionic personality disorder and dissociative disorder, and these patients are also prone to conversion reactions, somatoform disorders, anxiety reactions, and panic attacks.

Psychopathic Deviation (Pd; 4)

Elevations on the Psychopathic Deviation (Pd) Scale, or Scale 4, must also be interpreted in the light of Antisocial Practices (ASP), Anger (ANG), and Family Problems (FAM) content scales and usually reflect poor social maladjustment. In general, patients with elevations on Scale 4 tend to be impulsive, rebellious, unreliable, and hostile; to have a low frustration tolerance; to show poor judgment; to be hedonistic and resentful; and to be hostile toward authority (see Pd2, page 36) and social constraints; to be aggressive, high risk takers, and high in sensation seeking. Although outgoing, sociable, and even likable, they are deceptive, manipulative, and superficial in their relationships. They are extremely narcissistic and self-centered and show superficial emotions of shame and guilt, usually when in an unavoidable situation (arrest, mandated treatment, etc). They use people for their own gain, show little regard for the feelings of others, and have few, if any, emotional attachments to others. They tend to be dramatic, emotional, and erratic. These patients seem not to profit from experience. They act without thinking about the consequences of their behavior. They get easily restless and agitated. They seem to behave as if social rules do not apply to them. They show poorly controlled anger (see ANG on page 44), and show childish demands for attention. They generally are free from disabling anxiety or depression (see Scales 2 on page 18, 7 on page 28, ANX [Anxiety] on page 42, and DEP [Depression] on page 43). They are likely to have disrupted family relations and have histories of school, work, marital, and/or legal difficulties. Alcoholism/drug addiction (see MAC-R on page 49, AAS on page 51, and APS on page 50), pathological gambling, sexual perversions, aggressive outbursts, and assaultive crimes—including murder and sexual abuse perpetration— have been associated with high Scale 4 scores. These patients tend to have poor work histories, lack clear goals, and drift from job to job. When stressed, they may resort to substance abuse to reduce tension. However, Scale 4 may assess a generalized propensity toward antisocial behavior rather than psychopathic traits per se.

This code has appeared in sexual offenders. In an offender population, inmates with this code had histories of being pampered and babied by their caretakers and were overprotected. If they were married, they formed dependent relationships on their wife. This code type is quite frequent among offenders, particularly among child abusers and rapists. It is also common among drug addicts, alcoholics, and pathological gamblers.

- Elevations on Scale 4 are usually viewed as a negative treatment indicator and suggest poor prognosis for psychotherapy. Such patients may appear to accept psychological feedback but do not internalize it. Instead, they tend to blame others for their problems and accept no responsibility for doing the things necessary to change their behavior. They usually enter treatment under duress or as a manipulation (to beat a court case). Clinical lore suggests they are more responsive to peer and group confrontation and exposure of their manipulations. However, this profile is very stable and patients with high Scale 4 scores rarely change over time.

- Scores in the range of 55–60 suggest energy, drive, ambition, assertiveness, independence, adventurousness, sociability, and generally positivity. However, when frustrated, these patients can become aggressive.

- Low scores on Scale 4 among men suggest patients who are less likely to appear depressed, to be easily annoyed, to be moody, to use profanity, to express resentment, and to have criminal records. They also seem more able to tolerate a boring lifestyle. Women with low scores on Scale 4 are more likely to be cooperative, pleasant, and relaxed and are less likely to have temper tantrums, to tell people off, to argue over minor issues, to be overly sensitive to rejection, to nag and act in a hostile and unfriendly manner, and to feel irritable, resentful and grouchy. Partners rate high-scoring men as moody, irritable, resentful, attention craving, and generally unpleasant to be around. Partners rate high-scoring women as having temper tantrums, as having a tendency to yell frequently and get angry, as feeling that others do not care about them, as being hostile, and as easily getting upset.

Low scores (T < 40) reflect rigid and conventional behavior with generally moralistic behavior. The individual may also be passive and unassertive.

Diagnoses associated with Scale 4 elevations include antisocial personality disorder, adult antisocial behavior, narcissistic personality disorder, and substance use disorder.

Note: The score on this scale may be elevated without the patient's having antisocial/psychopathic traits. Patients experiencing family problems (see FAM on page 46) can produce high Scale 4 scores but will not have elevations on the ASP Scale. For example, scores on this scale are often elevated among patients experiencing marital problems or undergoing divorce. Partners rated them as moody, craving attention, resentful, and irritable (for both genders). They generally have negative emotionality, poor interpersonal adjustment, and poor conflict-management skills. Also, college students obtain higher Pd scores (e.g., T = 55 to 60). In a college population, elevated scores on Scale 4 suggest rebellion and conflict.

Masculinity/Feminity (Mf; 5)

Note: The Mf scale was not an original part of the MMPI clinical scales. After Scales 1 through 4 and 6 through 9 had been developed, Starke Hathaway and J. Charnley McKinley wanted to develop a scale that would differentiate homosexuals without other psychopathology from heterosexuals without psychopathology. Recall that in the late 1930s, homosexuality was considered a psychopathology, whereas today it has been removed from official psychiatric nomenclature.

The criterion group consisted of 13 "homoerotic inverts," but the authors were never able to find a set of items that differentiated homosexuals from heterosexuals. Accordingly, they developed a scale that differentiated the more feminine from the more masculine men on the basis of their responses to stereotypic interests and occupations. Although they intended to develop a scale that would differentiate lesbians from heterosexual women, learning that they could not do so with men led them to give up the quest for a similar scale for women. Instead, they merely changed the direction of scoring for the women. Hence, low scores for both men and women suggest gender identification patterns opposite those of stereotypic men and women.

A Spike 5 profile usually suggests an absence of significant psychopathology and is consider a normal limit profile code. One may also think of the underlying dimension of Scale 5 as flexibility or inflexibility as related to gender role.

Men with elevated scores on Mf may show an "unusual" male interest pattern, such as:

- Stereotypic "feminine" interests
- Conflicts over their sexual identity
- A homosexual behavior pattern
- Passivity and effeminacy
- Aesthetic, cultural, and intellectual interests
- Inner directedness
- A high valuation of cognitive pursuits
- A concern with philosophical problems
- Peaceability, tolerance, idealisism, curiosity, caution, nurturance, ambition, capability, sensitivity, empathy, and social perceptivity (or any combinations of the above)

High scores also correlated with emotional distress, including anxiety, depression, guilt feelings, and tension. However, when stressed, these men tend to seek social support.

Women with elevated Scale 5 scores may

- Have "unusual" female interest patterns
- Be overly aggressive and "masculine" (e.g., assertive, competitive, tough, independent, dominant)—or may be dominant in a lesbian relationship
- Appear active, brusque, vigorous, rebellious, unemotional, competitive, and assertive

High scores also correlate with emotional distress, including anxiety, depression, guilt feelings, and tension. When stressed, these women tend to seek social support. They feel distressed when not in control.

In a college population, elevations on Scale 5 are rare among women. College women with high Mf scores described themselves as exploitative, self-confidant, tender, and emotional but were rated as bold and unsympathetic by peers. College men with elevated Scale 5 scores described themselves as undemanding and shy and were rated as emotional by their peers.

Clinically elevated scores on the Mf Scale have been reported for both men and women undergoing gender reassignment surgery. High-scoring men in this group were seen as more prone to worry and interested in aesthetics when compared with normal men. High-scoring women were seen as more active, adventurous, and more masculine compared with normal women.

Low Mf scores in men may indicate

- Exaggerated "masculine" traits
- An orientation toward action and doing
- A lack of empathy toward others
- An enjoyment of mechanics-related activities

These men appear crude, "macho," rugged, and vulgar; have limited intellectual interests; and perhaps doubt their masculinity such that they have to exaggerate it to others. They are reckless, coarse, hasty, and lack originality. Extremely low Scale 5 scores in men suggest doubts about their masculinity to the point where they have to prove how masculine they are.

College men with low Mf scores have been judged as domineering and impersonal; their wives have described them as well-mannered. They describe themselves as being balanced, practical, cheerful, and self-confidant; as preferring action to thinking; as being somewhat self-indulgent; as having a narrow range of interests; and as being unwilling to face problematic situations.

Women with low Mf scores may

- Show an exaggerated "female" demeanor (think of the character Melanie Wilkes in *Gone with the Wind* for a clear illustration of a "low 5" woman)
- Be more oriented toward feelings and emotional expression
- Defer to men for decision making
- Present as self-pitying, self-sacrificing, sensitive, modest, and idealistic yet be fault-finding
- Be masochistic and self-sacrificing or caught up in a sense of duty
- Be interested in child-rearing and homemaking activities
- Be passive, submissive, dependent, helpless, self-pitying, and passive-aggressive

College women with low Mf scores described themselves as tender, idealistic, sensitive, and emotional, whereas raters described them as bold and unsympathetic. These women see themselves as capable, competent, considerate, easygoing, insightful, assertive, and conscientious. They do report stereotypic female interests.

Some psychologists believe that Scale 5 lacks interpretive meaning. Preliminary research with MMPI-2 Scale 5 with normal men does not support the usefulness of Scale 5 with this population. For additional information, refer to interpretations for GM and GF (see page 53).

Paranoia (Pa; 6)

Depending on elevation, the Paranoia (Pa) Scale measures interpersonal sensitivity of the negative variety, suspiciousness, and self-righteousness. Elevations on Scale 6, particularly when T > 80, is associated with paranoid symptoms and the presence of a thought disorder, including delusions of persecution or grandeur; ideas of reference; angry, argumentative, belligerent, and resentful behaviors; rigid thought patterns; a guarded interpersonal demeanor; and possible fear of a physical attack on the patient. Those scoring high on this scale tend to harbor grudges, show hostility and jealousy, appear aloof and intractable, and keep others at bay with their projections and externalization of blame. Their major defenses are denial and projection. They tend to feel mistreated and picked on. They have ideas of reference and delusions of grandeur or persecution.

Women who score high on Scale 6, when stressed, tend to blame themselves for the situation and become emotionally detached. This code has also appeared among women in marriage counseling.

Scores from T = 65 to T < 80 suggest paranoid predisposition. These patients tend to be overly sensitive and feel they get a raw deal in life. They are resentful, hostile, and argumentative; externalize blame; show rigidity of thinking; and have undue sensitivity. They overreact to criticism, are guarded in interpersonal relations, and do not trust others, fearing that others will take advantage of them.

Women with low scores on Scale 6 are less likely to have many fears and bad dreams, to be moody, to worry about the future, to be bored and restless, to break down and cry easily, and to lack control over their emotions.

- In nonclinical populations, $T > 65$ to $T < 75$ can indicate a person who is sensitive and emotional, empathic, curious, tolerant, creative, energetic, industrious, sentimental, softhearted, peaceful, and reserved. In some cases, scores at this level suggest a person who has been humiliated, shamed, coerced, or threatened with maltreatment.
- A score in the range of 55 to 65 suggests an inquiring and investigative attitude. The person is likely to be curious, questioning, perceptive, and not naive.
- In a college population, high Scale 6 scores suggest people who are sensitive, generous, cooperative, individualistic, and rational. High Scale 6 scores have also appeared in college counseling centers among students who are underachievers.
- Regarding T scores < 35, clinical lore suggests that in some cases, clinically paranoid patients see through the items and systematically deny the paranoid content, which results in abnormally low scores on Scale 6. In such cases, in a clinical setting, scores of $T < 35$ should be interpreted with descriptors for clinical elevations. If the person is not paranoid, then low scores in this range suggest interpersonal insensitivity, naiveté, gullibility, and an overly trusting attitude. Low scores may also suggest a lack of sensitivity to the needs of others.

Diagnoses associated with Scale 6 elevations include paranoid personality disorder or paranoia, or paranoid schizophrenia (if Scale 8 scores are elevated).

Psychasthenia (Pt; 7)

Elevations on Scale 7 suggest ruminative, intellectualizing, and ritualistic behaviors, phobias, and problems in concentration. They show obsessive-compulsive thinking and behaviors, along with anxiety, worries, agitation, and tension that are obsessive in quality. They are fearful and indecisive, feel guilty, and are troubled by disturbing thoughts. They report a lack self-confidence, and use intellectualization and rationalization as main defenses. They also worry about being inundated with anxiety to such a great degree that it becomes debilitating. These people neither relate well nor are comfortable in social interactions or assertive in social situations. They may be overly perfectionistic and rigid in thinking and action. They have strong feelings of insecurity. (Also, see FRS and OBS on page 42). When stressed, high-scoring Scale 7 patients tend to emotionally distance themselves from the stressful situation and engage in wishful thinking.

In a college population, men with high Scale 7 scores were described as sentimental and reasonable, whereas women with high scores were described as sensitive, prone to worry, and high strung.

The presence of an elevated 7 in profiles is thought to be a good predictor of response to clinical interventions, as patients do not like the feeling of anxiety and are motivated towards symptom reduction. There are effective treatment plans for a variety of anxiety disorders.

Moderate scores on Scale 7 may measure organizational ability. These people are likely to be methodical and punctual and show systematic and convergent thinking.

Low-scoring men on Scale 7 are less likely to have many fears or to worry about their health. Low-scoring women are less likely to blame others when things go wrong; are more cheerful and self-confidant; and are less likely to report nervousness, bad dreams, or multiple fears. These people also appear relaxed and secure.

Diagnoses associated with elevations on Scale 7 include anxiety disorder and obsessive-compulsive disorder. Binge eating has also been associated with high Scale 7 scores among women with an eating disorder.

Schizophrenia (Sc; 8)

- For the Schizophrenia (Sc) Scale, or Scale 8, T scores > 80 suggest confusion, delusions (see Scale 6, page 27) and hallucinations (see BIZ, page 44), poor impulse control, poor contact with reality, and personality and behavioral deterioration, along with withdrawn and seclusive behavior and apathy. Things seem strange to them and people are difficult to understand. They feel different from others. At this level, Scale 8 measures mental and emotional confusion, organic scrambling of information processing of the kind that would be detected on neuropsychological testing, and perhaps a genetic vulnerability to schizophrenia (called schizotypy). The higher the scores are on Scale 8, the greater the degree of cognitive disturbance seen on psychiatric evaluation.

- Scores between T > 70 and T < 80 suggest a schizoid lifestyle (look for elevations on Scale 10), feelings of alienation and being misunderstood, unconventional behaviors, identity confusion, circumstantial thinking, bizarre behaviors such that they appear spacey to others, difficulty in forming and maintaining relationships, difficulties in thinking and concentration, difficulties in emotional expression (except for feelings of resentment, hostility, and aggression), and a chaotic lifestyle. These patients also have considerable sexual difficulties and may experience sexual perversions.

- T scores between 65 and 69 could also include endorsement of the neurological items on the MMPI-2, so both caution and a closer scrutiny of other MMPI-2 scales for differential diagnosis are suggested when scores are at this level. These patients lead an unconventional lifestyle; feel inferior, alienated, aloof, and self-preoccupied; and tend to distance themselves from others. They have poor behavioral controls.

- Moderate elevations on Scale 8 may suggest imagination, spontaneity, divergent thinking, and creativity with good ego strength (see K Scale, page 12), and for those more in touch with preconscious processes, an ability to mobilize this into original productions.

- In nonclinical college populations, moderate elevations suggest creativity, alienation, and unconventionality, and perhaps even giftedness. Patients attending a university counseling center with high scores in this range reported feeling socially isolated, having a stressful home life, and having heterosexual relationship difficulties.

Diagnoses associated with elevated Scale 8 scores often include schizophrenic spectrum disorders. High Scale 8 scores have appeared in psychiatric patients, emotionally disturbed convicts, incarcerated criminals, and some sex offenders.

Hypomania (Ma; 9)

- Elevations on the Hypomania (Ma) Scale, or Scale 9, describe patients who are hyperactive, expansive, and grandiose; have low impulse control, temper tantrums, and agitated behaviors; and tend to act out and be rebellious. They have disturbed relations with authority (see Pd2, page 36) and are euphoric, talkative, unrestrained, and sociable with elevated mood, labile affect, and rapid speech. They seem to live in a world of constant action. They present with excess energy and are action oriented but show low endurance. They may appear colorful, expressive—even ebullient—but at the same time are restless. They have many ideas and seem ambitious but fail to complete these plans, as they become easily bored. They are impatient and superficially involved with people, use them for their own gratification, and are narcissistic. They often have problems with alcohol, drug abuse; or both. These patients tend to use guile, charm, deceit, and manipulation to achieve their goals and they make few personal commitments.
- Elevations on Scale 9 in nonclinical populations suggest people who are enthusiastic, energetic, outgoing, pleasant, and gregarious. Sometimes, men with high Scale 9 scores are viewed as bossy and demanding of attention. High scores may also reflect zest, enthusiasm, eagerness, and generally talkative people.
- Men with low scores on Scale 9 are less likely to stir up excitement, swear and curse, talk back to others, and use

illicit drugs. Women with low scores are less likely to stir up excitement, talk back too much, and wear strange or unusual clothing.

- Very low scores (T < 35) suggest apathy, low energy, low self-esteem, lack of self-confidence, lack of drive and ambition, and withdrawal. If Scale 2 scores are significantly elevated, then a low Scale 9 score may suggest clinical depression with psychomotor retardation.

Diagnoses associated with these elevations include bipolar disorder, mania, cyclothymia, narcissistic personality disorder, and substance use disorders.

Social Introversion (Si; 10)

The Social Introversion (Si) Scale, or Scale 10, is extremely stable and shows a test–retest correlation of .74 after 30 years. It predicts school dropouts in adolescence.

- Elevations on the Social Introversion Scale, or Scale 10, reflect extreme withdrawal, introversion, timidity and shyness, submissive and overly compliant behavior, non-assertiveness, dependency, and an avoidance of interpersonal relationships. People with high Scale 10 scores are uncomfortable around members of the opposite gender, seem hard to get to know, are reluctant to display feelings, and feel more comfortable when alone. They lack self-confidence, have difficulty forming relationships, have a slow personal tempo, have easily hurt feelings, and are prone to depression. They are not aggressive nor competitive. They also are overly sensitive to the feelings of other people. Interestingly, some patients are shy among strangers but are more sociable among friends. Others describe them as cold and distant or submissive and compliant in interpersonal relationships. They prefer to be alone. Very high scores suggest a schizoid adjustment level.

- In a college population, high Scale 10 scores suggest people who are shy, withdrawn, modest, and socially uncomfortable but still capable of expressing emotional warmth.
- Low scores suggest people who are extroverted, friendly, and talkative and have good social skills. They are active and energetic, enjoy being around people, and enjoy competitive experiences. They have strong needs for affiliation and are gregarious and friendly. They enjoy social recognition and strive for it.
- Very low scores could reflect social manipulativeness, poor impulse control, superficial relationships, and immaturity.

Diagnoses associated with Scale 10 elevations include schizoid personality disorder and avoidant personality disorder.

HARRIS AND LINGOES SUBSCALES

The Harris and Lingoes Subscales, although clinically useful, are based on items of varying lengths. Some are based on as few as 6 items and psychometrically may be unreliable. Information on item length is provided in parentheses. Also, it is not possible to determine which of the descriptors listed below have been endorsed by the patient. Inspection of the critical items would help in this regard.

D1: Subjective Depression (32)

High D1 (Subjective Depression) Subscale scores report a variety of physical symptoms, including poor sleep, poor appetite, sweating, and lack of energy, along with psychological and mental difficulties in the areas of poor concentration, comprehension, and judgment; malaise; weakness; and nervousness. Patients say they are unhappy, feel useless, feel life is not worthwhile, avoid social situations, and feel less capable than others. They seem shy and uneasy in social situations, usually as a result of their depression.

Those with low scores mix well socially, report multiple interests, and have a good appetite.

D2: Psychomotor Retardation (14)

High D2 (Psychomotor Retardation) Subscale scores suggest lack of energy resulting in difficulty carrying out routine activities, reduced levels of interest and sociability, avoidance of confrontation, nervousness, and fears of losing one's mind. Those with high scores are indecisive, tend to avoid people, and appear withdrawn.

Low scores suggest adequate energy, enjoyable interests, and participation in recreation.

D3: Physical Malfunctioning (11)

Patients with high D3 (Physical Malfunctioning) Subscale scores report episodes of, among other things, nausea, vomiting, poor health, constipation, weight changes, seizures, respiratory disorders, and general complaints of poor health. They feel they will never get well and are quite pessimistic. They are preoccupied with their poor physical functioning.

Low scores suggest patients are well and feel good physically.

D4: Mental Dullness (15)

High scorers on the D4 (Mental Dullness) Subscale complain that life is not worthwhile; have reduced judgment, memory, comprehension, concentration, energy, work efficiency, enjoyment of recreational interests; report work tension and apathy; and lack self-confidence. They fear they are losing their mind. They feel inferior and have trouble with starting and finishing tasks. They have become disinterested in life's pleasures.

Low scores suggest enjoyment of recreation and a feeling of being capable of work.

D5: Brooding (10)

High scorers on the D5 (Brooding) Subscale complain of unhappiness, feel that life is not worthwhile, fear losing their mind, cry easily, brood, ruminate, and are easily hurt by criticism.

Low scores suggest a kind of cheerfulness, even when these patients experience distress.

Hy1: *Denial of Social Anxiety (6)*

High scorers on the Hy1 (Denial of Social Anxiety) Subscale report not being shy or bashful, can easily talk to new people, and initiate conversation. They allege an absence of anger and report they are quite friendly and very extroverted.

Low scores suggest feeling awkward and shy around strangers.

Hy2: *Need for Affection (12)*

High scores on the Hy2 (Need for Affection) Subscale suggest patients are saying, "I am a very nice person." These patients believe that people will not lie to get ahead. They rarely argue, believe that people will not use unfair means to gain an advantage, do not look for hidden motivation in people's behavior, are generally trustful, do not get mad easily, and will not go against the grain. They deny being resentful. They have very strong needs for attention and affection and believe that these needs will go unmet if they communicate more honest feelings to those closest to them. They avoid confrontations and are quite trusting.

Low scores suggest people who believe that the world is viscious and that one has to take care of oneself.

Hy3: *Lassitude-Malaise (15)*

High scorers on the Hy3 (Lassitude-Malaise) Subscale complain of poor concentration, poor sleep, restlessness, weakness, poor appetite, reduced work efficiency and tiring easily; report that their home life is unpleasant; and feel unhappy and in poor physical health. They feel they lead a dull life and are plagued by distress. They feel physically uncomfortable.

Low scores suggest patients who feel healthy, happy, and engaged in several activities that are a joy to them.

Hy4: Somatic Complaints (17)

Those patients who score high on the Hy4 (Somatic Complaints) Subscale complain of vague physical symptoms with multisite involvement, including headaches, jumping and twitching muscles, fainting and dizziness, chest pains and shortness of breath, poor eyesight, hands that are not warm enough, a hot and sweaty feeling, and a lump in their throat.

Hy5 Inhibition of Aggression (7)

High scorers on the Hy5 (Inhibition of Aggression) Subscale often deny feeling irritable, hostile, or aggressive; deny identifying with criminal or detective stories involving violence; are decisive; and are bothered by what others think of them.

Pd1: Familial Discord (9)

Patients scoring high on the Pd1 (Familial Discord) Subscale report their home life is unpleasant, with much family discord and family quarrels and little expression of love. Their report that their family objects to their choice of friends and choice of work and feel they get little sympathy. They report their family engages in constant fault finding. They very much want to leave home.

Low scores suggest a happy home life that is seen as supportive and appreciated.

Pd2: Authority Problems (8)

High scores on the Pd2 Authority Problems Subscale reflect episodes of bad school behavior and a dislike of school, patients who had past troubles with the law, those with troubles due to sexual behavior, those who are not easily downed in arguments, and those who feel that their behavior is not controlled by others. These patients have difficulty adhering to behavioral standards imposed by others. They usually resent authority and report they have been in trouble with the law. Of interest is the fact that high scorers may not be aware of their anger.

Low scores suggest compliance with authority and denial of prior troubles with authority figures.

Pd3: Social Imperturbability (6)

High scorers on the Pd3 (Social Imperturbability) Subscale are socially facile, are not shy, find it easy to talk with people, are generally independent, and are comfortable in embarrassing social situations. They can start conversations easily.

Low scores suggest a reticence in social situations.

Pd4: Social Alienation (13)

Patients scoring high on the Pd4 (Social Alienation) Subscale feel isolated, misunderstood, and unhappy; believe they get a raw deal out of life; regret past behavior; have been disappointed in love; have had an unsatisfactory sex life; believe someone has it in for them; and believe they have not been successful because of the actions of others. These patients feel quite resentful and blame others for their problems.

Low scores suggest that patients feel they have been treated fairly, feel understood, and have few regrets.

High scores correlate with poor socialization, whereas low scores correlate with successful completion of a correctional halfway house program.

Pd5: Self-Alienation (12)

Patients scoring high on the Pd5 (Self-Alienation) Subscale feel unhappy and hopeless, feel they have lived the wrong kind of life, regret past behaviors, have problems in concentration, and report strange and peculiar experiences. They are quite remorseful but blame others for their problems.

Low scores suggest patients who feel happy, get many pleasures out of life, and have little guilt.

High scores correlate with measures reflecting poor interactions with employers and parents, whereas low scores are associated with successful completion of a correctional halfway house program.

Pa1: Persecutory Ideas (17)

High-scoring patients on the Pa1 (Persecutory Ideas) Subscale report a number of delusions, including the belief that people are influencing and controlling their mind, trying to hypnotize them, and talking about them behind their back; beliefs that they are being followed, being plotted against, and being punished without cause; and a belief that they have enemies who wish to harm them, particularly when the Pa1 score is T > 65.

Pa2: Poignancy (9)

Patients scoring high on the Pa2 (Poignancy) Subscale are strongly affected by feelings, cry easily, feel more intensely than others do, are more sensitive than others, and feel misunderstood. They are hyper-sensitive, feel aggrieved, and are high strung.

Pa3: Naiveté (9)

High scores on the Pa3 (Naiveté) Subscale suggest patients who believe that people are basically honest, who believe that others would not lie or use unfair influence to gain an advantage, and who feel people are not really bossy. They tend to be moral, virtuous, and very trusting.

Sc1: Social Alienation (21)

High scorers on the Sc1 (Social Alienation) Subscale report feeling unloved or misunderstood, experiencing family conflict, avoiding social relationships, and believing that others are against them. They feel lonely, that they get a raw deal in life, that they are not successful because of other people, and that they are punished without cause; believe people treat them like a baby; and do not make friends easily.

Low scores suggest people who feel attached to their home life, understood, and that they are treated fairly.

Sc2: Emotional Alienation (11)

High scores on the Sc2 (Emotional Alienation) Subscale suggest depression, suicidal thoughts, despair, and apathy. Those with high scores believe they are condemned, may wish they were dead, and report they enjoy hurting people they love. They feel life is a strain.

Low scores suggest people who feel that life is a pleasure.

Sc3: Lack of Ego Mastery, Cognitive (10)

High scores on the Sc3 (Lack of Cognitive Ego Mastery) Subscale suggest patients who report a fear of losing their mind, problems with concentration and memory, strange thought processes, and difficulty in concentration, memory, and comprehension. They also report strange and peculiar experiences.

Sc4: Lack of Ego Mastery, Conative (14)

High scores on the Sc4 (Lack of Conative Ego Mastery) Subscale suggest depression, despair, excessive worry, hopelessness, inability to cope, and a feeling that life is not worthwhile. The scale detects primarily depression and anxiety. High-scoring patients report poor concentration, feel that life is a strain, feel they are a condemned person, do not care what happens to them, and wish they were dead.

Sc5: Lack of Ego Mastery, Defective Inhibition (11)

High scores on the Sc5 (Lack of Ego Mastery—Defective Inhibition) Subscale reflect fear of losing control over one's emotions, restlessness, irritability, and periods of dissociation. Patients with high scores become easily excited, are touchy, would like to do something shocking, fear people will hurt them, believe people are hypnotizing them, and fear using a knife. Elevations on this subscale could signal a serious potential for dangerous outbursts. These patients may have crying spells. The subscale has been able to discriminate psychotic from nonpsychotic patients.

Low scores suggest consistent composure, well-controlled behavior, and a slowness to get upset.

Sc6: Bizarre Sensory Experiences (20)

High scores on the Sc6 (Bizarre Sensory Experiences) Subscale reflect complaints pertaining to unusual physical sensations and thoughts and hallucinations. Patients with high scores report strange and peculiar experiences, blank spells, and twitching and jumping muscles; experience peculiar odors; feel that everything tastes the same; and hear strange things when alone. High scores have been shown to discriminate psychotic from nonpsychotic patients. However, these symptoms may be produced by functional processes, neurological disorders, and drug-induced syndromes.

Ma1: Amorality (6)

Patients who score high on the Ma1 (Amorality) Subscale feel it is acceptable to grab everything they can and that it is okay to take advantage of people, enjoy clever criminals, are not disgusted when a criminal is legally freed, and believe it is okay to lie to get out of trouble. They tend to be selfish, dishonest, and cynical and get satisfaction out of manipulating others.

Ma2: Psychomotor Acceleration (11)

Patients with high scores on the Ma2 (Psychomotor Acceleration) Subscale report that they work under a great deal of tension, have racing thoughts, are restless, get frequently excited, need to stir up excitement when bored, and would like to do something dangerous just for the thrill of it.

Ma3: Imperturbability (8)

Patients with high Ma3 (Imperturbability) Subscale scores do not worry about their looks, do not mind putting on stunts at parties, find no difficulty in meeting and talking with new people, and would not be nervous if they got into trouble with the law. They deny social anxiety.

Ma4: Ego Inflation (9)

Patients with high Ma4 (Ego Inflation) Subscale scores believe they are important people, feel inspired, feel they are punished without cause, feel people treat them like a child, keep talking to others until others lose patience, and believe people should try to understand their dreams. They are also stubborn and resent demands placed on them by others.

Si1: Shyness/Self-Consciousness (14)

The Si1 (Shyness/Self-Consciousness) Scale measures shyness and anxiety in social situations. Patients with high scores report they are shy in social situations, feel uneasy around others, deny sociability, do not speak unless spoken to, get easily embarrassed, and do not make friends easily. They have low self-esteem.

Si2: Social Avoidance (8)

The Si2 (Social Avoidance) Scale measures an active effort to avoid social situations and escape from social events. High-scoring patients report they are unfriendly; dislike crowds, parties, dances, and social gatherings; are socially withdrawn; and avoid social groups.

Si3: Alienation—Self and Others (17)

The Si3 (Alienation—Self and Others) Scale measures alienation and low self-esteem. Patients with high scores feel alienated from others, are apprehensive, mistrust people, are publicly more self-conscious, have a poor self-image, feel disappointed by others, give up easily when things go wrong, shrink from problems or difficulties, and feel unhappy.

CONTENT SCALES

Anxiety (ANX)

High scorers on the Anxiety (ANX) Scale report symptoms of physio-logical arousal, including shortness of breath, sleep disturbances, prob-lems in concentration, edginess, a pounding heart, shortness of breath, and excessive tension, and they fear they are losing their mind. They feel that life is a strain, lack self-confidence, and feel overwhelmed by their daily responsibilities. Women view such husbands as generally maladjusted and not helpful. Men view high-scoring wives as hostile, irritable, argumentative, uncooperative, and overbearing.

Fears (FRS)

High scores on the FRS (Fears) Scale suggest the presence of many phobias and the endorsement of specific fears. These could include fear of the sight of blood, animals, leaving home, darkness, high places, and perhaps even being indoors. Preliminary research suggested no behavioral correlates for high-scoring men, but high-scoring women were seen as maladjusted, nervous, and fearful. This content scale has two subscales: Generalized Fears and Multiple Fears.

Low scores suggest better overall adjustment.

Obsessiveness (OBS)

High scores on the Obsessiveness (OBS) Scale suggest excessive rumi-nations over trivial things, worries, irrational thoughts, and indeci-siveness that results in others' becoming inpatient with them. They may also report strongly compulsive behaviors. They become over-whelmed by their own obsessive thinking. Spouses view them as generally maladjusted, lacking in self-confidence, generally disinterested, fearful, and indecisive. Men viewed their high-scoring wives as helpless, whereas women viewed their high-scoring husbands as fearful and semantically distressed.

Low scores suggest better overall adjustment.

Depression (DEP)

High scores on the Depression (DEP) Scale suggest clinical depression, symptoms of which include a depressed affect with depressive cognitions and feelings of hopelessness, worthlessness, and helplessness. High-scoring patients have difficulty concentrating, feel unworthy, lack sufficient energy, and cry easily. They brood, feel blue much of the time, and feel unhappy. Many also report wishing they were dead (refer to critical items for suicidal ideation) and feeling that others close to them are not supportive. High-scoring men are viewed by their spouses as overly sensitive to rejection, indecisive, passive, tense, and generally disinterested, whereas high-scoring women are viewed by their spouses as maladjusted, nervous, irritable, angry, emotional, demanding, moody, depressed, resentful, and uncooperative. They report social withdrawal. This content scale has four subscales: Lack of Drive, Dysphoria, Self-Depreciation, and Suicidal Ideation.

Low scorers report they are happy and optimistic, feel good about themselves, and are generally satisfied.

Health Concerns (HEA)

High scores on the Health Concerns (HEA) Scale reflect item endorsements of a variety of health problems and symptoms. These could include neurological symptoms (seizures, dizziness, muscle paralysis), cardiovascular symptoms (heart pains, chest pains), respiratory symptoms (hay fever, asthma, coughs), gastrointestinal symptoms (constipation, nausea, vomiting, stomach pains), and sensory symptoms regarding sight and hearing. These patients believe they are sicker than the average person. They feel weak, tired, and fatigued.

This content scale has three subscales: Gastrointestinal Symptoms, Neurological Symptoms, and General Health Concerns.

Bizarre Mentation (BIZ)

High scores on the Bizarre Mentation (BIZ) Scale reflect reports of auditory and visual hallucinations and the presence of thought disorders of the paranoid kind, including ideas of persecution or grandiosity. Patients with high scores report strange and peculiar thoughts. They may also experience paranoid ideations. Preliminary data suggest no behavioral correlates for men. High-scoring women were seen as maladjusted, fearful, mistrusting, and having poor judgment. **Note:** Elevated BIZ scores can be due to functional psychoses, neurological disorders, or organicity or can be substance induced. This content scale has two subscales: Psychotic Symptomology and Schizotypal Characteristrics.

Anger (ANG)

Patients with high scores on the Anger (ANG) Scale report problems in controlling their temper when frustrated or stressed. They report themselves as irritable, hotheaded, grouchy, easily annoyed, moody, inpatient, hotheaded, and lacking in self-control. They sometimes feel like throwing objects or smashing things and have temper tantrums. High scores on the ANG Scale could mean either current feelings of anger or a predisposition to the external expression of anger, when provoked. These patients may become physically abusive. This content scale has two subscales: Explosive Behavior and Irritability.

High-scoring men are viewed by their spouses as being hostile, overbearing, maladjusted, easily annoyed, frequent users of profanity, overly aggressive, unpleasant, stubborn, and suspicious. High-scoring women were viewed by their spouses as antisocial.

Low scores suggest better overall adjustment.

Cynicism (CYN)

High scores on the Cynicism (CYN) Scale suggest patients who are disbelieving, who look for the hidden motivation in other people's behavior, and who have negative attitudes toward others. These people are also cautious and distrust others. They view others as uncaring, selfish, and dishonest. High-scoring men are viewed by their spouses as maladjusted, hostile, overbearing, whiny, demanding, and as often lossing their temper. This content scale has two subscales: Misanthropic Beliefs and Interpersonal Suspiciousness.

Low scores suggest better overall adjustment.

Antisocial Practices (ASP)

Preliminary studies of high scores on the Antisocial Practices (ASP) Scale indicate good correlations with reports of illicit drug use, legal problems, profanity, antisocial threats, dishonesty, deceitfulness, aggression, externalization of blame, and impulsivity. Such patients may also report negative attitudes, including condoning antisocial behavior in others. These are core psychopathic traits; hence, the scale provides incremental validity over that obtained by Scale 4 (Pd). High-scoring women are viewed by their spouses as maladjusted, histrionic, unfriendly, unsociable, suspicious, nervous, and as having poor judgment. High-scoring men were described by their spouse as taking drugs, having a criminal history, being demanding and profane, and as not being religious. High-scoring women were viewed as lying, disinterested, threatening, and uncooperative. This content scale has two subscales: Antisocial Attitudes and Antisocial Behavior.

Type A (TPA)

Patients with high scores on the Type A (TPA) Scale describe themselves as fast working, intolerant of interruptions, irritable, overly direct, overbearing, hard driving, aggressive, competitive, work oriented, and easily annoyed. Hostility is the underlying negative emotion in these patients. High-scoring men were viewed by their spouses as critical, angry, bossy, irritable, tense, argumentative, and negative. High-scoring women were viewed by their spouses as restless, tense, and jittery. In women, there is more of a general maladjustment component tapped by this scale. This content scale has two subscales: Impatience and Competitive Drive.

Low scores suggest better overall adjustment

Low Self-Esteem (LSE)

Patients with high scores on the Low Self-Esteem (LSE) Scale are self-abasing and overly self-critical, have a low opinion of themselves (they feel unattractive, useless, and somewhat of a burden to others), tend to give up easily, are overly sensitive to rejection, and lack self-confidence. The LSE scale provides a good assessment of global self-esteem. One study found three distinct components, labeled Ineptitude, Negative Self-Value, and Negative Comparisons with Others.

Social Discomfort (SOD)

High scores on the Social Discomfort (SOD) Scale reflect social discomfort around people and in social situations. Patients with high scores tend to be shy and perhaps avoidant. They dislike going to parties and to other social functions. They are bashful, avoidant, quiet, reticent, and self-conscious and report having few friends. An introverted lifestyle is suggested by high scores. These people prefer to be alone. This content scale has two subscales: Introversion and Shyness.

Low scores suggest gregariousness, a fun-loving approach to life, an enjoyment of going to parties, and an extroverted personality.

Family Problems (FAM)

High scores on the Family (FAM) Problems Scale suggest families (either nuclear or current marriage/cohabitation partner) described as lacking in love, support, and sympathy and as having considerable family tension, discord, arguments, and problems. Patients with high scores feel their early family life was abusive, that their marriage is unsatisfactory, or both. High-scoring men were viewed by their spouses as unhelpful, maladjusted, antisocial, and hostile. High-scoring women were viewed by their spouses as hostile, unreliable, irresponsible, and maladjusted. This content scale has two subscales: Family Discord and Family Alienation.

Work Interference (WRK)

High scores on the Work Interference (WRK) Scale reflect patients who lack self-confidence, have problems with concentration and in dealing with pressure, are indecisive, and have trouble getting started. They may also report lack of support for their career choice and negative attitudes toward coworkers. They tend to be obsessive and have problems in concentration. These attitudes and behaviors most likely interfere with effective performance. High-scoring men were viewed by their spouses as having problems with adjustment; being unfriendly, distant, unambitious, indecisive, and lacking in self-confidence; and feeling rejected. High-scoring women were viewed by their spouse as being unfriendly, uncooperative, irresponsible, and unambitious and as having poor judgment. These women also feel easily rejected and tend to avoid other people.

Negative Treatment Indicators (TRT)

The Negative Treatment Indicators (TRT) Scale was developed to identify individuals with negative attitudes and beliefs about physicians and psychological treatment. High-scoring patients believe that no one understands them, are uncomfortable in discussing personal problems with others, and do not feel change is possible. Early research shows that high TRT scores correlate with anxiety, depression, apathy, low self-esteem, and limited coping skills. The scale has two subscales: Low Motivation and Inability to Disclose (personal information).

High-scoring men were viewed by their spouses as having psychological problems and were maladjusted, unhelpful, disinterested, and fearful of the future. They lacked self-confidence, were tense, and had poor judgment. The high-scoring women were also viewed by their spouses as maladjusted, nervous, lacking in energy and self-confidence, showing poor judgment, and being interpersonally avoidant.

In a chronic-pain population, the scale has been shown to be able to predict treatment-related changes and post-treatment functioning.

SUPPLEMENTAL/FREQUENTLY SCORED SCALES

Anxiety (A)

High Scale A (Anxiety) scores reflect general emotional distress, general maladjustment, anxiety, and a tendency to react emotionally when stressed. These patients tend to be inhibited, indecisive, uncertain, unhappy, compliant, suggestible, submissive, insecure, fussy, shy and retiring, pessimistic, self-doubting, hesitant, and overcontrolled; to have a slow personal tempo; to be apathetic and hesitant; to have difficulty concentrating; and to have problems coping with stress. They are plagued by self-doubts. High Scale A scores generally reflect conscious-state anxiety and not trait anxiety and should be construed as a measure of current maladjustment.

Low scores reflect restrained behavior, but these patients prefer action to thought. They are described as gregarious, outgoing, confident, extroverted, confidant, energetic, and competitive. Low scorers usually do not have serious problems with adjustment and are rated as less anxious than high scorers.

Repression (R)

High scores on the Repression (R) Scale suggest a conscious suppression of emotions and an overreliance on the defenses of denial and repression. These people tend to be rather submissive, try to avoid conflict, do not get easily angered (and even deny their angry feelings), are unexcitable, and do not enjoy either a variety of interests or being at social gatherings. They seem limited and conventional.

Low scorers appear outgoing, energetic, excitable, enthusiastic and expressive, outspoken, and self-indulgent but willing to discuss their problems. They are rated as higher in achievement motivation.

Ego Strength (Es)

High scores on the Ego Strength (Es) Scale reflect healthy emotional adjustment, positive psychological health, and good ego strength and ego resiliency. People with high scores are able to cope with stress and feel personally adequate. High scores also indicate a more favorable adjustment and are a sign of emotional stability. Although high scorers may be aware of a desire to act out feelings impulsively, they are able to control and contain their impulses. They are stable, effective, independent, realistic, alert, self-confidant, and resourceful and deal effectively with others. This is true if K Scale scores are in the acceptable range. If K scores are unduly elevated, then elevated Es Scale scores also indicate defensiveness.

Low scores suggest people who are fearful; worry excessively; lack self-control, feel inadequate; are passive, rigid, dependent, and submissive; and feel inadequate and worthless. Emotionally disturbed and psychologically maladjusted people score lower than normal on the Es Scale.

MacAndrew Alcoholism Scale–Revised (MAC-R)

By convention, raw scores are used, rather than T scores, to interpret this scale. For men, a cutoff score of > 26 is suggested, whereas for women a cutoff score of > 24 is recommended. The higher the score, the higher the probability that the patient is a polysubstance abuser. Because some research suggests that the concurrent validity for minorities (e.g., blacks) is lower with the MAC-R than for whites, it is suggested that the raw cutoff be increased by 2 points for minorities.

This scale should be construed as a substance abuse scale and is not specific to alcoholism. Addicts and polysubstance abusers also get elevated scores on the MAC-R. The scale may also detect someone in recovery, because scores on the MAC-R are generally stable over time. Also, some research suggests that elevated scores predict future problems with substance abuse.

High scores also suggest certain personality traits, such as extroversion, boldness, competitiveness, and sensation seeking. These patients have high needs for affiliation, change, exhibition, and play. They are extroverted, gregarious, and rebellious; resent authority; often have alcohol-related legal problems; and often become belligerent and aggressive when drunk. This scale also seems to assess a personality style characterized by sociability, boldness, rebelliousness, and reward-seeking and pleasure-seeking behaviors. This style may be prodromal to the subsequent development of alcoholism; hence, a high score could mean problem substance abuse or a personality style that puts a person at risk for developing a substance abuse problem.

Men with elevated MAC-R scores were rated by their spouses as having temper tantrums, abusing illicit substances to excess, being profane, having had trouble with the law, not using sound judgment, driving recklessly, and lying. Wives with elevated MAC-R scores were rated by their spouses as drinking alcohol excessively to the point where they pass out, having been in trouble with the law, taking too many risks, and disregarding the feelings of others.

Low scores suggest a lack of self-confidence. Alcoholics with low MAC-R scores have a lower need for variety and stimulation and need immediate pleasure. They are less outgoing and often prefer to drink alone but still have histories of serious consequences associated with their alcoholism. Their behavior may be a kind of punishment avoidance.

Among nonalcoholics, low scorers on the MAC-R were rated as having fewer antisocial character traits and having lower levels of narcissism, suspiciousness, and defensiveness.

Addiction Potential Scale (APS)

The Addiction Potential Scale (APS) is new to the MMPI-2. It is designed to identify those individuals at risk for developing a substance abuse problem; it was not meant to identify patients with a current substance abuse problem. Elevated scores are associated with a lifestyle that often accompanies substance abuse. African

American men tend to score lower on this scale compared with white men.

Addiction Admission Scale (AAS)

The Addiction Admission Scale (AAS) is new to the MMPI-2 and was created to highlight a patient's willing endorsement of MMPI-2 items regarding problematic substance abuse. Elevated scores suggest the patient is willing to admit, on the test, to a substance abuse problem. Low scores suggest a patient does not have a substance abuse problem or is not willing to admit it.

Overcontrolled Hostility (OH)

Elevated scores on the Overcontrolled Hostility (OH) Scale suggest a tendency to chronically contain hostility, even in the face of extreme provocation, but with the possibility of occasionally erupting into uncontrolled aggression when a situation reaches a critical threshold. High-scoring patients tend to be passive, self-effacing, and unassuming and cope with frustrations by binding tensions. They are dependent, lack overt anxiety, and have rigid inhibitions against the expression of aggression of any kind. In fact, they deny or repress any interpersonal conflict and profess social conformity. Most of the time, these patients would not be described as aggressive by others, yet as tension builds up and when provoked, they may react violently. These patients even describe themselves as having few angry feelings and their OH score may indicate how they respond to provocation: by inhibiting their frustrations and denying their hostility.

Scores on the OH Scale are often elevated in child custody litigants, suggesting they are controlling their hostility. They are also often elevated in personnel screening contexts. Among such applicants, a high score suggests not suppressed hostility but rather good socialization and well-controlled behavior.

There is little research in the area of predictive validity with this scale. Most of the research has established the scale's concurrent validity.

Dominance (Do)

Extremely high scores on the Dominance (Do) Scale suggest people who are willing to step on other people to get what they want.

High scores indicate people who are prosocial and want to exert a positive influence on their surrounding environment. They are dominant in a positive sense; present take-charge attitudes; have self-assurance and poise; and generally are confident, resourceful, and effective people who address problems in a realistic manner. They have strong opinions, persevere in goal attainment, and are seen as optimistic. They have a good sense of morality and a willingness to face reality.

Low scores suggest submissiveness, feelings of inadequacy and unassertiveness, and a desire for others to take charge.

Social Responsibility (Re)

Patients with high scores on the Social Responsibility (Re) Scale are socially responsible, trustworthy, and dependable; accept the consequences of their behavior; and have high integrity and a strong sense of justice, morality, and social obligation. In a college setting, it has been suggested that high scores on the Re Scale reflect people who have accepted a previously held value system but that low scores reflect rejection of this value system. In noncollege settings, low scores suggest social irresponsibility; low scorers are undependable, unreliable, and lack integrity.

College Maladjustment (Mt)

The College Maladjustment (Mt) Scale helps to identify college students with current emotional difficulties, but it does not predict future adjustment problems. High scorers are maladjusted, anxious, and pessimistic. They complain of problems with memory and concentration, anxiety and nervousness, excessive worry, and social isolation. They tend to be pessimistic and anxious, procrastinate, and feel much of life is a strain. They tend to develop somatic symptoms when stressed.

Low scores suggest good emotional adjustment in college and conscientiousness.

Gender Masculine (GM) and Gender Feminine (GF)

Because of possible changing gender roles and interest patterns, the MMPI-2 restandardization committee developed two new scales based on contemporary endorsement frequencies.

In men, high Gender Masculine (GM) Scale scores are correlated with self-confidence and persistence toward goal attainment. In women, such scores are correlated with a lack of worrying, with honesty, with a willingness to try new things, and with self-confidence.

In men, high Gender Feminine (GF) Scale scores correlate with hypercritical behavior, refraining from use of profanity, poor temper control, and bossiness. For both genders, they also correlate with misuse of nonprescription drugs and religiosity.

Higher GM and GF scores suggest less psychopathology and correlate with psychological well-being.

It is suggested that use of these two scales in combination would add to interpretive refinement as to masculine or feminine psychological identity as follows:

- High GM, GF: androgyny
- High GM, low GF: stereotypical masculinity
- Low GM, high GF: stereotypical femininity
- Low GM, low GF: nondifferentiation

Posttraumatic Stress—Keane (PK)

The Posttraumatic Stress—Keane (PK) Scale was originally developed to detect posttraumatic stress disorder (PTSD) among Vietnam veterans. Subsequent research suggested it has utility in detecting PTSD in civilian trauma (e.g., rape) as well. Patients with high scores on the scale experience emotional distress associated with trauma. They may have insomnia or experience nightmares; may have unwanted and intrusive thoughts; may feel guilty (perhaps survivor guilt); may have startle responses to stimuli associated with past trauma; and may be anxious, depressed, or both. High PTSD scores may also reflect general maladjustment and emotional distress not associated with trauma.

Posttraumatic Stress—Schlenger (PS)

The Posttraumatic Stress—Schlenger (PS) Scale was also developed to detect PTSD in combat veterans. Characteristics of patients with elevated scores on this scale are probably similar to those for patients with elevated scores on the PK Scale. Both PK and PS Scales are highly correlated with each other.

Marital Distress Scale

The Marital Distress Scale is new to the MMPI-2. Elevated scores are associated with serious relationship problems in a marital dyad or sustained, committed relationship.

Critical Items

Many firms providing computerized scoring print out critical items responded to by the client in the endorsed direction. It is suggested that the clinician inspect these critical items and follow up as necessary.

Interpreting MMPI-2 Code Types: Two-Point Codes

Two-point codes are MMPI-2 profiles in which only two clinical scale scores are $T > 65$ and the other clinical scale scores are $T < 65$. There is a long history of MMPI/MMPI-2 research on these code types conducted according to stringent rules. This often meant that scores on the validity scales and the clinical scales had to be in certain ranges before they were said to represent a two-point code. Over time, these interpretive rules were relaxed such that clinicians were using the top two scales in the profile as a two-point code, even though scores for several clinical scales were T > 65. Technically, such profiles are referred to as high-ranging codes and the scales should be interpreted singly.

More recently, the concept of well-defined code types has been introduced. Here it is argued that if the scores for the top two scales in the profile are substantially above the other clinical scales, which might also be T > 65, these are well-defined code types where traditional two-point code interpretations can be applied. This is somewhat controversial and the reader is advised to consider such code types as hypotheses that have not been substantiated as well as to consider the two-point code types developed on the basis of stringent rules.

By convention, information presented without specification of gender is presumed to be applicable to both genders. Where specific information is available by gender, the reference is to men with the code or women with the code. Where information is reported for one gender but not for the other, no information has been reported in the literature for that code by specific gender.

12/21

Patients classified as fitting code 12/21 may be described as anxious, fearful, tense, insecure, denying angry feelings, not living up to their daily responsibilities, passive, and dependent. They tend to somaticize their problems and exaggerate the severity of their problems, seek medical solutions to their problems, and resist psychological treatment. Their complaints center around headaches, backaches, stomachaches, blackouts, cardiac complaints, or gastrointestinal problems. Even when these complaints are valid, these patients exaggerate their level of symptom expression. These patients are often disgruntled and dissatisfied with the kind of medical care they are receiving and crave more personal attention from caregivers. They tend to be shy in social situations and are introverted and self-conscious. They feel hostile toward those they perceive as not giving them enough attention. They show low initiative and are depressed, withdrawn, and seclusive.

Diagnoses associated with this code type include somatoform disorder, major depression, anxiety disorders, and psychological factors affecting physical condition.

College students with this code are described as shy, introverted, unhappy, tense, experiencing social discomfort, insecure, and worried, particularly about heterosexual relationships. College women with this code are also seen as indecisive, are prone to experience test anxiety and experience an emotional block during exams, and feel insecure in social situations.

13/31

The 13/31 profile is most common in medical settings and more common in women. These patients are anxious and fearful, present with a variety of hypocondriacal symptoms and complaints, but deny the possibility of a psychological conflict as the source of their problems. They see themselves as normal and responsible. Repression and displacement are the primary defenses. Their symptoms can include almost any body system but primarily include reports of chronic back pain, numbness, blurred vision, headaches, dizziness, tremors, insomnia, and general fatigue. Their daily efficiency and ability to respond to daily responsibilities have been greatly reduced. These patients get considerable secondary gain from their chronic complaints; they almost demand sympathy and attention from those around them, yet they continue to complain, and interventions are never enough. They are essentially insecure and manifest unconscious hostility through symptom expression. They have a defeatist attitude toward treatment and tend to doctor-shop for medical answers. However, they do not see themselves as emotionally dependent, in contrast to the view of those closest to them. They have a strong histrionic component to their personality and behavior. Accordingly, they have a strong need for attention and feel insecure if they are not to focus of discussion. They are immature, dependent (though they do not recognize this), selfish, and extroverted. They rarely express anger and hostility, instead displacing these emotions onto their bodily complaints and acting in a passive-aggressive or passive-dependent manner. They irritate others around them with their constant complaints and irritability. They often have a low sex drive and have problems with heterosexual relations. When the code type is 31′, these patients are more likely to show the histrionic features than when the code type is 13′.

Diagnoses associated with this code include somatoform disorder, major depression, psychological factors affecting physical condition, and histrionic personality disorder.

14/41

The 14/41 profile is more common in men than in women. These patients have excessive and even severe somatic complaints, personality problems, and long-standing relationship problems. Aggressive behavior may also be a part of the current or past history. They are socially extroverted and manipulative and may exaggerate their symptomatic expression to get drugs. They may be described as pessimistic, negative, demanding, grouchy, indecisive, and disobedient of rules and regulations; have poorly defined goals; have difficulty establishing lasting relationships with members of the opposite gender; and often have family and relationship problems. They often report nonspecific headaches.

Diagnoses associated with this code type include personality disorders.

15/51

Patients with a 15/51 code are described as passive, dependent, indecisive, fussy, dissatisfied, and constantly complaining, but they rarely act out. In men, this code suggests a general failure to identify with cultural masculine roles, and their characterological style may be used to avoid family and work responsibilities. In women, this code suggests a great deal of unnecessary suffering.

16/61

Patients with a 16/61 code present with many somatic symptoms, have disturbed interpersonal relationships, are hostile but do not recognize their hostility, and blame others for their problems. Depending on the elevation of Scale 6, they may manifest paranoid traits and symptoms. (This code type is rare.)

17/71

Patients with a 17/71 code report myriad physical complaints that result in a great deal of anxiety, stress, and tension. They are insecure and bothered by obsessive thoughts. They fear they are losing their mind. They tend to be introverted and spend an inordinate amount of time worrying about their personal deficiencies.

18/81

Patients with an 18/81 code are poorly socialized and are likely to have had chronic interpersonal problems. They feel alienated and keep others at a distance. This often results in problems with the opposite gender. They tend to be distractible and confused, demonstrate a thought disorder, experience periods of disorientation, and have flat affect. They may become suddenly belligerent. Somatic delusions may be a part of the clinical picture. They tend to harbor anger and resentment and are prone to periodic explosive behavior. They are quite maladjusted. Any physical symptoms expressed are likely to be of a bizarre nature and may include somatic delusions. Others see them as odd, strange, or bizarre. They are likely to have poor work histories and lead a nomadic existence. This code type was found among a group of substance abusers with a history of suicide attempt but was absent from substance abusers who had no history of suicide attempt.

19/91

Patients with a 19/91 code are tense and restless, are overly concerned with their physical symptoms, feel in distress, and are quite agitated. They have a high level of energy and irritability. Usually they are extroverted and tend to have many ideas and plans but little history of accomplishment or endurance. They tend to have a passive-dependent or passive-aggressive personality style, though they deny having personality problems and may even appear socially extroverted. They generally view themselves as happy and do not see themselves as difficult to get along with, despite these very complaints from those closest to them.

This profile has appeared among lesbian and heterosexual women without a history of sexual abuse. It is also common among drug abusers who are detoxifying, particularly from opiate dependence.

Diagnoses associated with this code type include organic brain dysfunction.

23/32

The 23/32 code type is associated with anxiety and depression. These patients lack energy, have multiple somatic complaints (particularly issues with fatigue, gastric complaints, headaches, and dizziness), feel helpless and socially inadequate and insecure, are immature and dependent, and tend to elicit helping behaviors from others. They appear anxious, fearful, insecure, and generally dissatisfied. They dwell on vague somatic complaints and tend to resist psychological treatment. These physical complaints are often of a histrionic quality. They appear, passive, compliant, and obedient and often assume a martyr-like role in the form of self-sacrificing behaviors. They tend to blame themselves when things go wrong. There may be sexual adjustment problems. They tend to avoid social situations and feel uncomfortable in heterosexual relationships. Men with this code often are ambitious and serious about their responsibilities and may present with business problems and interpersonal problems. Women with this code report sexual difficulties, are overly sensitive to criticism, and report they are chronically unhappy.

This code type has appeared in patients with female orgasmic dysfunction, frigidity, sexual dysfunction, impotence or frigidity, sexual maladjustment, and a variety of other sexual difficulties and in patients with marital difficulties. However, some women reporting no sexual abuse history had a 23 code type.

Diagnoses associated with this code include somatoform disorder, major depression, psychological factors affecting physical condition, and histrionic personality disorder.

24/42

The 24/42 profile reflects both anger and depression. Patients with this profile have difficulty controlling their impulses; tend to be uncomfortable in social situations, particularly with women; and are passive-dependent. They may make a good impression at first, as they seem sociable and outgoing, but their unreliability will frustrate others, as will their manipulations. They are likely to have a history of problems with the law, to act out, and to show a lack of respect for social rules and standards. Outwardly, they appear energetic, social, and gregarious, but inwardly, they feel inadequate and self-conscious. They feel distressed, worthless, and guilty over their behavior, but the cycle is a repetitive one and is likely to repeat itself. Any professed guilt or remorse is more commonly due to being in a situation (often legal) in which they face undesirable consequences. These expressions are not internalized guilt. These patients tend to feel angry at society for putting them in their current situation and angry at themselves for allowing this to happen to them. Patients with this profile have been known to make suicidal threats as a manipulation. Men with this code may have histories of severe rejection or feelings of parental deprivation as a child, particularly from fathers with histories of alcohol abuse. As adults, these patients are sensitive to rejection and feel a lack of approval from significant others. They also tend to have poor vocational and marital adjustment. These patients have histories of social, family, legal, and marital problems.

College students with this code type report many problems with their family, have poor heterosexual relationships, dislike rigid rules, and have low self-esteem.

This profile has appeared in substance abusers, DUI/DWI (driving under the influence/driving while intoxicated) offenders, shoplifters, prisoners, sexual offenders, and bulimic women. Diagnoses associated with this code also include major depression and antisocial personality disorder.

25/52

Men with code 25/52 are typically passive, dependent, idealistic, and noncompetitive and resent demands placed on them, such as family responsibilities. They generally have good verbal skills and are friendly and cooperative. Although only a minority of men with this code type are homosexuals, all seem to have problems with heterosexual relationships, suggested by divorce, separation, and marital discord, along with expressions of sexual dissatisfaction in their relationships. They tend to avoid interpersonal emotional involvement. Although depression may be the primary clinical symptom, others present primarily with anxiety. This depression is usually mild and situational in nature. They use intellectualization as a main defense. Acting out is very unlikely. They show problematic dating histories and report poor heterosexual adjustment.

In college university health clinics, 25 men with this code type reported infrequent dating. They typically have a high incidence of job dissatisfaction and job-related injuries. One study found this code type only in inpatients. A dependent personality style/disorder is suggested by this code type, as is some type of depressive disorder.

26/62

Patients with a 26/62 code are moody and depressed and overreact to criticism. They appear bitter and resentful, angry, argumentative, agitated, and touchy; have a "chip on the shoulder" attitude; and have paranoid traits. When criticized, they become passive but harbor angry resentments at those who are being "unreasonable." They also tend to be openly hostile and resentful toward others. They usually present with interpersonal difficulties and feel they have been treated unfairly. Malevolent projections are frequent. The code type suggests chronic maladjustment.

Diagnoses associated with this code type include paranoid personality disorder or depression.

27/72

The 27/72 code is one of the more common MMPI-2 code types, particularly in psychiatric outpatient settings. These patients tend to be anxious, depressed, fearful, tense, high strung, and overly sensitive; chronically feel fatigue, tension, and exhaustion; and often feel hopeless, blameworthy, in emotional discomfort, helpless, and inadequate. They are pessimistic and preoccupied with their deficiencies. They tend to be perfectionistic, religious, meticulous, hyper-responsible, and compulsive and may have many phobias (check FRS content scale) and obsessive thinking (check OBS content scale). Their behavior may be dominated by feelings of neurotic guilt. Their interpersonal relationships show a pattern of dependency. They report problems being assertive and try to solicit nurturance from others. They feel inadequate and appear docile and passive. Many report suicidal ideation.

This profile has appeared among a sample of lesbian and heterosexual women without a history of sexual abuse.

Diagnoses associated with this code type include anxiety disorder, obsessive-compulsive disorder or some form of depression, dependent personality disorder, and substance abuse, particularly alcoholism.

28/82

The 28/82 code type is found mainly is psychiatric populations. These patients have problems being assertive and are seen as dependent and submissive, yet they tend to avoid close interpersonal relationships and keep people at a distance. They appear both irritable and resentful, are pervasively unhappy and high strung, and are manifestly depressed. They appear conflicted with and in a profound state of inner turmoil that seems inescapable. Some have reduced speech and retarded stream of thought. They have problems concentrating and making decisions and appear withdrawn. Many have sexual conflicts. They are prone to obsessional thinking (check OBS content scale). They report social withdrawal, problems in anger modulation, and difficulty in interpersonal relationships. Suicidal ideation may be present. If the code type is 82′, then psychotic symptoms may predominate the clinical picture.

Diagnoses associated with this code type have included bipolar disorder, brief reactive psychosis, schizophrenia, schizoaffective type (particularly when scale elevations are T > 80), and personality disorder. In such cases, the psychotic manifestations of this code type predominate and might include symptoms of delusions, hallucinations, difficulties with impulse control, interpersonal difficulties, poor family relationships, social withdrawal, and bizarre mentations. (Refer to Scale F and BIZ for confirming evidence). In ranges of T = 65 to 70, the patient may be endorsing the neurological symptoms in Scale 8 and may feel distressed by them. In such cases, the descriptors for this code type would only be partially applicable. This code has also appeared in a sample of bulimic women.

29/92

Depression, agitation, irritability, and restlessness predominate the clinical picture for patients with code 29/92. They tend to be narcissistic and may experience depression following a narcissistic injury. They are tense and jumpy, ruminate about issues of self-worth, and may oscillate from being happy and optimistic to being negativistic, sullen, and explosive. They feel inadequate and worthless. They are prone to emotional outbursts. They report many somatic symptoms and may use substances to excess. This code type has been found among drug abusers with a history of suicide attempt but was not present among drug abusers without such a history.

Diagnoses associated with this code type include organic brain dysfunction, narcissistic personality disorder, clinical depression, and bipolar disorder.

20/02

The 20/02 code type reflects shyness, introversion, and mild depression. People with this code are withdrawn, socially inhibited, timid, and unhappy; lack self-confidence; feel socially inept and inadequate; and lack interpersonal warmth. They tend to be passive.

This code was seen in a group of nonpurging bulimics.

Diagnoses associated with this subtype include depression and schizoid personality disorder.

34

Although people with code 34 have chronic feelings of anger and hostility and have become sensitive to criticism and rejection, they tend to be reluctant to admit to any psychological problems, even when such problems are quite evident to others. They exhibit more passive and indirect expressions of their anger. They may appear dramatic, erratic, and emotional. Issues of anger control often precipitate a visit to a mental health provider. Legal problems often are associated with this code. These patients are quite immature, and this code has been associated with marital dysfunction, family problems, sexual promiscuity, substance abuse, and divorce. This code suggests patients will inhibit their anger and not act it out; however, some may be unable to inhibit their anger and may experience an episode of violent acting out.

This code has appeared among both lesbian women with a history of sexual abuse and those without it. This code type, at subclinical levels, has been reported among child custody litigants. Diagnoses associated with this code type include histrionic personality disorder, passive-aggressive personality disorder, or antisocial personality disorder.

35/53

Men with the 35/53 code type are described as manipulative, demanding, and immature and as having exploitive interpersonal relationships. These men describe themselves as having a nervous temperament yet are also passive, inhibited, and insecure. They seem shy and uncomfortable in social situations. They often have histories of job conflict and job-related disabilities. Women with this code type get easily irritated and have a poor self-concept and poor body image. Overt homosexuality is rare, but both men and women with this code report marital problems. Prior psychiatric histories for this code type are rare.

This profile has appeared in a sample of lesbian and heterosexual women without a history of sexual abuse and in heterosexual women with a history of sexual abuse.

36/63

Patients with the 36/63 code harbor hostile feelings and resentment, usually toward family members, and are hypersenstive to criticism. They are suspicious, mistrustful, and defiant but have marked difficulty in overtly expressing anger—of which they are not aware—and blame others for their troubles. This anger is often expressed instead in indirect ways. They are hypersensitive to criticism, self-centered, and resentful of authority figures. Their personality style interferes with their developing a sense of intimacy. They can be power hungry and ruthless in business. They may have many somatic complaints but deny any psychological problems.

This code has appeared in lesbian women without a history of sexual abuse. At subclinical levels, this is the code most frequently seen among child custody litigants. The code is more common in women.

37/73

The 37/73 code is relatively uncommon and is associated with anxiety, tension, and somatic complaints in a histrionic personality, along with excessive ruminations. These patients have unresolved issues with dependency but lack insight. They are chronic worriers who feel excessively guilty unless they address all their daily responsibilities. They have difficulty relaxing.

This code has appeared among lesbians with a history of sexual abuse.

Diagnoses associated with this code type include anxiety disorder.

38/83

Patients with a 38/83 code have a noticeable thought disorder that may include unconventional or autistic thinking and irrelevant and even incoherent speech, and they are seen by others as peculiar. Delusions and hallucinations can be expected. Their emotional tone is one of depression and they often feel hopeless. They can be described as tense, resentful, alienated, fearful (particularly of getting involved in dependent relationships), and obsessional. They report an insecurity over sexual expression and have excessive needs for attention and affection, yet they are uninvolved, apathetic, and passively resistant to interpersonal relations: Underneath, they are quite immature, self-centered, and dependent. These patients have a major thought disorder, and many have sexualized psychotic episodes. They may have brief psychotic episodes with symptoms of highly sexualized content. Some women with this code have histories of sexual abuse and tend to dissociate this traumatic experience. In such cases, they may not have psychotic symptoms and traits common with this profile.

This profile has appeared among heterosexual women without a history of sexual abuse.

Diagnoses associated with this code type include some form of psychosis or schizophrenia, some type of dissociative disorder, and somatoform disorders.

39/93

Patients with a 39/93 code are extroverted and dramatic but superficial. They tend to be aggressive and irritable and report anxiety attacks and acute distress accompanied by a variety of somatic complaints. Their typical behavior is characterized by high energy, optimism, and drive, and they expect both praise and recognition for their efforts. Much of their motivation is a desire to gain attention and approval. They are gregarious, extroverted, and outgoing people who act to draw attention to themselves, yet they are usually unaware they are behaving in this way. They may also be emotionally labile and mercurial.

This profile has appeared among a sample of lesbian women without a history of sexual abuse. It also appeared at a college counseling center where women presented with difficulties with their instructors to whom they were sexually attracted.

43

Patients with a 43 code have chronic feelings of anger and hostility that are prone to be acted out in violent ways. They have intense anger but are unable to appropriately express negative feelings. It has been speculated that these patients may be more prone to the overcontrolled hostility dynamic (see Scale OH, page 51). They allow others to take advantage of them and frustrate them to the extreme, whereupon their hostility builds to such a point that it is expressed directly through extreme aggression, including murder. They may have long periods of time where they demonstrate socially appropriate behavior, and they tend to be quiet and withdrawn, but then they erupt in violence. These patients are emotionally maladjusted and unstable; they have marital problems; are prone to alcoholism and sexual promiscuity, and make suicide attempts and homicidal threats. Offenders with a 43 code type are often incarcerated for violent acts and have criminal histories of violent and assaultive crimes.

This code has appeared in a sample of bulimic women. In those cases, the appearance of the code would suggest a cycle of rigid overcontrol to uncontrolled acting out, which includes bingeing/purging and perhaps substance abuse. Because bulimics do not see this behavior as problematic, they are relatively free from depression and anxiety. This profile may also suggest a mild suicide risk. It also appears in forensic and offender populations.

45/54

Men with the 45/54 code type seem to be looking for nurturance; are passive, dependent, submissive individuals; and appear to have issues with dominance and dependence. They often will present with histories of divorce, separation, or marital discord. They resent the demands placed on them. They usually are insecure over the gender role and need to reassure themselves about their identity. Although not all men with this code type are homosexual, a substantial number are. Others exhibit sexual confusion and seem to have a fear of rejection by women. One study reported that men with this code type have a higher than expected incidence of absence of fathers from the home during developmental years. The code type may also suggest nonconformity in behavior and dress. In a college university health clinic, 45 men usually presented with specific distress over a breakup with a girlfriend. Women with this profile may have adopted the masculine role in a lesbian relationship, or the appearance of this code may suggest identification with "male" interests and values.

This profile has been found among both heterosexual women with a history of sexual abuse and heterosexual women without such a history. It has also appeared in lesbian women with a history of sexual abuse and in women who have committed murder.

A diagnosis frequently associated with this code is dependent personality. It is important to rule out sexual disorder not otherwise specified (NOS) and adjustment disorder. If Scale 4 scores are higher than those for Scale 5, a history of criminal activity is more likely than when Scale 5 scores are higher than those for Scale 4.

46/64

The 46/64 profile is more common among women than among men. Patients with this profile have chronic anger and resentment but often express it in passive-aggressive ways. They resent demands placed on them and tend to be manipulative. They are often dramatic, sullen, emotional, rebellious, hostile, irritable, aggressive, erratic, and egocentric. They seek attention and will engage in dramatic behaviors to get it. They are seen as argumentative and derogatory toward authority. They blame others for their troubles, feel emotionally abandoned, and deny psychological problems. They resent any demands placed on them while they also demand sympathy and

attention from others. They feel neglected, rejected, and unfairly criticized. They are seen by others as immature, insecure, narcissistic,
sullen, and manipulative, with poor judgment and exaggerated needs
for attention and affection. Many patients with this code report problematic childhoods, behavior problems, and adult substance abuse. As
Scale 6 scores become more elevated, more paranoid features are associated with the clinical profile. Women with this code type appear
overly dependent on men.

This code has appeared in a sample of bulimics and in drug
addicts with a history of suicide attempt(s). It has also appeared in
male child sex offenders and in both lesbians and heterosexual women
with a history of sexual abuse (particularly if Scale 5 scores are low).
This code, at subclinical levels, has been reported among child custody litigants.

Women with this code type have difficulties in social relationships and are quite dependent and demanding of attention and affection in their relationships. Many have reported a history of
physical/sexual abuse. The profile has been called that of a battered
woman syndrome.

Diagnoses associated with this code type include passive-aggressive personality disorder, narcissistic personality disorder, and paranoid
personality disorder.

47/74

Patients with a 47/74 code tend to act out in repetitive fashion, especially around issues of substance abuse and sex. Even though they may
profess superficial and even sincere remorse, this guilt, whether real or
actual, does not change their behavior, which oscillates between total
disregard for the consequences of the behavior to excessive concerns
and guilt over their behavior. Their psychology is organized around
self-indulgence and impulsivity. The anxiety associated with this code
should be thought of as state anxiety rather than trait anxiety, whereby
the patient is temporarily feeling anxious because of some negative
environmental consequence of his behavior. These patients have
underlying issues with dependence and independence and have strong

needs for reassurance. They tend to ruminate over their conflicts and find rules, regulations, standards, and restrictions imposed by others irritatingly inhibiting. They may present with vague somatic complaints. Mental health clinicians may meet these patients during the remorse phase of their cyclical behavior, but the long-term prognosis is poor.

Diagnoses associated with this code type include personality disorder (usually antisocial and/or narcissistic), eating disorder (usually bulimia), and perhaps an anxiety disorder.

48/84

The 48/84 code type is relatively more common in women than in men. High-scoring patients often have identity problems and are seen as peculiar. They are rebellious; feel inadequate, alienated, irritable, angry, argumentative, promiscuous, and distrustful; and behave unpredictably. They see the world as quite threatening. They are likely to show a history of being in constant trouble. These patients are emotionally distant from others and chronically unhappy. They present with a variety of social, sexual, and familial maladjustments. Many have serious concerns about their sexual identity. Behavioral controls are quite tenuous. They have poor social judgment and are quite prone to act out. They are impulsive. Men with this code often have criminal histories comprising brutal, viscious, and unplanned assaultive crimes, including homosexual attacks and rape. They may be trying to demonstrate a kind of sexual adequacy when, underneath, they feel they have difficulty performing sexually. Women with this code have low self-concepts and are sexually promiscuous. They often are involved with men who would be considered losers. Suicide ideation and attempts have been associated with this code type. (See items 150, 506, 520, and 524).

This code also appeared in a group of bulimic women in several studies. It is also common in both male and female drug addicts and in an offender population, particularly in rapists, child sex abusers and other sex offenders, prostitutes, and murderers. In women, the code has been found in multiple personality disorders.

Diagnoses associated with this code are antisocial, histrionic, or narcissistic personality disorders; borderline personality disorder; and even schizophrenia.

49/94

The 49/94 code is particularly frequent in an offender population (child abusers and rapists, murderers, career criminals, and those convicted of violent crimes) and among drug addicts. These patients have long-standing problems with impulsivity. They are self-centered, irresponsible, moody, and rebellious; show poor judgment; and do not plan for the future. They blame others for their problems and seem indifferent to anxiety or stress. They also can appear friendly, extroverted, and very self-confident, but they rarely change their behavior and they keep others at a distance except when using others to meet their needs. Often, they are simply provocative and resist demands put on them. Sexual promiscuity is common. Offenders with this profile may have committed violent crimes, including rape and assault. The profile has also been seen in child sex offenders and in both lesbian and heterosexual women with a history of sexual abuse.

Diagnoses most frequently associated with this code are antisocial personality disorder and narcissistic personality disorder. The code has also appeared in a sample of bulimics and in male and female drug addicts.

56/65

Men with the 56/65 code are described as being aloof, guarded, resistant, impulsive, irritable, abrasive, and easily angered and as having poor social skills and disrupted heterosexual relationships. They have feelings that are easily hurt and seem afraid of emotional involvement with people, yet they feel they mix in with others quite easily. They view women as domineering and rarely marry. One study reported that men with this code were often raised in matriarchal households and had fathers who were absent from the home early on.

This profile has appeared among lesbian women without a history of sexual abuse.

57/75

Men with the 57/75 code complain of marital conflict and sexual conflicts and a variety of interpersonal and heterosexual difficulties. They lack self-confidence and assertiveness in sexual situations and have difficulty expressing their needs to their sexual partners. They are shy, bashful, and easily embarrassed. They lack spontaneity and have a ruminative cognitive style. They complain of inefficiency and reduced ability to work at their desired level of performance. Anxiety and depression are the predominant symptoms. They tend to ruminate over their perceived shortcomings and feel inadequate in heterosexual relations.

This profile has appeared among lesbian women with a history of sexual abuse.

In a university health clinic, most of a group of 57 men complained of academic difficulties, interpersonal problems with women, or a recent breakup with a girlfriend.

58/85

Men with the 58/85 code seem to lead a chaotic and stress-filled lifestyle and are described as immature, confused, unhappy, alienated, and passive. Many have histories of a problematic relationship with a father or father figure who was rejecting and abusive. Though they describe their mothers as domineering, they feel closer to their mothers and seem to delay separating from the nest. Marriage is rare for this code type. Divorce, mental illness (often beginning in childhood), and physical abuse are common with this code type. They appear eccentric and have sexual conflicts. Many are essentially asexual. They are shy and lack a stable identity and have problems forming meaningful interpersonal relationships. A schizoid personality disorder is suggested by this code type. Also, rule out sexual disorder NOS.

Women with this code are more likely to be psychotic with symptoms of hallucinations, thought broadcasting, and social isolation. The profile has appeared in lesbians with a history of sexual abuse and in heterosexual women without a history of sexual abuse.

59/95

Men with the 59/95 code are seen as hyperactive, grandiose, impulsive, and, at higher elevations, as delusional with ideas of reference and persecution. They lack assertiveness. They often have histories that include involvement with the criminal justice system or report illegal activities. They generally have unstable relationships with women. Many report feeling happy about themselves and do not report any psychological distress. They see themselves as self-confidant and self-assured.

67/76

Patients with a 67/76 code are anxious, tense, overly sensitive, and restless; brood; and feel resentment. They have interpersonal relationship problems and feel (often inaccurately) that they have been wronged. They use projection as their main defense, and they express their hostility verbally and directly. This profile has appeared among lesbian women without a history of sexual abuse.

68/86

Patients with a 68/86 code have long-standing psychological problems of a severe nature, including psychotic and/or delusional experiences and florid psychological/psychiatric symptomology. They appear confused, maladjusted, and disorganized. They have poor social skills and problem-solving skills and are poorly sexualized. They avoid emotional contact with others because they distrust others and are markedly suspicious. They appear shy, avoidant, introverted, inhibited, withdrawn, and schizoid when not in a florid state of psychosis. They have trouble distinguishing between fantasy and reality and their emotional life is unstable. They report delusions and hallucinations and spend a great deal of time in daydreams, fantasy, and nonnatural causation, such as astrology and numerology. They feel inferior, but many present with delusions of grandiosity and many paranoid symptoms and confusion. They are moody, show poor judgment, and are generally apathetic and uncooperative—not out of resistant but more from ego deficits. They are likely to have poor job histories. Conflict concerning sexuality is usually present.

The diagnosis most often associated with this code is paranoid schizophrenia or other varieties of schizophrenia.

69/96

Patients with a 69/96 code are seen as guarded, dependent, overly sensitive to criticism, tense, jumpy, excitable, loud, rigid, and anxious. Their anger may take the form of irritability and frustration. Angry outbursts are common, as they feel vulnerable to perceived threats. They have a difficult time trusting others and are markedly suspicious and often disoriented, having obsessions and ruminative ideations. They have strong paranoid features to their personality, such as moodiness, grandiosity, suspiciousness, and excessive religiosity, and they use projection as their main defense. Patients with this code have sexual conflicts and show poor heterosexual adjustment. They are afraid of emotional involvement and keep others at an emotional distance. However, they are prone to have emotional outbursts and may present with a thought disorder. This code has appeared in male child sex offenders. Patients with this code type are high in the grandiose factor of narcissism.

Men at a university mental health clinic with this code were described as having flat affect, poor memory, and a family history positive for schizophrenia, and reported numerous compulsions and phobias. Women at a college university mental health clinic with this code were described as being somewhat autistic with flat affect and having a thought disorder.

Diagnoses associated with this code type include bipolar—manic disorder and schizoaffective disorder. Both thought disorder and mood disorder diagnoses are possible with this code type. This code has also appeared in a sample of bulimics.

78/87

These patients present in a great deal of psychological distress. They show chronic worry and anxiety or may even be in a panic state. They are overly ruminative, ideational, and introverted. They may report sexual conflicts and gender role inadequacy. They show poor heterosexual adjustment and are often unable to be dominant in relationships. They feel depressed, high strung, inferior, and overly introspective; show poor judgment; and are passive in relationships. They tend to be obsessional and introspective in a negative sense and are indecisive. They seem hard to get to know and withdraw into a fantasy life. These patients are prone to experience psychological crises. They are unable to concentrate, lack self-confidence, and feel inadequate, especially in heterosexual relationships. The profile is common among men who were sexually abused as a child and has appeared in both lesbian and heterosexual women with histories of sexual abuse. Patients with this code type are high on the depletion factor (an unconscious feeling of inadequacy and unhappiness that has been hypothesized to underlie narcissism).

Men at a university mental health clinic with this code were described as having flat affect, poor memory, and a family history positive for schizophrenia and reported numerous compulsions and phobias. Women at a university mental health clinic with this code were described as being somewhat autistic with flat affect and having a thought disorder.

Diagnoses associated with this code include schizophrenia, psychosis NOS, affective disorders, anxiety disorders, obsessive-compulsive disorder, schizoid personality disorder, and substance use disorders, particularly alcoholism.

This code type has appeared in men who have sexually assaulted children.

89/98

The 89/98 code is associated with significant psychological disturbance and serious psychological maladjustment. These patients tend to be schizoid, spending a great deal of time in personal fantasy, ruminations, delusional thinking, and daydreaming. They have little capacity to form meaningful interpersonal relations and they withdraw from others. They are very self-centered, and others view them as odd, indecisive, hostile, restless, hyperactive, impulsive, emotionally labile, negativistic, uncooperative, and perplexed. Flights of ideas and general confusion may also be possible. These patients tend to become disorganized under stress. They distrust others' motivations and fear deep emotional involvement with people, so they keep others at a distance. They have poor sexual adjustment. They demand a great deal of attention and express resentment and hostility when their perceived needs are not met. They are hyperactive, grandiose, emotionally labile, agitated, boastful, unmanageable, tense, restless, and evasive. They may have religious delusions. They may have flights of ideas, labile affect, bizarre speech, and paranoid delusions. They are prone to act out.

This profile has appeared among lesbian and heterosexual women with histories of sexual abuse.

Diagnoses associated with this code type include bipolar disorder—manic and some form of schizophrenia. This code type is most representative of narcissistic personalities in nonclinical samples.

Interpreting MMPI-2 Code Types: Three-Point Codes

Three-point codes are MMPI-2 profiles in which scores for three clinical scales are $T > 65$ and scores for other clinical scales are $T < 65$.

123

The 123 profile is more common in medical problems and reflects depression with multiple somatic complaints, particularly pain, dizziness, headaches, and gastrointestinal problems but may also include musculoskeletal or cardiorespiratory systems as well. These symptoms are largely hypocondriacal in nature. This results in reduced psychological functioning. Patients with this code show a conflict between dependency and assertion. They lack insight into the psychological nature of their somatic complaints and experience high levels of physiological distress. They tend to be passive-dependent, anxious, fearful, apathetic, and depressed. It is important for them to be liked and approved by people, so they act in a very conforming manner. Still, they try to control others close to them by complaining about their health problems. They believe others simply do not understand how sick they are feeling. They are also dissatisfied, insecure, tense, worrisome, and depressed. They are easily hurt by criticism and react to it by becoming depressed. They have a low sex drive and experience sexual aversion, are sexually inhibited, and have an overall poor sexual adjustment. They tend to use passive-aggressive means to maintain and satisfy their dependency needs. Defenses primarily include denial and repression. These patients become irritable and hostile when they perceive that their illnesses are not getting the proper attention. There is a large secondary gain associated with these symptoms, so these patients often demand attention and sympathy. However, the underlying dynamic may be to express unconscious hostility toward others through constantly reporting physical ailments and blaming others for their problems.

This code type is seen most often in purging bulimics and in sexual inhibition in women. It has been found among heterosexual women without a history of sexual abuse. These patients are also prone to develop conversion disorders. Women with this code report higher than average parental rejection, particularly by fathers. Their family of origin is often dysfunctional. Also, women with this code may report sexual conflicts and marital problems. Men with this code also report problems with ulcers.

Diagnoses associated with this code type include affective disorders, somatoform disorder, and histrionic personality disorder.

124

Patients with a 124 code report a variety of physical symptoms that do not correspond to findings on objective physical evaluation. These patients tend to somaticize, are irritable and shy, tend to be depressed, and deny emotional problems. They tend to be passive-dependent and lean on others for support. They seem incapable of dealing with environmental pressures or stress and feel inadequate. They also have problems in controlling the expression of hostile feelings, generally through bitterness and irresponsibility rather than through overt antisocial behavior. (This is true as long as scores on the ASP Scale are in the normal range.)

128

Patients with a 128 code appear anxious, fearful, and dependent. They are unhappy, depressed, and pessimistic and may be chronically depressed, particularly by physical symptoms that they feel have not been satisfactorily addressed by the medical establishment. Their hypochondriacal character structure results in their "defeating" medical interventions, and they continue to whine and complain about diffuse physical complaints. They believe people understand neither their problems nor how truly sick they are. If Scale 8 scores are particularly high, then these patients may have periods of unreality and manifest psychotic processes. Somatic delusions may be a part of the clinical picture. These patients tend to have chronic problems with psychological adjustment and are preoccupied with feeling depressed, unreal, alienated, and misunderstood. They tend to be quite withdrawn, shy, and introverted, with no energy for life.

Diagnoses associated with this code type include affective disorders, psychological factors affecting physical condition, somatoform disorder, schizotypal personality disorder, and psychotic disorder NOS.

129

Patients with a 129 code often experience acute distress and present with a variety of medical complaints and symptoms. A neurological examination is recommended because this code has been associated with organic brain disease.

136

Patients with a 136 code tend to develop gastrointestinal problems, headaches, or both in response to stress and to be hypersensitive to criticism and demands. They are egocentric, narcissistic, and quick to express their anger and have little insight into how others see them. Their suspiciousness and anger is more pronounced as Scale 6 scores become more elevated.

138

Patients with a 138 code often have bizarre symptoms and strange ideas and beliefs often centering around religion and sex. Conversion disorders may be present, as may borderline or psychotic features. This profile has appeared among heterosexual women with a history of sexual abuse.

A diagnosis associated with schizophrenia is often seen in patients with this code type.

139

Patients with a 139 code exhibit an overreliance on physical symptoms, report numerous somatic complaints, are whiny and complaining, and handle hostile feelings by making others around them feel miserable. They have a cynical and defeatist view toward treatment. Additionally, they have a demanding and egocentric personality; are self-indulgent, tense, and restless; have a low frustration tolerance; are irritable; and are prone to emotional outbursts and temper tantrums. Their interpersonal relationships are characterized by attempts at dominance, either directly or through the elicitation of sympathy through their physical complaints. As such, their relationships are often stormy and divorce is frequent. They are guileful and deceitful and can manipulate to the point of arousing the ire of those closest to them. These patients are also emotionally labile and have temper tantrums.

This profile has appeared among heterosexual women with a history of sexual abuse.

Diagnoses associated with this code include somatoform disorder, personality disorders, and organic brain dysfunction.

148

The 148 code profile has appeared among heterosexual women with a history of sexual abuse.

178

The 178 code profile has appeared among heterosexual women with a history of sexual abuse.

234

Patients with a 234 code experience agitation, dysphoria, pessimism, and depression. They tend to be impulsive, immature, and self-centered and present with many familial and social maladjustments. Antisocial behavior is common.

246

Patients with a 246 code feel depressed, helpless, agitated, dysphoric, pessimistic, negative, and inadequate and cope poorly with stress. They are immature, restless, sensitive, hostile, jealous, and suspicious; feel they have been treated unfairly; and may act out in suicidal gestures, depending on the perniciousness of their misperceptions. They may express guilt, but it is short lived. Their main defenses include projection, rationalization, and acting out. They have many antisocial traits, including problems with impulse control, egocentricity, irritability, excitability, argumentativeness, and general rebelliousness. They seem to have strong dependency needs that are denied. Although they are essentially insecure, they do not recognize this. They often have strong a sense of entitlement. The code type has been found in a sample of cocaine abusers.

Diagnoses associated with this code include some form of personality disorder (antisocial, passive-aggressive, paranoid) and some form of psychosis.

247

Patients with a 247 code tend to report anxiety and depression and are tense, fearful, pessimistic, dissatisfied, and unhappy with life. They tend to overreact, cry easily, and feel weak and drained. Their mood is dominated by anxious thoughts and feelings of inadequacy. They tend to ruminate and have obsessional thoughts (check the OBS content scale). They have intense dependency needs and would like to be taken care of. However, these patients internalize their anger and resentment about not having their needs fulfilled, thereby adding to their depression. They are often unable to express angry feelings toward family and significant others. They suffer from basic insecurity and have unresolved needs for attention and exaggerated needs for affection. They appear very emotionally dependent and passive-aggressive but are erratic and unpredictable. They overreact to minor problems and treat everything as an emergency. They chronically ruminate over their situational distress and usually express their resentment in passive-aggressive ways.

Diagnoses associated with this code type include substance use disorders, passive-aggressive personality disorder, antisocial personality disorder, and some form of depression.

248

Patients with a 248 code tend to be erratic, agitated, distressed, and unpredictable, having poor ego controls. They are angry, resentful, argumentative, hostile, moody, and distrustful and may have ideas of reference and feel alienated. They are immature, self-centered, pessimistic, and restless and cope poorly with stress. They have long-standing and severe adjustment difficulties, perhaps because they are suspicious of other people, fear emotional involvement, and hence avoid close interpersonal relationships. They have a high rate of sexual maladjustment, including sexual offenses with children and adults. Many have unfulfilled needs for affection and are severely maladjusted. These patients tend to deteriorate under stress and become psychotic. Some of these descriptors are akin to a passive-aggressive (negativistic) personality disorder as well to paranoid traits. These patients act out in antisocial ways and use rationalization, projection, and acting out as their main defenses. Suicide ideation and attempts, or both, have been reported for patients with this code type (refer to MMPI-2 items 150, 506, 520, and 524).

In an offender population, inmates with this code experienced parental dominance and rejection and perceived they lacked affection during childhood.

This code has appeared among lesbian and heterosexual women with a history of sexual abuse. Women who reported only sexual abuse had a code type of 248, women who reported only physical abuse had a code type of 284, and women who reported both physical and sexual abuse had a code type of 428. The code 248 profile is also common among mothers of child psychiatry patients.

If the code is 284, then schizoid traits predominate the clinical picture. These include feelings of alienation, strange and bizarre thoughts, general psychosocial maladjustment, and loss of impulse control, including anger and rebelliousness.

Diagnoses associated with this code type include borderline personality disorder, schizophrenia, and a personality disorder (antisocial/ narcissistic).

249

Patients with a 249 code are self-centered, immature, and impulsive and have many psychopathic character traits. They are likely to have family, social, and legal problems, which may be a source of distress, because they report some dysphoria, pessimism, and depression. These patients also tend to have substance abuse problems.

The most probable diagnosis is antisocial personality disorder.

258

Patients with a 258 code tend to be tense, depressed, lethargic, and apathetic—even anhednoic. Life for them is a drudgery. They tend to be withdrawn, feel unworthy, and function at a very low level. They are often passive and compliant in interpersonal relationships, and many have problems expressing anger. If married, they usually are dissatisfied in their marriage, mostly because they feel insecure in relationships and have many psychosocial skill deficits. Suicide ideation is a possibility. These patients probably have an affective disorder, so thought disorder needs to be ruled out.

268

The 268 code profile has appeared among both heterosexual women with a history of sexual abuse and those without such a history.

273

Patients with a 273 code have a history of significant stress and show patterns of clinging dependency. They appear helpless, docile, and passive and tend to relate in a manner that pulls for therapeutic rescue. Depression and anxiety are the most prominent affects; these patients expect others to take care of them.

274

Patients who score high for code 274 present primarily with anxiety and chronic depression symptoms; feel inadequate, unworthy, and guilty; and appear dependent on others. They may have problems with alcohol but do not admit they are dependent. This code type has been found in a group of agoraphobics with panic attacks.

278

The code 278 profile appears more often in psychiatric settings. These patients appear anxious and fearful and have strong dependency conflicts. They tend to lead schizoid lifestyles and experience a great deal of emotional distress. They feel fearful and guilty. Depression, despair, and hopelessness are common, along with suicide ideation, which is often verbalized to others. They feel fatigued, inadequate, and inferior; lack social skills; and tend to be shy, withdrawn, introverted, and socially isolated. They usually have histories of long-standing interpersonal problems. They have difficulty expressing hostile feelings until their defenses fail. Significant mental symptoms usually accompany this profile type. These patients have flat affect, ruminate, report a loss of interest, have ideas of reference and magical thinking, are socially impaired, report peculiar experiences, and are prone to acute psychotic episodes. Hallucinations and thought disorders are likely. Their ruminations and obsessions may be a defense against psychotic processes. They have a chaotic and disorganized lifestyle and are often personally isolated, having few friends. Obsessional thinking predominates in their life. Many feel their parents were emotionally rejecting, and they often report sexual problems and a history of poor heterosexual relationships.

Men at a college counseling center who produced this code were described as depressed and emotionally flat, with bizarre, tangential, or disrupted thought processes. They complained of depression and difficulty concentrating and reported much suicidal ideation but had not made any suicide attempts (see MMPI-2 items 150, 506, 520, and 524). They described themselves as having gone through childhood as loners and had few sexual relationships. They were considered latent schizophrenics. Many were not overtly psychotic. Several were concerned about homosexual thoughts.

College women with this code had similar symptoms and traits. Additionally, they reported family histories of psychological difficulties in near relatives and were more often considered neurotic rather than psychotic. They also had much suicidal ideation, but many had also made an actual past attempt.

Diagnoses associated with this code type include borderline personality disorder, schizotypal personality disorder, and some form of psychosis, usually schizophrenia. Schizotypal personality disorder becomes more likely when the code type is 287.

348

The code 348 profile has appeared among heterosexual women without a history of sexual abuse.

349

Patients with a 349 code have many psychopathic traits, including impulsivity, immaturity, self-centeredness, irresponsibility, and undependability. They also show features of underlying dependency that most patients with antisocial characters do not display. They have strong needs for attention and are probably very gregarious and socially outgoing, but they are also manipulative and have superficial relationships. These patients are extremely prone to act out.

354

Patients with a 354 code act in passive-aggressive ways in an attempt to control socially unacceptable impulses, including fears of homosexuality. They frequently present with sexual maladjustment and are pessimistic and anxious. They are also self-centered, impulsive, immature, attention seeking, and insecure in their gender role. They tend to have marital, family, and social problems.

456

Men with a 456 code have many psychopathic traits and are chronically maladjusted. They are immature, self-centered, hedonistic, irresponsible, and manipulative. However, they seem to be insecure in their masculine role and may present in one of two ways: (1) as excessively macho, as if to overdramatize their masculinity, or (2) as passive, effeminate men in behavior and dress who act very dependent on others and act out when they do not get their way. Also, these patients are unduly suspicious, resentful, and rigid in thinking and behavior. They are prone to develop rage reactions, in part because of low defenses and also because of their malevolent projections and unreasonable suspiciousness, as they blame others for their personal troubles.

457

Men with a 457 code appear to be quite insecure in a male gender role and may assume a feminine demeanor or mannerisms, including dependency, passivity, and homosexuality. They are impulsive, act out, are irresponsible, and tend toward promiscuity but dislike confrontations and report much tension, anxiety, and fatigue and many worries. These patients are chronically maladjusted and find it difficult to successfully manage their daily affairs. They are narcissistic and alienate others with their self-centeredness and their manipulativeness.

459

Men with a 459 code are psychologically maladjusted and have many undesirable personality traits of an antisocial variety, including irresponsibility, lack of empathy, manipulativeness, hedonism, self-centeredness, and acting-out tendencies. They appear to have problems with the traditional gender role and may have adopted a feminine identification in manner and dress, up to and including homosexuality. They dislike confrontation and are more passive except when stressed and frustrated, at which time they become agitated, restless, grandiose, and hyperactive. They can exploit interpersonal relations, and this tends to drive others away. They also tend to be promiscuous.

462

Patients with a 462 code seem absorbed in their own psychological distress. They appear quite agitated and very dramatically seek attention and sympathy. They tend to manipulate and externalize blame. They have issues with authority and actively resist any signs of dependency. Sexual and marital maladjustments are likely. When their demands for attention are unmet, they sulk and get depressed. They feel guilty after they express their feelings.

463

Patients with a 463 code are highly manipulative and demand a great deal of attention. They are overly sensitive to rejection and have underlying dependency needs. They make excessive demands on people and are extremely sensitive to perceived slights and to signs of rejection or inattention. They may use physical complaints to secure the attention they need. When this is not successful, they may act out to get attention.

468

The 468 code usually suggests a severe emotional disorder. These patients are emotionally maladjusted, get upset easily, are guarded, feel alienated, and often are exposed to acute situational crises. They tend to be overly suspicious, angry, overly sensitive, and evasive. They show a variety of paranoid symptoms and traits and ruminate about real or imagined injustices. Their anger is quickly rationalized with self-justifications. They show poor judgment, severe relationship difficulties, sexual maladjustment, and may report suicidal ideation.

This profile appeared in a group of battered women.

469

Patients with a 469 code have many psychopathic personality traits, including self-centeredness, impulsivity, and social and familial maladjustments. They also feel hostile and jealous, believe they have been treated unfairly, and are suspicious and overly sensitive, with many malevolent projections. Many try to control their perceived agitation through passive-aggressive means. However, some have acted out precipitously and violently, such that this code type is considered one that puts a person at risk of dangerous acting out. Some, however, make superficial suicidal gestures and attempts to gain attention from others. They are chronically maladjusted, despite appearing self-confident, and present airs of exaggerated self-importance.

478

Men with a 478 code appear, dramatic, emotional, and erratic. They are chronically insecure, feel socially alienated, and exhibit acting-out behaviors. They show poor judgment, tend to manipulate others, lack empathy, and resent authority. They have serious concerns over issues of masculinity and feel inadequate. They have deficient social skills, avoid close relationships, and tend to be socially withdrawn. They are quite anxious.

Diagnoses associated with this code type include borderline personality disorder and substance use disorders. This profile has also appeared among incestuous fathers.

489

Patients with a code 489 profile have severe characterological problems associated with impulsivity, irresponsibility, acting-out tendencies, immaturity, poor judgment, hostility toward authority figures, and difficulty in adhering to social norms; are undersocialized; and have impaired empathic abilities. They have mostly psychopathic traits with poor behavioral controls and usually have histories involving delinquency and antisocial behavior. Although some may appear charismatic, they have tendencies to violence. They are emotionally unstable, argumentative, and unpredictable. They are likely to be seen by others as odd.

This profile has been found in male child abusers.

496

Patients with a 496 code have many psychopathic personality traits, including impulsivity, hedonism, egocentricity, grandiosity, irritability, and a nomadic restlessness, and are prone to explode when stressed or frustrated. They are likely to have problems with social, familial, and legal issues, as well as vocational maladjustments. They are likely to exploit interpersonal relationships, and those who know them best will attest to their cunning and insincere behaviors. These patients avoid deep emotional attachments and use others for personal gain. They also are very suspicious and overly sensitive, have many malevolent projections, and are very excitable and irascible. Projection and acting out are used as main defenses. They feel they have been wronged or slighted and attack those who are the objects of their projections. Assaults and homicidal behaviors should be ruled out.

498

Patients with a 498 code are chronically maladjusted. They show a mixture of psychopathic personality traits, such as irresponsibility, hedonism, impulsivity, self-centeredness, and manipulativeness, yet they also have tendencies to be withdrawn, aloof, and unpredictable. They are quite insecure in interpersonal relationships and tend to avoid deep emotional attachments. Most relationships are used to satisfy their own needs. Their thinking may be tangential and confused and their behavior is generally erratic. They become emotionally upset when stressed or when they do not get their way. These patients are at risk for substance abuse.

678

Patients with a 678 code are usually experiencing a psychotic disorder characterized by florid psychotic processes, personality decompensation, and social withdrawal. They may become belligerent and act out aggressively and may even engage in assaultive behavior motivated by delusions. They are quite confused, do not separate fantasy from reality, and have either flat or hostile affect. Their thinking is confused and bizarre and manifested by a thought disorder. They feel others either do not understand them or are trying to control them. Their acting out aggressively is a preemptive strike taken before others inflict harm on them. Chronic psychological adjustment problems are associated with this code.

In forensic settings, this is a frequently occurring code, irrespective of gender and psychiatric diagnosis. This profile has appeared among heterosexual women with a history of sexual abuse.

A psychotic diagnosis usually is associated with this code.

689

The code 689 profile has appeared among heterosexual women without a history of sexual abuse.

Interpreting MMPI-2 Code Types: Four-Point Codes

Four-point codes are MMPI-2 profiles with scores for four clinical scales of T > 65 and with those for the other clinical scales of T < 65. There are only a few four-point codes that have any empirical base.

1234

Patients with a 1234 code have chronic psychological adjustment problems and histories of acting-out behaviors, including outbursts of anger often precipitated by alcohol abuse or alcoholism. These patients are immature, dependent, easily frustrated, quite irritable, demanding, and irresponsible. They have many somatic complaints, but these could be explained by chronic drinking. They show brief expressions of guilt when sober, but sobriety lasts for only a short period. They can become physically abusive, particularly when intoxicated. They are likely to have vocational, interpersonal, marital, and financial troubles. This profile corresponds closely to the character style described by psychoanalysts as the orally fixated character.

Diagnoses associated with this profile almost always includes some type of alcohol abuse or alcohol dependence diagnosis and passive-aggressive personality disorder.

1237

Refer to the interpretation for 123 code type (see page 76). In addition to this, these patients are anxious, tense, fearful, feel inadequate, are dependent in interpersonal relations, and unable to cope with daily stress. Men with this code are often alcoholic and have married stronger women to perpetuate their dependent role.

2874

The code 2874 profile has been found among patients with severe alcoholism, including marked impairment over controlling alcohol intake, increased alcohol tolerance, and repeated alcohol withdrawal. These patient demonstrate depression, alienation, anxiety impulsiveness, and much psychological turmoil. If a patient does not manifest these late-stage alcoholism symptoms, then this profile may be a marker for an early identification for an individual at risk to possibly develop one of the more severe forms of alcoholism.

References

Allen, J. P. (1991). Personality correlates of the MacAndrew Alcoholism Scale: A review of the literature. *Psychology of Addictive Behavior, 5*, 59–65.

Allen, J. P., Faden, V. B., Miller, A., & Rawlings, R. (1991). Personality correlates of chemically dependent patients scoring high versus low on the MacAndrew Scale. *Psychological Assessment, 3*, 273–276.

Anderson, W. P., & Holcomb, W. R. (1983). Accused murderers: Five MMPI personality types. *Journal of Clinical Psychology, 39*, 761–768.

Anderson, W. P., & Kunce, J. T. (1984). Diagnosic implications of markedly elevated MMPI Sc scale scores for nonhospitalized clients. *Journal of Clinical Psychology, 40*, 925–930.

Arbisi, P. A., & Ben-Porath, Y. S. (1995). An MMPI-2 Infrequent Response Scale for use with psychopathological populations: The Infrequency-Psychopathology Scale F(p). *Psychological Assessment, 7*, 424–431.

Archer, R. P., Griffin, R., & Aiduk, R. (1995). MMPI-2 clinical correlates for ten common codes. *Journal of Personality Assessment, 65*, 391–407.

Baer, R. A., Wetter, M. W., & Berry, D. T. (1992). Detection of underreporting of psychopathology on the MMPI: A meta-analysis. *Clinical Psychology Review, 12*, 509–524.

Balogh, D. W., Merritt, R. D., Lennington, L., Fine, M., & Wood, J. (1993). Variants of the 2–7–8 code type: Schizotypal correlates of high point 2, 7, or 8. *Journal of Personality Assessment, 61*, 474–488.

Bathhurst, K. D., Gottfried, A. W., & Gottfried, A. E. (1997). Normative data for the MMPI-2 in child custody litigation. *Psychological Assessment, 9*, 205–211.

Bayer, M. B., Bonta, J. L., & Motiuk, L. L. (1985). The Pd subscales: An empirical evaluation. *Journal of Clinical Psychology, 41*, 780–788.

Bell-Pringle, V. J., Pate, J. L., & Braun, R. C. (1997). Assessment of borderline personality disorder with the MMPI-2 and the Personality Assessment Inventory. *Assessment, 4*, 131–139.

Ben-Porath, Y. S. (1996). Assessing coping styles with the MMPI-2. *Topics in MMPI-2 Interpretation* (No. 13). Minneapolis: MMPI Workshops.

Berry, D. T., Baer, R. A., & Harris, M. (1991). Detection of malingering in the MMPI: A meta-analysis. *Clinical Psychology Review, 11*, 585–598.

Brehms, C., & Lloyd, P. (1995). Validation of the MMPI-2 Low Self-Esteem content scale. *Journal of Personality Assessment, 65*, 550–556.

Brown, R. A., & Goodstein, L. D. (1962). Adjective Check List correlates of extreme scores on the MMPI Depression scale. *Journal of Clinical Psychology, 18*, 477–481.

Butcher, J. N. (1990). *The MMPI-2 in psychological treatment*. New York: Oxford University Press.

Butcher, J. N., Dahlstrom, W. G., Graham, J. R., Tellegen, A., & Kaemmer, B. (1989). *MMPI-2: Minnesota Multiphasic Personality Inventory-2: Manual for administration and scoring*. Minneapolis: University of Minnesota Press.

Butcher, J. N., Graham, J. R., Williams, C. L., & Ben-Porath, Y. S. (1989). *Development and use of the MMPI-2 content scales*. Minneapolis: University of Minnesota Press.

Butcher, J. N., & Han, K. (1995). Development of an MMPI-2 scale to assess the presentation of self in a superlative manner: The S scale. In J. N. Butcher & C. D. Spielberger (Eds.), *Advances in personality assessment* (Vol. 20, pp. 25–50). Hillsdale, NJ: Lawrence Erlbaum Associates.

Butcher, J. N., & Williams, C. L. (1992). *Essentials of MMPI-2 and MMPI-A interpretation*. Minneapolis: University of Minnesota Press.

Caldwell, A. B. (1988). *MMPI supplemental scale manual*. Los Angeles: Caldwell Report.

Caron, G. R., & Archer, R. P. (1997). MMPI and Rorschach characteristics of individuals approved for gender reassignment surgery. *Assessment, 4*, 229–241.

Castlebury, F. D., & Durham, T. W. (1997). The MMPI-2 GM and GF scales as measures of psychological well-being. *Journal of Clinical Psychology, 53*, 879–893.

Clark, M. E. (1994). Interpretive limitations of the MMPI-2 Anger and Cynicism scales. *Journal of Personality Assessment, 63*, 89–96.

Clark, M. E. (1996). MMPI-2 Negative Treatment Indicator content and content component scales: Clinical correlates and outcome prediction for men with chronic pain. *Psychological Assessment, 8*, 32–38.

Craig, R. J.(1984a). A comparison of MMPI profiles of heroin addicts based on multiple methods of classification. *Journal of Personality Assessment, 48*, 115–121.

Craig, R. J. (1984b). MMPI substance abuse scales on drug addicts with and without concurrent alcoholism. *Journal of Personality Assessment, 48*, 495–499.

Craig, R. J. (1988). Psychological functioning of cocaine free-basers derived from objective psychological tests. *Journal of Clinical Psychology, 44*, 599–606.

Craig, R. J., & Olson, R. (1990). MMPI comparisons of cocaine abusers and heroin addicts. *Journal of Clinical Psychology, 46*, 230–237.

Craig, R. J., & Olson, R. (1990). MMPI characteristics of drug abusers with and without histories of suicide attempts. *Journal of Personality Assessment, 55*, 717–728.

Craig, R. J., & Olson, R. (1992). MMPI subtypes for cocaine abusers. *American Journal of Drug and Alcohol Abuse, 18*, 197–205.

Dahlstrom, W. G. (1992). Comparability of two-point high-point code patterns from original MMPI norms to MMPI-2 norms for the restandardization sample. *Journal of Personality Assessment, 59,* 153–164.

Dubinsky, S., Gamble, D. J., & Rogers, M. L. (1985). A literature review of subtle-obvious items on the MMPI. *Journal of Personality Assessment, 49,* 62–68.

Duckworth, J. C., & Anderson, W. P. (1995). *MMPI and MMPI-2: Interpretation manual for counselors and clinicians* (4th ed.). Bristol, PA: Accelerated Development.

Engels, M. L., Mosian, D., & Harris, R. (1994). MMPI indices of childhood trauma among 110 female outpatients. *Journal of Personality Assessment, 63,* 135–147.

Erickson, W. D., Luxenberg, M. G., Walbek, N. H., & Seely, R. K. (1987). Frequency of MMPI two-point code types among sex offenders. *Journal of Consulting and Clinical Psychology, 55,* 566–570.

Friedman, A. F., Webb, J. T., & Lewak, R. (1989). *Psychological assessment with the MMPI.* Hillsdale, NJ: Lawrence Erlbaum Associates.

Gartner, J., Hunt, S. W., & Gartner, A. (1989). Psychological test signs of borderline personality disorder: A review of the empirical literature. *Journal of Personality Assessment, 57,* 46–51.

Gilberstadt, H. (1969). *Comprehensive MMPI code book for males.* Minneapolis: Veterans Administration.

Gilberstadt, H., & Duker, J. (1965). *A handbook for clinical and actuarial MMPI interpretation.* Philadelphia: W.B. Saunders.

Goldwater, L., & Duffy, J. F. (1990). Use of the MMPI to uncover histories of childhood abuse in adult female psychiatric patients. *Journal of Clinical Psychology, 46,* 392–398.

Gottesman, I. I., & Prescott, C. A. (1989). Abuses of the MacAndrew MMPI Alcoholism Scale: A critical review. *Clinical Psychology Review, 9,* 223–242.

Graham, J. R. (1978). Review of Minnesota Multiphasic Personality Inventory Special scales. In P. McReynolds (Ed.), *Advances in psychological assessment* (Vol. 4, pp. 11–55). San Francisco: Jossey-Bass.

Graham, J. (1993). *MMPI-2: Assessing personality and psychopathology* (2nd ed). New York: Oxford University Press.

Graham, J. R., Ben-Porath, Y. S., & McNulty, J. L. (1997). Empirical correlates of low scores on MMPI-2 scales in an outpatient mental health setting. *Psychological Assessment, 9,* 386–391.

Graham, J. R., & Strenger, V. E. (1988). MMPI characteristics of alcoholics: A review. *Journal of Consulting and Clinical Psychology, 56,* 197–205.

Greene, R. L. (1991). *The MMPI-2/MMPI: An interpretive manual.* Boston: Allyn & Bacon.

Griffith, P. L., Myers, R. W., Cusick, G. M., & Tankersley, M. J. (1997). MMPI-2 profiles of women differing in sexual abuse history and sexual orientation. *Journal of Clinical Psychology 53,* 791–800.

Hall, G. C., Graham, J. R., & Shepherd, J. B. (1991). Three methods of developing MMPI taxonomies of sexual offenders. *Journal of Personality Assessment, 56,* 2–13.

Hall, G. C., Shepherd, J. B., & Mudrak, P. (1992). MMPI taxonomies of child sexual and nonsexual offenders: A cross-validation and extension. *Journal of Personality Assessment, 58,* 1127–1137.

Hathaway, S. R., & McKinley, J. C. (1943). *The Minnesota Multiphasic Personality Inventory.* New York: Psychological Corporation.

Hodo, G. L., & Fowler, R. D. (1976). Frequency of MMPI two-point codes in a large alcoholic sample. *Journal of Clinical Psychology, 32,* 487–489.

Kalichman, S. C. (1988a). Empirically derived MMPI profile subgroups of incarcerated homicide offenders. *Journal of Clinical Psychology, 44,* 733–738.

Kalichman, S. (1988b). MMPI profiles of women and men convicted of domestic homicide. *Journal of Clinical Psychology, 44,* 847–853.

Keane, S. P., & Gibbs, M. (1980). Construct validation of the Sc scale of the MMPI. *Journal of Clinical Psychology, 36,* 152–158.

Keiller, S. W., & Graham, J. R. (1993). The meaning of low scores on MMPI-2 clinical scales for normal subjects. *Journal of Personality Assessment 61,* 211–223.

Kelley, C. K., & King, G. D. (1979). Behavioral correlates of the 2–7–8 MMPI profile type in students at a university mental health center. *Journal of Consulting and Clinical Psychology, 47,* 679–685.

Kelley, C. K., & King, G. D. (1980). Two- and three-point classification of MMPI profiles in which scales 2, 7, and 8, are the highest elevations. *Journal of Personality Assessment, 44,* 25–33.

Khan, F. I., Welch, T. L., & Zillmer, E. A. (1993). MMPI-2 profiles of battered women in transition. *Journal of Personality Assessment, 60,* 100–111.

King, G. D., & Kelley, C. K. (1977). MMPI behavioral correlates of Spike-5 and two-point code types with Scale 5 as one elevation. *Journal of Clinical Psychology, 53,* 180–185.

Kirkland, K. D. & Rauer, C. A. (1982). MMPI traits of incestuous fathers. *Journal of Clinical Psychology, 38,* 645–649.

Kunce, J., & Anderson, W. (1976). Normalizing the MMPI. *Journal of Clinical Psychology, 32,* 776–780.

Levitt, E. E. (1989). *The clinical application of MMPI special scales.* Hillsdale, NJ: Lawrence Erlbaum Associates.

Leonard, S. T., & Dorfman, W. I. (1996). The role of the Minnesota Multiphasic Personality Inventory in the assessment of the sexual dysfunctions: A review. *Clinical Psychology Review, 16,* 317–335.

Levenson, M. R., Aldwin, C. M., Butcher, J. N., DeLabry, L., Wirkman-Daniels, K., & Bosse, R. (1990). *Journal of Studies on Alcohol, 51,* 457–462.

Lewak, R. W., Marks, P. A., & Nelson, G. E. (1990). *Therapist's guide to the MMPI and MMPI-2: Providing feedback and treatment.* Muncie, IN: Accelerated Development.

Lilienfeld, S. O. (1996). The MMPI-2 Antisocial Practices content scale: Construct validity and comparison with the psychopathic deviate scale. *Psychological Assessment, 8,* 281–293.

Long, K. A., & Graham, J. R. (1991). The Masculinity-Femininity scale of the MMPI-2: Is it useful with normal men? *Journal of Personality Assessment, 57,* 46–51.

MacAndrew, C. (1981). What the MAC scale tells us about men alcoholics: An interpretive review. *Journal of Studies on Alcohol, 42,* 604–625.

Marks, P. A., Seeman. W., & Haller, D. L. (1974). *The actuarial use of the MMPI with adolescents and adults*. New York: Oxford University Press.

McFall, M. E., Moore, J. E., Kivlahan, D. R., & Capestany, F. (1988). Differences between psychotic and non-psychotic patients on content dimensions of the MMPI Sc scale. *Journal of Nervous and Mental Disease, 176,* 732–736.

McGrath, R. E., & O'Malley, W. B. (1986). The assessment of denial and physical complaints: The validity of the Hy scale and associated MMPI signs. *Journal of Clinical Psychology, 42,* 754–760.

Morey, L. C., Roberts, W. R., & Penk, W. (1987). MMPI alcoholic subtypes: Replicability and validity of the 2-8-7-4 subtype. *Journal of Abnormal Psychology, 96,* 164–166.

O'Sullivan, M. J., & Jemelka, R. P. (1993). The 3-4/4-3 MMPI code type in an offender population: An update on levels of hostility and violence. *Psychological Assessment, 5,* 493–498.

Parmer, J. C. (1991). Bulimia and object relations: MMPI and Rorschach variables. *Journal of Personality Assessment, 56,* 266–276.

Peterson, C. D., & Dahlstrom, W. G. (1992). The derivation of gender-role scales GM and GF for MMPI-2 and their relationship to Scale 5 (Mf). *Journal of Personality Assessment, 59,* 486–499.

Post, R. D., Clopton, J. R., Keefer, G., Rosenberg, D., Blyth, L. S., & Stein, M. (1986). MMPI predictors of mania among psychiatric inpatients. *Journal of Personality Assessment, 50,* 248–256.

Preng, K. W., & Clopton, J. R. (1986). The MacAndrew Scale: Clinical application and theoretical issues. *Journal of Studies on Alcohol, 47,* 228–232.

Pryor, T., & Wiederman, M. W. (1996). Use of the MMPI-2 in the outpatient assessment of women with Anorexia Nervosa or Bulimia Nervosa. *Journal of Personality Assessment, 66,* 363–373.

Raskin, R., & Novacek, J. (1989). An MMPI description of the narcissistic personality. *Journal of Personality Assessment, 53,* 66–80.

Rathvan, N., & Holmstrom, R. W. (1996). An MMPI-2 portrait of narcissism. *Journal of Personality Assessment, 66,* 1–19.

Root, M. P., & Friedrich, W. N. (1989). MMPI code-types and heterogeneity in a bulimic sample. *Psychotherapy in Private Practice, 7,* 97–113.

Shretlen, D. J. (1988). The use of psychological tests to identify malingered symptoms of mental disorder. *Clinical Psychology Review, 8,* 451–476.

Sieber, K. O., & Meyers, L. S. (1992). Validation of the MMPI-2 Social Introversion subscales. *Psychological Assessment, 4,* 185–189.

Streit, K., Greene, R. L., Cogan, R., & Davis, H. G. (1993). Clinical correlates of MMPI depression scales. *Journal of Personality Assessment, 60,* 390–396.

Svanum, S., & Ehrmann, L. C. (1992). Alcoholic subtypes and the MacAndrew Alcoholism Scale. *Journal of Personality Assessment, 58,* 411–422.

Tanner, B. A. (1990). Composite descriptors associated with rare MMPI two-point code types: Codes that involve Scale 5. *Journal of Clinical Psychology, 46,* 425–431.

Timbrook, R. E., Graham, J. R., Keiller, S. W., & Watts, D. (1993). Comparison of the Weiner-Harmon Subtle-Obvious Scales and the standard validity scales in detecting valid and invalid MMPI-2 profiles. *Psychological Assessment, 5,* 53–61.

Todd, A. I., & Gynther, M. D. (1988). Have MMPI mf scale correlates changed in the past 30 years? *Journal of Clinical Psychology, 44,* 505–510.

Trimboli, F., & Kilgore, R. (1983). A psychodynamic approach to MMPI interpretation. *Journal of Personality Assessment 47,* 614–626.

Vincent, K. R., Castillo, I., Hauser, R. I., Stuart, H. J., Zapata, J. A., Cohn, C. K., & O'Shanick, G. J. (1983). MMPI code types and DSM-III diagnoses. *Journal of Clinical Psychology, 39,* 829–842.

Walters, G. D. (1983). The MMPI and schizophrenia: A review. *Schizophrenia Bulletin, 9,* 226–246.

Walters, G. D., & Greene, R. (1983). Factor structure of the Overcontrolled-Hostility scale of the MMPI. *Journal of Clinical Psychology, 39,* 560–562.

Walters, G. D., Greene, R. L., & Solomon, G. S. (1982). Empirical correlates of the Overcontrolled-Hostility Scale and the MMPI 4-3 high-point pair. *Journal of Consulting and Clinical Psychology, 50,* 213–218.

Ward, L. C., & Dillon, E. A. (1990). Psychiatric symptom correlates of the Minnesota Multiphasic Personality Inventory (MMPI) Masculinity-Femininity scale. *Psychological Assessment, 2,* 286–288.

Wong, M. R. (1984). MMPI Scale Five: Its meaning, or lack thereof. *Journal of Personality Assessment, 48,* 279–284.

Wright, P., Nussbaum, D., Lynett, E., & Buis, T. (1997). Forensic MMPI-2 profiles: Normative limitations impose interpretive restrictions with both males and females. *American Journal of Forensic Psychology, 15,* 19–37.

Yanagida, E. H., & Ching, J. W. (1993). MMPI profiles of child abusers. *Journal of Clinical Psychology, 49,* 569–576.

CHAPTER 2

Millon Clinical Multiaxial Inventory–III[1]

Background and History

IN 1980 the American Psychiatric Association revised its diagnostic nomenclature and adopted a multiaxial system. AXIS II was assigned personality disorders. This was an important conceptual development, because the idea is that one cannot fully understand a clinical syndrome unless one takes into consideration the personality in which it is embedded. Since the introduction of AXIS II, there has been a spate of structured psychiatric interviews and psychological inventories to use in diagnosing personality disorders. Among these, the Millon Clinical Multiaxial Inventory (MCMI), as revised, has become the most popular and the most researched inventory for the assessment of personality disorders.

The MCMI, as revised, emanated from Millon's biopsychosocial and bioevolutionary theory of personality development. It was not meant to be congruent with various official diagnostic classification systems. However, over time, revisions of the MCMI have

---

[1] Some of the material in this section is an expanded version of material from *Psychological Assessment with the Millon Clinical Multiaxial Inventory (II): An Interpretive Guide* and from *MCMI II/III Interpretive System,* both by Robert J. Craig, Ph.D., copyright 1993 by Psychological Assessment Resources, Inc., and reproduced by special permission of the publisher, Psychological Assessment Resources, Inc., 16204 North Florida Avenue, Lutx, Florida 33549. Further reproduction is prohibited without permission of Psychological Assessment Resources, Inc.

become closely aligned with the *Diagnostic and Statistical Manual of Mental Disorders* (fourth edition, or *DSM-IV*), although there are still disorders of personality (e.g., aggressive/sadistic and self-defeating) that are not a part of the *DSM-IV* Also, *DSM-IV* now includes, in the appendix, a passive-aggressive (negativistic) personality disorder that brings the definition of this disorder more in line with the way Millon has historically conceptualized it, so, at its heart, the MCMI-III is a test for personality disorders and a few major clinical syndromes.

Test Development

Millon used a three-step, state-of-the-art test development methodology to create and revise the MCMI. For step 1, the *substantive validity* phase, Millon created an item pool that was generated according to his theoretical model of personality development. These items were then submitted to a group of experts who were familiar with his theoretical model and asked them to rate each item in terms of its degree of correspondence and fit to this model. Items that were poorly related to the model were deleted from further consideration. Other items were reduced on rational grounds. The *structural validity* of the test was then established by assessing item endorsement patterns, internal consistency estimates, scale intercorrelations, temporal stability, and factor analysis. Finally, the test was submitted for *external validity* by assessing its convergent and discriminant validity. For convergent validity, the MCMI was correlated with measures of similar constructs using other tests. For discriminant validity, the MCMI was correlated with measures that should have no real relationship with MCMI scales. When all this information had been ascertained, only then was the test published and available to consumers.

Millon has revised the MCMI whenever *DSM* has been revised. The current version, MCMI-III, is relatively congruent with *DSM-IV*. This revised test now includes new scales for depressive personality disorder and for posttraumatic stress disorder. A few critical items are included in the test pertaining to eating disorders and childhood abuse but are not scored on any scale.

Base Rate Scores

Millon has persuasively argued that personality disorders are not normally distributed in the general population. In fact, the prevalence of these disorders rarely exceeds 3% to 5% and most occur at rates of only 1% to 2%. Therefore, it is inappropriate to convert raw scores of a distribution that is normally distributed, so Millon created the base rate (BR) score to reflect the skewed nature of the distribution in the population. A BR > 84 indicates that point in the distribution of scores at which the patient had all the characteristics that define the disorder at a diagnostic level. BR scores between 75 and 84 indicate the presence of traits associated with the disorder but below the diagnostic level. A BR of 60 is the mean BR score of everyone in the standardization sample, whereas a BR of 35 is the average score of people in nonclinical populations who participated in the test development phase. BR scores < 75, as a general rule, are not considered diagnostically significant and hence are not interpreted.

Interpreting the MCMI-III

MODIFIER (VALIDITY) INDEX

Validity Index

The Validity Index (VI) consists of three items of an improbable nature that, if endorsed as true, suggest invalidity. Although Millon suggests that the profile is invalid if two or more of these items are endorsed as true, I recommend not interpreting the profile even if one of the items is marked true. The examiner needs to visually inspect the MCMI-III test answer sheet for items 65, 110, and 157 to see if any one is marked as true. The VI should be sensitive to random responding, confusion, or reading disorders.

Disclosure (Scale X)

Scale X assesses whether the patient is reporting a sufficient amount of information to produce a valid profile. It functions in a way analogous to the K Scale on the Minnesota Multiphasic Personality Inventory–2 (MMPI-2). Low scores suggest defensive reporting, whereas high scores suggest an unusually open and self-revealing attitude.

- Raw score < 34; This profile cannot validly be interpreted because the patient showed a strong tendency to deny personal problems, symptoms, and negative feelings and responded to the test with a defensive response set. The patient is denying the existence of psychological problems such that the MCMI-III may not be the most appropriate test to use for this particular assessment. It is suggested that the clinician review this matter with the patient to ascertain if the patient does not in fact have any psychological difficulty or whether the patient would be willing to report more accurately the extent of current problems on repeat test administration. Often, if the clinician explains the purpose of testing and how this test will be used in the best interest of helping the patient, then a repeat testing may produce a more valid picture of current psychological functioning.
- Raw score > 178: This profile cannot validly be interpreted because the patient showed a strong tendency to endorse so many personal problems, symptoms, and negative feelings that the information in the profile cannot be considered reliable.

Desirability (Scale Y)

Scale Y assesses whether the endorsed items on the MCMI-III are essentially of a more desirable (e.g., nonpathological) nature. Although low scores are generally not significant, a BR > 74 suggests the patient is presenting him- or herself as morally virtuous with few, if any, psychological problems. Scores on Scale Y do not invalidate a profile, because adjustments are made on scales known to be affected by high or low scores on Scale Y.

Debasement (Scale Z)

Scale Z determines whether the endorsed items are placing the patient in an unfavorable light (e.g., endorsing pathological items). It functions in an analogous manner to the F Scale on the MMPI-2. Low scores on Scale Z are generally not significant, whereas a BR between 75 and 84 suggests the patient is depreciating and devaluing him- or herself, has many emotional and behavioral problems, and is unusually self-disclosing. A BR > 84 suggests particular emotional distress that may be a cry for help—the patient is responding to the items in such a way as to call attention to his or her situation. Scores on Scale Z do not invalidate the profile, as adjustments are made on scales known to be affected by elevated scores on Scale Z.

Validity Scale Configurations

- Scores low for Scales X and Y with high Scale Z scores: suggests moderate exaggeration of current emotional problems
- Scores low for Scales X and Z and high for Scale Y (giving the appearance of an arrow pointing right): suggests emphasis on looking psychologically healthy
- Scores low for Scale Y and high for Scales X and Z (giving the appearance of an arrow pointing left): suggests emphasis on looking psychologically maladjusted
- Scale Z BR > 85 and Scale Y BR < 40: suggests symptom exaggeration

ONE-POINT CODES

One-point MCMI-III codes are those in which scores for only one Clinical Personality Pattern Scale or one Severe Personality Pathology Scale are BR > 74. When BR > 84, the patient has all of the defining features that characterize the disorder and would meet the criteria for that personality disorder. When BR is between 75 and 84, the patient has most but not all of the defining features and traits of the disorder but is below the diagnostic threshold.

Schizoid (Scale 1A: Passive-Detached)

Patients scoring high on Scale 1A appear apathetic, dull, quiet, colorless, vague, aloof, and introverted. They seem lost in their surroundings, blending into the background or engaging in vague pursuits. They show limited enthusiasm for most activities, preferring a solitary life and rarely initiating conversation. They seem indifferent to social relationships and do not seek out social contact. They seem to have a low need for social involvement, appear to require little affection, and lack both warmth and emotional expression. They manifest an emotionally bland appearance with flattened affect, combined with a lack of sensitivity to their own feelings and those of others. They lack an outward expression of aggression. They are often asexual, perhaps as a result of their relationship deficits. They are quite content to be passive, detached, and distant in their relationships. They have few friends, preferring the life of a loner. The detachment is not a defense mechanism. They are comfortable this way and prefer it, at least at the conscious level. Underneath this detachment lies a rich fantasy life and excessive daydreaming. Intrapsychically, they are in a chronic dilemma: They cannot be in a relationship without fearing engulfment, but they cannot be without a relationship without feeling intense aloneness. If this patient is married or in a committed relationship, problems are likely to arise, including spousal complaints of a lack of involvement and intimacy. Others see these people as strange and spacey. Relationship deficits are likely to be serious. These patients have low self-esteem, but more often, they have difficulty expressing how they feel about themselves. Their thinking can be obscure at times, with cognitive slippage occasionally manifested in speech. Their thoughts are vague and unfocused. Depersonalization, feelings of emptiness, and identity diffusion are also part of their personality structure. These patients tend to drift through marginal aspects of society. When social demands become inescapable, they are prone to anxiety reactions, somatoform disorders, and brief reactive psychoses.

Diagnosis, BR > 84: schizoid personality disorder

Diagnosis, BR 75 to 84: personality disorder not otherwise specified (NOS), schizoid personality traits

Suggested treatment goals:

- Develop ways to experience pleasure
- Increase social participation
- Increase social relatedness
- Reduce anxiety in social situations
- Become more active

Avoidant (Scale 2A: Active-Detached)

Patients with a BR > 84 present as socially awkward, withdrawn, introverted, and self-conscious. Because they are hypersensitive to rejection and both fear and expect negative evaluations, they either try to maintain a good social appearance despite their underlying fear or withdraw from social contacts. Tension, anxiety, and anger may also be present, but all stem from the same issue—a desire for social acceptance and a fear of rejection. Most often, these patients maintain a social distance to avoid any further experience of being rejected. They are devastated by perceived signs of disapproval and tend to withdraw, thus reducing the chance to enhance relationships. This circumstance results in social isolation despite a very strong need for social relatedness. These patients can put on a pleasant appearance to mask their underlying social anxiety, but they have a pervasive belief that others will be disparaging of them. Their essential conflict is a strong desire to relate but an equally strong expectation of disapproval, depreciation, and rejection. This conflict results in keeping others at a distance and in loneliness, isolation, and continued shyness and timidity. They are at risk for social phobias.

Diagnosis, BR > 84: avoidant personality disorder

The behavior of patients with a BR between 75 and 84 is characterized by and motivated by a fear of rejection, thus leading to either a physical or emotional withdrawal in public to avoid social disapproval. Independent action may be stymied and emotions are suppressed because of insecurity. These patients feel inadequate, so they probably avoid actions that will lead to autonomy. Many such patients can hide their social anxiety and appear to be without problems. Closer scrutiny and a trusting relationship with the clinician may cause them to reduce their defensiveness and admit to their fears, since these fears are at the conscious level. Others act in a fearful, dependent, and avoidant manner such that their hesitancies and dependency are quite obvious to a casual observer.

This patient may not have all of the characteristics that define an avoidant personality disorder, but the presence of avoidant characteristics is strongly indicated in the profile.

Diagnosis: personality disorder not otherwise specified (NOS), avoidant personality traits

Suggested treatment goals:

- Reduce sensitivity to rejection
- Reduce anxiety in social situations
- Reduce expectations of ridicule and abuse
- Develop rewarding pleasurable activities
- Understand how behavioral withdrawal perpetuates fear of rejection

Depressive (Scale 2B: Passive-Detached)

Patients scoring high on Scale 2B are generally gloomy, pessimistic, overly serious, quiet, passive, and preoccupied with negative events. They often feel inadequate and have low self-esteem. They tend to unnecessarily brood and worry and, though they are usually responsible and conscientious, they are also self-reproaching and self-critical, regardless of their level of accomplishment. They seem to be down all the time and are quite hard to please. They seem to find fault in even the most joyous experience. They are often described negatively rather than positively. They feel it is futile to try to make improvements in themselves, in their relationships, or in any significant aspect of their life because their incessant pessimism leads them toward a defeatist outlook. Their depressive demeanor often makes others around them feel guilty, because these patients are overly dependent on others for support and acceptance. They have difficulty expressing anger and aggression and perhaps introject it onto themselves. Interestingly, even though their mood is often one of dejection and their cognitions are often dominated by negative thoughts, they do not consider themselves to be depressed.

This personality style is present even in the absence of clinical depression. The melancholic, sober demeanor of these patients, combined with their passivity and self-doubts, puts them at risk for occupational and marital problems. They are also at risk for dysthymia, if stressed with issues of loss.

Caution: Should the patient have clinical depression (see Scales D, page 186, and CC, page 188), the personality profile described here may be a manifestation of depression and not the patient's basic personality style. If this is true, then the symptoms and behaviors should abate when the depression has been successfully treated.

Diagnosis, BR between 75 and 84: personality disorder not otherwise specified (NOS), Depressive personality traits.

Suggested treatment goals:

- Reduce dysphoric mood, behavior, and cognitions
- Relate in a more cheerful manner
- Display humor
- Reduce passivity
- Expand activities designed to provide pleasure
- Reduce self-perpetuating activities that reinforce a sense of depression and dejection

- Understand the unconscious dynamics and seek a more realistic way to seek support
- Increase self-esteem

Dependent (Scale 3: Passive)

Patients with a BR > 84 tend to lean on other people for security, support, guidance, and direction. Such patients are passive, submissive, dependent, and self-conscious and lack initiative, confidence, and autonomy. Their temperament is pacifying and they try to avoid conflict. They acquiesce to maintain nurturance, affection, protection, and security. They can be expected to be obliging, docile, and placating, seeking relationships in which they can lean on others for emotional support. They have excessive needs both for attachment and to be taken care of, and they feel helpless when alone. They willingly submit to the wishes of others in order to maintain this security and this behavior tends to elicit helping and nurturing behaviors in those around them. When threatened with a loss of security, they seek out other relationships or institutions to take care of them. Their basic conflict is a fear of abandonment. This fear leads them to be overly compliant to ensure enduring protection for themselves. Their need for support is overwhelming. They prefer the dependent state and are genuinely docile. They have a self-image as a weak and fragile person, avoiding responsibilities and thereby precluding any chance of autonomy. When stressed (with a disruption of security), they are prone to develop anxiety and depressive disorders and substance abuse problems.

Note: Millon's theory argues that this style is not a veneer that masks deeply held resentments. Traditional psychodynamic theory posits that these people are quite angry and resentful toward those who provide them with the needed safety and security.

The core motivation for the dependent personality is to obtain and maintain nurturing and supportive relationships. It is quite possible that a person can act both passively and assertively to accomplish this central goal.

It has been theorized that some form of overprotection during childhood produces this style, in that these patients were not given the opportunity to learn autonomous behaviors.

Diagnosis, BR > 84: dependent personality disorder

The personality of patients with a BR between 75 and 84 shows markedly dependent features. This style reflects a conflict between dependence and independence that results in a fear of independence and a desire to withdraw from interpersonal relationships. This dependence–autonomy conflict is enhanced by a belief that reliance on others will bring disappointment and possible rejection, yet independent action will result in failure, shame, and ridicule. This conflict requires these patients to suppress any angry resentment they may feel to maintain relationships with those who can satisfy their basic needs. Patients who score at this level may be described as passive, docile, serene, quiet, compliant, obliging, and submissive.

When stress is minimal, these patients appear genuinely well adjusted, with few interpersonal difficulties, particularly if they are in a dominant/adaptive relationship in which the partner assumes primary responsibility and control for decision making. When stressed, particularly by threats to dependency security, these patients can be expected to engage in behaviors that will restore their basic dependency and to seek out people or institutions that will care for their needs. However, if unsuccessful, such patients are at risk for developing an anxiety disorder, a depressive disorder, or both. These patients may not meet all the criteria for a diagnosis of dependent personality disorder, but dependent traits are a salient aspect of the clinical presentation.

Diagnosis, BR between 75 and 84: personality disorder not otherwise specified (NOS), dependent traits

Suggested treatment goals:

- Become more assertive
- Reduce submissive behaviors
- Practice independent behaviors
- Increase self-reliance
- Reduce the need for support from others

- Increase self-perception of personal adequacy
- Reduce clinging behaviors

Histrionic (Scale 4: Active Dependent)

Patients who score at the level of a BR between 75 and 84 have very high needs for attention and praise, and they engage in self-dramatizing, gregarious, and socially engaging behaviors to maintain their security. Millon believes that the underlying fear of such patients is one of abandonment, so they demonstrate an admiration of significant others to assure themselves that they will not be left alone. Sometimes they will act in a subservient and overly compliant manner to maintain their security. Conflicts are avoided in favor of interpersonal harmony, even at the expense of their own values and beliefs. Marital problems may result from this particular personality style.

This patient may not meet the diagnostic criteria for a histrionic personality disorder, but histrionic traits are a part of the personality pattern.

Caution: See **Caution** paragraph in the section below.

Diagnosis, BR between 75 and 84: personality disorder not otherwise specified (NOS), histrionic traits

Expect patients with a BR > 84 to be overly dramatic, with strong needs to be the center of attention. Such patients are seductive—through speech, style, dress, or manner—and seek constant stimulation and excitement in an exhibitionistic atmosphere, requiring praise and attention. They are emotionally labile, are easily excited, and have frequent emotional outbursts. They are very gregarious, assertive, and socially outgoing, but they manipulate people to draw their approval and affection. They have strong needs for constant social acceptance. They are socially facile and seductively engaging, such that others are drawn to their enchanting manner. Relationships are often shallow and strained, however, as a result of their repeatedly dramatic and emotional outbursts and their self-centeredness. Denial and repression are their main defenses. They court the favor of others, but beneath this persona of confidence and self-assurance is a fear of autonomy and independence that mandates a constant need for acceptance and approval. They tend to displace anxieties when stressed. They are at risk for somatoform disorders and marital problems.

Millon has subdivided the histrionic personality disorder into six subtypes. These patients closely resemble the theatrical histrionic subtype. The cardinal features of this subtype are excessively dramatic, theatrical, and attention-getting behaviors designed to bring attention and approval. They are pure histrionics in the classic sense. They publicly profess undying adoration and approval toward their valued object, but this is easily seen as superficial and phony by those around them. Their unconscious use of denial, however, precludes them from this self-observation.

Caution: Empirical research has shown that Scale 4 (1) correlates positively with measures of mental health and negatively with measures of mental disorders; (2) infrequently appears in MCMI code types in psychiatric patients, except for substance abuse; and (3) is frequently the scale with the most elevated scores among nonclinical patients who have taken this test, particularly among women. These people would have a gregarious, extroverted, and socially engaging personality *style* but not a histrionic disorder. The clinician needs to evaluate which of these two possibilities is applicable to the particular patient.

Diagnosis, BR > 84: histrionic personality disorder
Suggested treatment goals:

- Reduce dramatic and theatrical behaviors
- Develop more authentic relationships through balanced interpersonal conduct
- Reduce manipulative and/or seductive behaviors
- Reduce excessive needs to seek attention and approval
- Reduce emotional overreacting

Narcissistic (Scale 5: Passive Independent)

Patients with high scores on Scale 5 are quite self-centered, expect people to recognize their special qualities, and require constant praise and recognition. They have excessive expectations of entitlement and demand special favors. Grandiose statements of self-importance are readily elicited, and they consider themselves particularly attractive. They appear egocentric, arrogant, haughty, conceited, boastful, snobbish, pretentious, and supercilious. They will exploit people and manipulate them with an air of superiority. Although they can be momentarily charming, they have a deficient social conscience and think only of themselves. They show a social imperturbability and are likely to disregard social constraints. They exploit social relationships, are indifferent to the rights of others, relate in an autocratic manner, and expect others to focus on them. Even though this basic style often alienates other people, they respond with a sense of contempt and indifference because their inflated sense of self needs no confirmation from other people. Because of their grandiosity and arrogance, they rarely show signs of self-doubt. If they are humiliated or experience a narcissistic injury, they are prone to develop an affective disorder and perhaps a paranoid disorder. Many substance abusers also have a narcissistic personality style.

Millon has subdivided the narcissistic personality disorder into four subtypes. Patients with high scores on Scale 5 closely resemble the elitist narcissistic subtype. Patients of this subtype present a pure form of narcissism. The cardinal feature of this subtype is these patients' strong desire for public accolades and even celebrity status and for recognition of their special talents and accomplishments. However, an objective review of their life would suggest a large discrepancy between their actual deeds and the braggadocio about those deeds. They show the typical traits of the prototypical narcissist but feel excessively privileged. They are quite grandiose and self-aggrandizing.

Caution: Empirical research has shown that Scale 5 (1) correlates positively with measures of mental health and negatively with measures of mental disorders; (2) infrequently appears in MCMI code types in psychiatric patients, except for substance abuse; and (3) is frequently the scale with the most elevated scores among non-clinical patients who have taken this test, particularly among men. These people have a confidant demeanor with high self-regard, seem socially charming, and perhaps even have a personality style of attention seeking but not a narcissistic personality disorder. The clinician needs to evaluate which of these two possibilities is applicable to the particular patient.

Diagnosis, BR > 84: narcissistic personality disorder

Diagnosis, BR between 75 and 85: personality disorder not otherwise specified (NOS), narcissistic traits

Suggested treatment goals:

- Reduce self-centeredness
- Take the other person's perspective into consideration
- Accept self on a more realistic basis
- Reduce grandiosity
- Learn how other people react and feel about narcissistic behavior; accept constructive feedback
- Prevent the development of a depressive disorder by reducing risk for narcissistic injury

Antisocial (Scale 6A: Active Independent)

Patients with high scores on Scale 6A are quite narcissistic, fearless, pugnacious, daring, blunt, aggressive and assertive, irresponsible, impulsive, ruthless, victimizing, intimidating, dominating, often energetic and competitive, but quite determined and independent. They are argumentative, self-reliant, revengeful, and vindictive. They are chronically dissatisfied and harbor resentment toward people who challenge, criticize, or express disapproval over their behavior. They are characteristically touchy and jealous, brood over perceived slights and wrongs, and provoke fear in those around them through their intimidating social demeanor. They tend to present with an angry and hostile affect. They are suspicious and skeptical of the motives of other people, plan revenge for past grievances, and view others as untrustworthy. They avoid expressions of warmth, gentleness, closeness, and intimacy, viewing such involvement as a sign of weakness. They often ascribe their own malicious tendencies to the motives of others. They feel comfortable only when they have power and control over others. They are continually on guard against anticipated ridicule and act out in a socially intimidating manner, desiring to provoke fear in others and to exploit others for self-gain. These patients are driven by power, by malevolent projections, and by an expectation of experiencing suffering at the hands of others, so they react to maintain their autonomy and independence. Millon believes their behavior is motivated by an expectancy that people will be rejecting and that other people are malicious, devious, and vengeful, thus justifying a forceful counteraction to maintain their own autonomy. They are alert for signs of ridicule and contempt, and they react with impulsive hostility in response to felt resentments. They are prone to substance abuse, relationship difficulties, vocational deficits, and legal problems.

Millon has subdivided the antisocial personality disorder into five types. Scale 6 patients closely resemble the covetous antisocial type. The cardinal feature of this subtype of patients is their incessant greediness. These patients feel constantly deprived and are motivated by envy and retribution to appropriate others' possessions. They tend to maintain a lifestyle of ostentatious displays of material possessions and concentrate their efforts at gaining power. They are completely self-centered and have little or no guilt or remorse for the anguish their deceit and exploitiveness have caused in others. These patients feel constantly deprived and use external signs of self-worth to satisfy an unconscious need for love and attention, which they feel they have not received in life. Thus, this style represents a pure form of the psychopathic personality.

Note: It is possible to have an antisocial character style without engaging in antisocial (criminal) behavior.

Diagnosis, BR > 84: antisocial personality disorder

Diagnosis, BR between 75 and 84: personality disorder not otherwise specified (NOS), antisocial personality traits

Suggested treatment goals:

- Reduce antisocial behaviors
- Become more empathic
- Reduce manipulation and conning behaviors

- Reduce aggressive behaviors
- Channel negative emotions toward prosocial activities
- Reduce impulsivity
- Learn to appropriately express anger
- Do not violate the rights of others

Aggressive/Sadistic (Scale 6B: Active-Discordant)

Patients with high scores on Scale 6B may not be publicly antisocial, but their clinical features are quite similar to those of the antisocial personality style and may be considered as a more pathological variant of the antisocial style. They engage in behaviors that are abusive and humiliating and may violate the rights and feelings of others. They are aggressive, forceful, commanding, militant, domineering, hardheaded, hostile, dominating, intimidating, pervasively destructive, and brutal. They become combative when provoked, and they are antagonistic and disagreeable people. They tend to be touchy, excitable, and irritable and react angrily when confronted. In psychoanalytic terms, they are sadistic personalities. Some are able to sublimate these traits into socially approved vocations. When their autonomy is threatened, they are prone to spouse abuse and explosive outbursts that may result in legal problems.

Millon has subdivided the aggressive/sadistic personality disorder into four subtypes. Patients scoring high on Scale 6B closely resemble the explosive sadist subtype. Although these patients retain the essential features of the parent prototype, the cardinal feature of patients of the explosive sadistic subtype is their uncontrollable rage, usually expressed at those weaker than themselves. These patients erupt in violent behavior with unpredictable belligerent acts that are often irrational and of ferocious intensity. Although the effects of such behavior are to intimidate and control people, the actual motivation for the explosiveness is to release anger and tension associated with a feeling of humiliation and betrayal.

Diagnosis, BR > 74: personality disorder not otherwise specified (NOS), aggressive personality traits

Suggested treatment goals:

- Reduce/eliminate physical and/or verbally aggressive behavior
- Control temper
- Reduce hostile and volatile moods
- Interpret the environment as less menacing
- Acquire prosocial behaviors
- Reduce emphasis on controlling others
- Do not harm anyone
- Manage anger more appropriately

Compulsive (Scale 7: Passive-Ambivalent)

Patients with high scores on Scale 7 are behaviorally rigid, constricted, conscientious, polite, organized, meticulous, punctual,
respectful, often perfectionistic, formal, prudent, overconforming,
cooperative, compliant with rules, serious, moralistic, self-righteous
and self-disciplined, efficient, and relatively inflexible. They place
high demands on themselves. They are emotionally restrained, suppressing strong resentments and anger, and they appear tense and
grim but emotionally controlled. They are socially conforming and
prone to a repetitive lifestyle, as a result of engaging in a series of
patterned behaviors and rules that must be followed. They have fears
of social disapproval and are a model of propriety and restraint. They
show excessive respect for authority yet may treat subordinates in an
autocratic manner. They operate from a sense of duty that compels
them not to let others down, thus risking the condemnation of
authority figures. They show an anxious conformity. They strive to
avoid criticism but expect it because of what they perceive to be
their personal shortcomings. They fear making mistakes because of
expected disapproval. Their behavior stems from a conflict between
a felt hostility that they wish to express and a fear of social disapproval should they expose this underlying oppositional resentment.
This circumstance forces them to become overconforming, thus
placing high demands on themselves that serve to control this
intense anger, which occasionally breaks through into their behavior. Obsessive thinking may or may nor be present.

Millon has subdivided the compulsive personality disorder into five subtypes. Patients with high Scale 7 scores closely resemble the conscientious Compulsive. Although their behavior is an example of a relatively pure form of the prototypal compulsive personality style, the cardinal feature of patients of this subtype is their excessive compliance, obedience, conformity, and desire to please authority figures. They impress people with their conscientiousness, but underneath their obedience is a fear of making mistakes and receiving disapproval. Their (largely unconscious) feelings of inadequacy and fear of failure compel them to maintain a rigid approach to life's tasks.

Caution: Empirical research has shown that Scale 7 (1) correlates positively with measures of mental health and negatively with measures of mental disorders; (2) infrequently appears in MCMI codetypes in psychiatric patients; (3) is frequently the scale with the most elevated scores among nonclinical patients who have taken this test, particularly among men; and (4) is the only study that has used the MCMI with patients with an obsessive-compulsive disorder who did not have elevations on Scale 7. Thus, patients with elevated scores on Scale 7 would be conscientious, rule bound, and orderly, suggesting a compulsive personality style but not a compulsive disorder. The clinician needs to evaluate which of these two possibilities is applicable to the particular patient.

Diagnosis, BR > 84: compulsive personality disorder

Diagnosis, BR between 75 and 84: personality disorder not otherwise specified (NOS), compulsive traits

Suggested treatment goals:

- Reduce rigidity
- Reduce compulsive behaviors
- Practice spontaneity and flexibility
- Reduce fears of disapproval
- Understand early childhood experiences that resulted in a compulsive personality style
- Reduce tendencies toward perfectionism if they interfere with life satisfaction
- Learn to take risks

Passive-Aggressive (Negativistic: Scale 8A: Active Ambivalent)

Patients with high scores on Scale 8A display a mixture of passive compliance and obedience at one time and oppositional and negativistic behavior the next time. They are moody, irritable, and hostile; manifest a grumbling, pessimistic demeanor; and are erratically and explosively angry and stubborn at one moment and feel guilty and contrite at the next moment. Disillusionment seems to permeate their lives. They feel misunderstood, so they vacillate between passive dependency and stubborn contrariness, which provokes discomfort and exasperation in those around them. They expect disappointment and maintain an unstable and conflictual role in relations with others. They sulk, feel unappreciated and/or feel they are being treated unfairly, constantly complain, and are persistently petulant and discontented. They often have problems with authority and, if employed, have job difficulties.

Commentary: Elevations on Scale 8A are a good indicator of problems with authority and with criminal behaviors or potential criminal behavior. Also, clinical elevations on this scale appear in a number of profile codes involving psychiatric patients. Patients with elevations on Scale 8A warrant close clinical evaluation.

Diagnosis, BR > 74: Personality not otherwise specified (NOS), passive-aggressive (negativistic) traits

Suggested treatment goals:

- Reduce negative behaviors
- Reduce argumentativeness
- Reduce moodiness
- Learn to appropriately express anger
- Learn to have a more thoughtful manner
- Learn to recognize and change manipulative behavior patterns
- Control emotions

Self-Defeating (Scale 8B: Passive-Discordant)

Patients with high scores on Scale 8B relate in a self-sacrificing, martyr-like manner, allowing others to take advantage of them. They seem to search for relationships in which they can lean on others for security and affection. Typically, they act in an unassuming manner, denigrating themselves into believing they deserve their fate. Thus, this pattern is repeated in most relationships, making them prone to being abused. It is conceptually similar to the analytic concept of masochism.

Diagnosis, BR > 74: personality disorder not otherwise specified (NOS), self-defeating (masochistic) traits

Suggested treatment goals:

- Become more assertive
- Reduce tendencies to be taken advantage of
- Develop a positive self-concept
- Reduce behaviors that provoke others
- Reduce dependency
- Reduce victimization, if applicable
- Reduce deferential interpersonal conduct
- Acknowledge and deal with feelings of resentment

Schizotypal (Scale S: Active-Dependent)

The profile pattern of patients with high scores on Scale S represents a more severe dysfunctional variant of the schizoid or the avoidant personality disorder. Millon subdivides this disorder into two types. The active variant is characteristically anxious, wary, and apprehensive, whereas the passive type is characteristically emotionally bland with a flat affect.

These patients have behavioral peculiarities and eccentricities and seem detached from the world around them, appearing strange and different. They tend to lead meaningless lives, drifting aimlessly from one activity to the next, remaining on the periphery of society. They are socially detached and isolated and show a pervasive discomfort with others. They have few, if any, personal attachments and rarely develop any intimate relationships. Their thinking is irrelevant, tangential, disorganized, or autistic and they are suspicious of others. Cognitive confusion and perceptual distortions are the rule. They are self-absorbed and ruminative with feelings of derealization.

They are prone to decompensate into schizophrenia if sufficiently stressed. If BR > 84, then because of the severity of the disorder, a clinical evaluation is needed to determine if the patient can function on a daily basis.

Diagnosis, BR > 84: schizotypal personality disorder

Diagnosis, BR between 75 and 84: personality disorder not otherwise specified (NOS) schizotypal traits

Suggested treatment goals for patient:

- Reduce intensity of thought disorder
- Improve relationship skills
- Increase social skills and social participation
- Become active in at least one desired activity

Suggested treatment goals for therapist:

- Monitor for possible deterioration and decompensation
- Evaluate the need for psychotropic medication
- Provide a supportive therapeutic environment

Borderline (Scale C)

Patients with high scores on Scale C have conflicting and ambivalent feelings, intensely resenting those on whom they depend yet being preoccupied with maintaining their emotional support. They show persistent attachment disorders with patterns of intense but unstable relationships. They tend to experience intense but labile emotions and frequent mood swings with recurring periods of depression, anxiety, or anger followed by dejection and apathy. They often will present with intense affect and with a history of impulsive behaviors. Manifestations of cheerfulness are often temporary coverups that mask deep fears of insecurity and fears of abandonment. They have strong dependency needs and are preoccupied with seeking attention and emotional support and need considerable reassurance. These people are particularly vulnerable to separation from those who emotionally support them. Feelings of idealization are usually followed by feelings of devaluation, and there is considerable interpersonal ambivalence. They lack a clear sense of their own identity, and this uncertainty leads them to constantly seek approval, attention, and reaffirmation. Splitting and projective identification are their major defenses. They often have a punishing conscience and are prone to acts of self-mutilation and suicidal gestures. They are also prone toward brief, psychotic episodes and substance abuse.

Diagnosis, BR > 84: borderline personality disorder

Diagnosis, BR between 75 and 84: personality disorder not otherwise specified (NOS), borderline traits

Suggested treatment goals:

- Reduce fears of abandonment
- Reduce dependent behaviors
- Reduce anxiety
- Learn to express anger more appropriately
- Relate to others on a more realistic basis
- Reduce impassivity
- Agree to work within the limits defined by the therapist

Paranoid (Scale P)

Millon believes that patients who have high scores on Scale P are conflicted between issues of control and affiliation. They vigilantly mistrust others and have an abrasive, hostile, irritable, touchy, and irascible demeanor that readily attacks and humiliates anyone whom they perceive as trying to control them. They may become belligerent, with such behavior stemming from distorted cognitions or actual delusions. They tend to magnify interpersonal slights, are prone to distort events to support their own suspicions, and strongly resist external influence. They are fiercely independent and tend to be provocative in interpersonal relationships, precipitating fear and exasperation in those around them. Their thinking is rigid and they often become argumentative. Projection is their main defense. They are particularly sensitive to perceived threats to their own sense of self-determination. Delusions of grandeur or persecution or ideas of reference may be present in the more extreme form of the disorder.

Diagnosis, BR > 84: paranoid personality disorder

Diagnosis, BR between 75 and 84: personality disorder not otherwise specified (NOS), paranoid personality traits

Suggested treatment goals:

- Learn to trust at least one person
- Reduce delusional thinking
- Reduce anger, hostility, and suspiciousness
- Reduce isolation
- Learn to express anger in a more socially approved way
- Develop a more realistic appraisal of personal environment

ONE-POINT CODE TYPES WITH ONE SUBSPIKE

One–point code types with one subspike are highlighted by scores for one clinical personality pattern scale of BR > 84 and for one clinical personality pattern scale of BR between 75 and 84. It is suggested that the reader review the interpretation for each of these scales as detailed under One-Point Codes (pages 106–124). Here, for illustration, only the interpretation for code type 1'2A (schizoid, avoidant) is presented.

1'2A

Patients with a 1'2A code appear apathetic, dull, quiet, colorless, vague, aloof, and introverted. They seem lost in their surroundings, blending into the background or engaging in vague pursuits. They show limited enthusiasm for most activities, preferring a solitary life and rarely initiating conversation. They seem indifferent to social relationships and do not seek out social contact. They seem to have a low need for social involvement, appear to require little affection, and lack both warmth and emotional expression. They manifest an emotionally bland appearance with flattened affect, combined with a lack of sensitivity to their own feelings and those of others. They lack an outward expression of aggression. They are often asexual, perhaps as a result of their relationship deficits. They are quite content to be passive, detached, and distant in their relationships. They have few friends, preferring the life of a loner. The detachment is not a defense mechanism. They are comfortable this way and prefer it, at least at the conscious level. Underneath this detachment lies a rich fantasy life and excessive daydreaming. Intrapsychically, they are in a chronic dilemma because they cannot be in a relationship without fearing engulfment yet cannot be without a relationship without feeling intense aloneness. If this patient is married or in a committed relationship, problems are likely to arise, including spousal complaints of a lack of involvement and intimacy. Others see these people as strange and spacey. Relationship deficits are likely to be serious. These patients have low self-esteem, but more often, they have difficulty expressing how they feel about themselves. Their thinking can be obscure at times, with cognitive slippage occasionally manifested in speech. Their thoughts are vague and unfocused. Depersonalization, feelings of emptiness, and identity diffusion are also part of their personality structure. These patients tend to drift through marginal aspects of society. When social demands become inescapable, they are prone to anxiety reactions, somatoform disorders, and brief reactive psychoses.

These patients' behavior is characterized by and motivated by a fear of rejection, thus leading to either a physical or emotional withdrawal in public to avoid social disapproval. Independent action may be stymied and emotions are suppressed because of insecurity. These patients feel inadequate and so probably avoid actions that will lead to autonomy. Many such patients are able to hide their social anxiety and appear to be without problems. Closer scrutiny and a trusting relationship with the clinician may cause them to reduce their defensiveness and admit to their fears, because these fears are at the conscious level. Others act in a fearful, dependent, and avoidant manner such that their hesitancies and dependency are quite obvious to a casual observer. These patients may not have all the characteristics that define an avoidant personality disorder, but the presence of avoidant characteristics is strongly indicated in the profile.

Diagnosis: schizoid personality disorder with avoidant personality traits

TWO-POINT CODES

Two-point codes are codes for which scores for two clinical personality pattern scales are BR > 84 and for which scores for the remaining clinical personality patterns are BR < 74. Because Millon subdivided prototype personality disorders into several subtypes with many represented by two-point codes, what are listed here are interpretations primarily for those subtypes that represent the more common MCMI two-point codes as well. If a patient has a one-point code with one subspike, it is recommended that the code types contained in this section also be considered.

12A', or 1S

Patients with a 12A' (or 1S) code appear apathetic, dull, quiet, colorless, vague, aloof, and introverted. They seem lost in their surroundings, blending into the background or engaging in vague pursuits. They show limited enthusiasm for most activities, preferring a solitary life and rarely initiating conversation. They seem indifferent to social relationships and do not seek out social contact. They appear both to have a low need for social involvement and to require little affection, and they lack both warmth and emotional expression. They manifest an emotionally bland appearance with flattened affect, combined with a lack of sensitivity to their own feelings and those of others. They lack an outward expression of aggression. They are often asexual, perhaps as a result of their relationship deficits. They are quite content to be passive, detached, and distant in their relationships. They have few friends, preferring the life of a loner. The detachment is not a defense mechanism. They are comfortable this way and prefer it, at least at the conscious level. Underneath this detachment lies a rich fantasy life and excessive daydreaming. Intrapsychically, they are in a chronic dilemma: They cannot be in a relationship without fearing engulfment, yet they cannot be without a relationship without feeling intense aloneness. If this patient is married or in a committed relationship, problems are likely to arise, such as spousal complaints of a lack of involvement and intimacy. Others see these people as strange and spacey. Relationship deficits are likely to be serious. These patients have low self-esteem, but more often, they have difficulty expressing how they feel about themselves. Their thinking can be obscure at times, with cognitive slippage occasionally manifested in speech. Their thoughts are vague and unfocused. Depersonalization, feelings of emptiness, and identity diffusion are also part of their personality structure. These patients tend to drift through marginal aspects of society. When social demands become inescapable, they are prone to anxiety reactions, somatoform disorders, and brief reactive psychoses.

These patients' behavior is also characterized by and motivated by a fear of rejection. This leads to either a physical or an emotional withdrawal in public to avoid social disapproval. Independent action may be stymied and emotions are suppressed because of insecurity. These patients feel inadequate, so they probably avoid actions that will lead to autonomy.

Millon has subtyped the schizoid personality disorder into four variants, reflecting more central personality difficulties within his domain model. Patients with a 12A′ code closely resemble the remote schizoid type. They are characterized by emotional distance, inaccessibility, and isolation. They seem to have few social interests and drift in and out of peripheral social roles, with little apparent interest in sexuality. They often rely on public institutions for self-care. They appear intellectually dull and have serious relationship difficulties.

Diagnosis: schizoid personality disorder

12B′

Patients with a 12B′ code appear apathetic, dull, quiet, colorless, vague, aloof, and introverted. They seem lost in their surroundings, blending into the background or engaging in vague pursuits. They show limited enthusiasm for most activities, preferring a solitary life and rarely initiating conversation. They seem indifferent to social relationships and do not seek out social contact. They appear both to have a low need for social involvement and to require little affection, and they lack both warmth and emotional expression. They manifest an emotionally bland appearance with flattened affect, combined with a lack of sensitivity to their own feelings and those of others. They do not outwardly express aggression. They are often asexual, perhaps as a result of their relationship deficits. They are quite content to be passive, detached, and distant in their relationships. They have few friends, preferring the life of a loner. The detachment is not a defense mechanism. They are comfortable this way and prefer it, at least at the conscious level. Underneath this detachment lies a rich fantasy life and excessive daydreaming. Intrapsychically, they are in a chronic dilemma: They cannot be in a relationship without fearing engulfment, yet they cannot be without a relationship without feeling intense aloneness. If these patients are married or in a committed relationship, problems are likely to arise, such as spousal complaints of a lack of involvement and intimacy. Others see these people as strange and spacey. Relationship deficits are likely to be serious. These patients have low self-esteem, but more often, they have difficulty expressing how they feel about themselves. Their thinking can be obscure at times, with cognitive slippage occasionally manifested in speech. Their thoughts are vague and unfocused. Depersonalization, feelings of emptiness, and identity diffusion are also part of their personality structure. These patients tend to drift through marginal aspects of society. When social demands become inescapable, they are prone to anxiety reactions, somatoform disorders, and brief reactive psychoses.

Millon has subtypes the schizoid personality disorder into four variants, reflecting more central personality difficulties within his domain model. Patients with a 12B' closely resemble the languid schizoid type. The cardinal feature of this schizoid subtype is slow motoric expression. These patients are characterized by a phlegmatic temperament, deficient energy level, a slow personal tempo, delayed reactivity to stimulus enrichment, and a weary exterior. They relate to others in a quiet, dependent style and rarely show affection.

Diagnosis: schizoid personality disorder

17'

Patients with a 17' code appear apathetic, dull, quiet, colorless, vague, aloof, and introverted. They seem lost in their surroundings, blending into the background or engaging in vague pursuits. They show limited enthusiasm for most activities, preferring a solitary life and rarely initiating conversation. They appear indifferent to social relationships and do not seek out social contact. They give the impression both of having a low need for social involvement and of requiring little affection and lack both warmth and emotional expression. They manifest an emotionally bland appearance with flattened affect, combined with a lack of sensitivity to their own feelings and those of others. They do not outwardly express aggression. They are often asexual, perhaps as a result of their relationship deficits. They are quite content to be passive, detached, and distant in their relationships. They have few friends, preferring the life of a loner. The detachment is not a defense mechanism. They are comfortable this way and prefer it, at least at the conscious level. Underneath this detachment lies a rich fantasy life and excessive daydreaming. Intrapsychically, they are in a chronic dilemma: They cannot be in a relationship without fearing engulfment, yet they cannot be without a relationship without feeling intense aloneness. If these patients are married or in a committed relationship, problems are likely to arise, such as spousal complaints of a lack of involvement and intimacy. Others see these people as strange and spacey. Relationship deficits are likely to be serious. These patients have low self-esteem, but more often, they have difficulty expressing how they feel about themselves. Their thinking can be obscure at times, with cognitive slippage occasionally manifested in speech. Their thoughts are vague and unfocused. Depersonalization, feelings of emptiness, and identity diffusion are also part of their personality structure. These patients tend to drift through marginal aspects of society. When social demands become inescapable, they are prone to anxiety reactions, somatoform disorders, and brief reactive psychoses. These patients are also behaviorally rigid, constricted, serious, and emotionally restrained, suppressing their strong resentments and anger, and they appear tense and grim.

Millon has subtyped the schizoid personality disorder into four variants, reflecting more central personality difficulties within his domain model. Patients with a 17′ code closely resemble the affectless schizoid type. The cardinal feature of this schizoid subtype is marked deficit in relational capacity, particularly as it pertains to the normal exchange of emotions and feelings. They seem cold, emotionally flat, and unperturbed by events that would normally stimulate the emotions.

Diagnosis: schizoid personality disorder

1S'

Patients with a 1S' code appear apathetic, dull, quiet, colorless, vague, aloof, and introverted. They seem lost in their surroundings, blending into the background or engaging in vague pursuits. They show limited enthusiasm for most activities, preferring a solitary life and rarely initiating conversation. They seem indifferent to social relationships and do not seek out social contact. They appear both to have a low need for social involvement and to require little affection, and they lack both warmth and emotional expression. They manifest an emotionally bland appearance with flattened affect, combined with a lack of sensitivity to their own feelings and those of others. They do not outwardly express aggression. They are often asexual, perhaps as a result of their relationship deficits. They are quite content to be passive, detached, and distant in their relationships. They have few friends, preferring the life of a loner. The detachment is not a defense mechanism. They are comfortable this way and prefer it, at least at the conscious level. Underneath this detachment lies a rich fantasy life and excessive daydreaming. Intrapsychically, they are in a chronic dilemma: They cannot be in a relationship without fearing engulfment, yet they cannot be without a relationship without feeling intense aloneness. If these patients are married or in a committed relationship, problems are likely to arise, such as spousal complaints of a lack of involvement and intimacy. Others see these people as strange and spacey. Relationship deficits are likely to be serious. These patients have low self-esteem, but more often, they have difficulty expressing how they feel about themselves. Their thinking can be obscure at times, with cognitive slippage occasionally manifested in speech. Their thoughts are vague and unfocused. Depersonalization, feelings of emptiness, and identity diffusion are also part of their personality structure. These patients tend to drift through marginal aspects of society. When social demands become inescapable, they are prone to anxiety reactions, somatoform disorders, and brief reactive psychoses.

Millon has subtyped the schizoid personality disorder into four variants, reflecting more central personality difficulties within his domain model. Patients with a 1S′ code closely resemble the Depersonalized schizoid type. The cardinal features of patients of this schizoid subtype are their disengagement both from their sense of self and from others, their sense of depersonalization, their disengagement, and their dissociated appearance. They occasionally seem oblivious to their surroundings, stare into space, appear to be in a dreamlike trance, or are simply inattentive and preoccupied. They have severe relationship deficits and seem lost within themselves.

Diagnosis: schizoid personality disorder

2A2B′

Patients with a 2A2B′ code present as socially awkward, withdrawn, introverted, and self-conscious. Because they are hypersensitive to rejection and both fear and expect negative evaluations, they either try to maintain a good social appearance despite their underlying fear or they withdraw from social contacts. Tension, anxiety, and anger may also be present, but all stem from the same issue—a desire for social acceptance and a fear of rejection. Most often, they maintain a social distance to avoid any further rejection. They are devastated by perceived signs of disapproval and tend to withdraw, thus reducing their chances of enhancing relationships. This circumstance results in social isolation despite a very strong need for social relatedness. These patients can put on a pleasant appearance to mask their underlying social anxiety, but they have a pervasive belief that others will be disparaging of them. Their essential conflict is a strong desire to relate but an equally strong expectation of disapproval, depreciation, and rejection. This conflict results in their keeping others at a distance but also results in loneliness, isolation, and continued shyness and timidity. They are at risk for social phobias.

Millon has subtyped the avoidant personality disorder into four variants, reflecting more central personality difficulties with his domain model. Patients with a 2A2B′ code closely resemble the self-deserting avoidant type. The cardinal features of these patients are social aversion and self-devaluation. To avoid public exposure and humiliation (because of anticipated rejection), these patients withdraw from social relationships. Their increasing loneliness results in increased melancholy, and their feelings of disconnection combined with self-devalution put them at risk for suicide.

Diagnosis: avoidant personality disorder

2A3

Patients with a 2A3 code present as socially awkward, withdrawn, introverted, and self-conscious. Because they are hypersensitive to rejection and both fear and expect negative evaluations, they either try to maintain a good social appearance despite their underlying fear or they withdraw from social contacts. Tension, anxiety, and anger may also be present, but all stem from the same issue—a desire for social acceptance and a fear of rejection. Most often, they maintain a social distance to avoid any further experience of being rejected. They are devastated by perceived signs of disapproval and tend to withdraw, thus reducing their chances of enhancing relationships. This circumstance results in social isolation despite a very strong need for social relatedness. These patients can put on a pleasant appearance to mask their underlying social anxiety, but they have a pervasive belief that others will be disparaging of them. Their essential conflict is a strong desire to relate but an equally strong expectation of disapproval, depreciation, and rejection. This conflict results in their keeping others at a distance but also results in loneliness, isolation, and continued shyness and timidity. They are at risk for social phobias.

Millon has subtyped the avoidant personality disorder into four variants, reflecting more central personality difficulties within his domain model. Patients with a 2A3 code closely resemble the phobic avoidant type. Patients of this subtype retain the essential core features of the avoidant type and have phobic anxieties such that they are chronically tense and anxious. Millon has described them as a mixture of avoidant and dependent personalities who are unable to control their anxieties over anticipated rejection. These patients often channel their fears onto an external object and also restrict their social relatedness to one or two people who will cater to their dependency needs. Although these patients may tolerate such support, they do so with considerable distrust and discomfort. Because of these cardinal features, it is suggested that the clinician explore for social phobias.

Diagnosis: avoidant personality disorder

2A8A'

Patients with a 2A8A' code present as socially awkward, withdrawn, introverted, and self-conscious. Because they are hypersensitive to rejection and both fear and expect negative evaluations, they either try to maintain a good social appearance despite their underlying fear or they withdraw from social contacts. Tension, anxiety, and anger may also be present, but all stem from the same issue—a desire for social acceptance and a fear of rejection. Most often, they maintain a social distance to avoid any further experience of being rejected. They are devastated by perceived signs of disapproval and tend to withdraw, thus reducing their chances of enhancing relationships. This circumstance results in social isolation despite a very strong need for social relatedness. These patients can put on a pleasant appearance to mask their underlying social anxiety, but they have a pervasive belief that others will be disparaging of them. Their essential conflict is a strong desire to relate but an equally strong expectation of disapproval, depreciation, and rejection. This conflict results in keeping others at a distance but also results in loneliness, isolation, and continued shyness and timidity. They are at risk for social phobias.

Diagnosis: avoidant personality disorder

The behavior of patients with a BR between 75 and 84 is characterized by and motivated by a fear of rejection, thus leading to either a physical or emotional withdrawal in public to avoid social disapproval. Independent action may be stymied and emotions are suppressed because of insecurity. These patients feel inadequate, so they probably avoid actions that will lead to autonomy. Many such patients can hide their social anxiety and appear to be without problems. Closer scrutiny and a trusting relationship with the clinician may cause them to reduce their defensiveness and admit to their fears, because these fears are at the conscious level. Others act in a fearful, dependent, and avoidant manner such that their hesitancies and dependency are quite obvious to a casual observer.

Millon has subtyped the avoidant personality disorder into four variants, reflecting more central personality difficulties within his domain model. Patients with a BR between 75 and 84 closely resemble the conflicted avoidant type. Patients of this subtype retain the essential core features of the avoidant type and have the features of the passive-aggressive (negativistic) personality. The cardinal feature of the conflicted avoidant patient is fear of both dependence and independence. Thus, the behavior of these patients is characterized by internal struggles to withdraw from social contacts and a desire to become involved in closer relationships. This conflict results in feelings of low self-esteem and a discontented, petulant exterior that may show paroxysmal hostility at the slightest provocation. This is followed by remorse, regret, then further acting out in an endless cycle of outbursts and moodiness. Their deep social mistrust and anticipated rejection and depreciation make it extremely difficult to retain stable interpersonal relationships.

Diagnosis: avoidant personality disorder

2AP

Patients with a 2AP code present as socially awkward, withdrawn, introverted, and self-conscious. Because they are hypersensitive to rejection and both fear and expect negative evaluations, they either try to maintain a good social appearance despite their underlying fear or withdraw from social contacts. Tension, anxiety, and anger may also be present, but all stem from the same issue—a desire for social acceptance and a fear of rejection. Most often, they maintain a social distance to avoid any further rejection. They are devastated by perceived signs of disapproval and tend to withdraw, thus reducing their chances of enhancing relationships. This circumstance results in social isolation despite a very strong need for social relatedness. These patients can put on a pleasant appearance to mask their underlying social anxiety, but they have a pervasive belief that others will be disparaging of them. Their essential conflict is a strong desire to relate but an equally strong expectation of disapproval, depreciation, and rejection. This conflict results in keeping others at a distance but also results in loneliness, isolation, and continued shyness and timidity. They are at risk for social phobias.

Millon has subtyped the avoidant personality disorder into four variants, reflecting more central personality difficulties within his domain model. Patients with a 2AP code closely resemble the hypersensitive avoidant type. This subtype retains the essential core features of the avoidant combined with more pervasive features of the paranoid personality style. The essential core feature of these patients is a pervasive apprehensiveness that people will be rejecting. The behavior of these patients is associated with an apathetic demeanor but also intense anger, fear, and resentment that may erupt in negative outbursts. These patients are easily threatened and use angry outbursts or an edgy demeanor to guard against anticipated rejection.

Diagnosis: avoidant personality disorder

2B2A

Patients with a 2B2A code are generally gloomy, pessimistic, overly serious, quiet, passive, and preoccupied with negative events. They often feel inadequate and have low self-esteem. They tend to unnecessarily brood and worry and, though they are usually responsible and conscientious, they are also self-reproaching and self-critical, regardless of their level of accomplishment. They seem to be down all the time and are quite hard to please. They seem to find fault in even the most joyous experience. They are often described negatively rather than positively. They feel it is futile to try to make improvements in themselves, in their relationships, or in any significant aspect of their life because their incessant pessimism leads them toward a defeatist outlook. Their depressive demeanor often makes others around them feel guilty, because these patients are overly dependent on others for support and acceptance. They have difficulty expressing anger and aggression and perhaps introject it onto themselves. Interestingly, although their mood is often one of dejection and their cognitions are often dominated by negative thoughts, they do not consider themselves depressed.

This personality style is present even in the absence of clinical depression. Their melancholic, sober demeanor, combined with their passivity and self-doubts, puts them at risk for occupational and marital problems. They are also at risk for dysthymia, if stressed with issues of loss.

Millon has subdivided the depressive personality disorder into five subtypes. These patients closely resemble the restive depressive subtype. Patients with a 2B2A code retain the essential features of the depressive personality style and have features of the avoidant personality style. The essential feature of this personality subtype is an agitated depression, vacillating between depressive despair and agitated anguish. These patients feel both shamed and helpless but turn their irritability and fears of rejection onto themselves. Unconsciously, their behavior is designed to elicit sympathy, support, nurturance, and reassurance from significant others.

Diagnosis: personality disorder not otherwise specified (NOS), depressive personality traits

Caution: Should these patients be clinically depressed (see page 186, Scales D, and CC, page 188), the personality profile described here may be a manifestation of depression and not their basic personality style. If this is true, then the symptoms and behaviors should abate when the depression has been successfully treated.

2B3

Patients with a 2B3 code are generally gloomy, pessimistic, overly serious, quiet, passive, and preoccupied with negative events. They often feel inadequate and have low self-esteem. They tend to unnecessarily brood and worry and, though they are usually responsible and conscientious, they are also self-reproaching and self-critical, regardless of their level of accomplishment. They seem to be down all the time and are quite hard to please. They seem to find fault in even the most joyous experience. They are often described negatively rather than positively. They feel it is futile to try to make improvements in themselves, in their relationships, or in any significant aspect of their life because their incessant pessimism leads them toward a defeatist outlook. Their depressive demeanor often makes others around them feel guilty, because these patients are overly dependent on others for support and acceptance. They have difficulty expressing anger and aggression and perhaps introject it onto themselves. Interestingly, although their mood is often one of dejection and their cognitions are often dominated by negative thoughts, they do not consider themselves depressed.

This personality style is present even in the absence of clinical depression. Their melancholic, sober demeanor, combined with their passivity and self-doubts, puts them at risk for occupational and marital problems. They are also at risk for dysthymia, if stressed with issues of loss.

Millon has subdivided the depressive personality disorder into five subtypes. Patients with a 2B3 code closely resemble the morbid depressive subtype. They retain the essential features of the depressive personality style and have features of the dependent personality style. The essential features of these patients are their pervasive dejection, despondency, hopelessness, and despairing demeanor. They often have sleep disorders, a downcast physical appearance, and near-continuous depressive conditions. More than any other depressive subtype, this personality style can easily evolve into a clinical depression. Unconsciously, their behavior is designed to elicit sympathy, support, nurturance, and reassurance from significant others.

Caution: Should these patients be clinically depressed (see Scales D, page 186, and CC, page 188), the personality profile described here may be a manifestation of depression and not their basic personality style. If this is true, then the symptoms and behaviors should abate when the depression has been successfully treated.

Diagnosis: *personality disorder not otherwise specified (NOS), depressive personality traits*

2B4 or 2B5

Patients with a 2B4 or 2B5 code are generally gloomy, pessimistic, overly serious, quiet, passive, and preoccupied with negative events. They often feel inadequate and have low self-esteem. They tend to unnecessarily brood and worry, and though they are usually responsible and conscientious, they are also self-reproaching and self-critical, regardless of their level of accomplishment. They seem to be down all the time and are quite hard to please. They seem to find fault in even the most joyous experience. They are often described negatively rather than positively. They feel it is futile to try to make improvements in themselves, in their relationships, or in any significant aspect of their life because their incessant pessimism leads them toward a defeatist outlook. Their depressive demeanor often makes others around them feel guilty, because these patients are overly dependent on others for support and acceptance. They have difficulty expressing anger and aggression and perhaps introject it onto themselves. Interestingly, although their mood is often one of dejection and their cognitions are often dominated by negative thoughts, they do not consider themselves depressed.

This personality style is present even in the absence of clinical depression. These patients' melancholic, sober demeanor, combined with their passivity and self-doubts, puts them at risk for occupational and marital problems. They are also at risk for dysthymia, if stressed with issues of loss.

Millon has subdivided the depressive personality disorder into five subtypes. Patients with a code 2B4 or 2B5 closely resemble the voguish depressive subtype. They retain the essential features of the depressive personality style and have features of the histrionic or narcissistic personality styles. These patients tend to adopt contemporary causes, particularly those of alienated subgroups, which allows them to ennoble their suffering and to identify with the larger subgroup, thereby allowing them to feel special. Even though they continue to feel lonely and unattached, their identification with socially unpopular movements provides them with a form of social attachment and a vehicle to express their disenchantment and unhappiness in a socially approved manner. Unconsciously, their behavior is designed to elicit sympathy, support, nurturance, and reassurance from significant others. This style may also emanate from a narcissistic injury that has resulted in primarily depressive features. A more thorough clinical evaluation is recommended.

Caution: Should these patients be clinically depressed (see Scales D, page 186, and CC, page 188), the personality profile described here may be a manifestation of depression and not their basic personality style. If this is true then the symptoms and behaviors should abate when the depression has been successfully treated.

Diagnosis: Personality Disorder not otherwise specified (NOS), depressive personality traits

2B8A

Patients with a 2B8A code are generally gloomy, pessimistic, overly serious, quiet, passive, and preoccupied with negative events. They often feel inadequate and have low self-esteem. They tend to unnecessarily brood and worry and, though they are usually responsible and conscientious, they are also self-reproaching and self-critical, regardless of their level of accomplishment. They seem to be down all the time and are quite hard to please. They seem to find fault in even the most joyous experience. They are often described negatively rather than positively. They feel it is futile to try to make improvements in themselves, in their relationships, or in any significant aspect of their life because their incessant pessimism leads them toward a defeatist outlook. Their depressive demeanor often makes others around them feel guilty, because these patients are overly dependent on others for support and acceptance. They have difficulty expressing anger and aggression and perhaps introject it onto themselves. Interestingly, although their mood is often one of dejection and their cognitions are often dominated by negative thoughts, they do not consider themselves to be depressed.

This personality style is present even in the absence of clinical depression. These patients' melancholic, sober demeanor, combined with their passivity and self-doubts, puts them at risk for occupational and marital problems. They are also at risk for dysthymia, if stressed with issues of loss.

Millon has subdivided the depressive personality disorder into five subtypes. Patients with a 2B8A code closely resemble the ill-humored depressive subtype. They retain the essential features of the depressive personality style and have features of the passive-aggressive (negativistic) personality style. These patients have difficulty finding pleasure in any activity and spend time grumbling and complaining about their sorry state in life. They appear irritable, sour, bitter, resentful, discontented, critical, and constantly dissatisfied. Unconsciously, their behavior is designed to elicit sympathy, support, nurturance, and reassurance from significant others.

Diagnosis: personality disorder not otherwise specified (NOS), depressive personality traits

Caution: Should these patients be clinically depressed (see Scale D, page 186, and CC, page 188), the personality profile described here may be a manifestation of depression and not their basic personality style. If this is true, then the symptoms and behaviors should abate when the depression has been successfully treated.

2B8B

Patients with a 2B8B code are generally gloomy, pessimistic, overly serious, quiet, passive, and preoccupied with negative events. They often feel inadequate and have low self-esteem. They tend to unnecessarily brood and worry and, though they are usually responsible and conscientious, they are also self-reproaching and self-critical, regardless of their level of accomplishment. They seem to be down all the time and are quite hard to please. They seem to find fault in even the most joyous experience. They are often described negatively rather than positively. They feel it is futile to try to make improvements in themselves, in their relationships, or in any significant aspect of their life because their incessant pessimism leads them toward a defeatist outlook. Their depressive demeanor often makes others around them feel guilty, because these patients are overly dependent on others for support and acceptance. They have difficulty expressing anger and aggression and perhaps introject it onto themselves. Interestingly, although their mood is often one of dejection and their cognitions are often dominated by negative thoughts, they do not consider themselves to be depressed.

This personality style is present even in the absence of clinical depression. These patients' melancholic, sober demeanor, combined with their passivity and self-doubts, puts them at risk for occupational and marital problems. They are also at risk for dysthymia, if stressed with issues of loss.

Millon has subdivided the depressive personality disorder into five subtypes. Patients with a 2B8B code closely resemble the self-derogatory depressive subtype. These patients retain the essential features of the depressive personality style and have features of the self-defeating (masochistic) personality style. These patients essentially express their anger, discontentment, and resentment in the form of self-derogatory statements and expressions of guilt that are unconsciously designed to elicit support and reassurance. Underneath such expressions is a fear of abandonment. Circumstances of perceived overburdened responsibilities are likely to exacerbate these behaviors.

Caution: Should these patients have a clinical depression (see Scales D, page 186, and CC, page 188), the personality profile described here may be a manifestation of depression and not their basic personality style. If this is true, then the symptoms and behaviors should abate when the depression has been successfully treated.

Diagnosis: personality disorder not otherwise specified (NOS), depressive personality traits

31

Millon has subdivided the dependent personality disorder into five subtypes. Patients with a 31 code closely resemble the ineffectual dependent subtype. They retain the essential features of the dependent personality and have the features of the schizoid personality.

The cardinal feature of these patients is a desire to avoid all demands and adult responsibilities that in any way would suggest independence and autonomy. Social withdrawal, communication deficits, absence of true intimate relationships, and avoidance of independent actions can be expected from them. The core motivation for the dependent personality is to obtain and maintain nurturing and supportive relationships. It is quite possible that a person can act both passively and assertively to accomplish this central goal. It has been theorized that some form of overprotection during childhood produces this style, in that these patients were not given the opportunity to learn autonomous behaviors.

     Diagnosis: dependent personality disorder

32A

Patients with a 32A code tend to lean on other people for security, support, guidance, and direction. Such patients are passive, submissive, dependent, and self-conscious and lack initiative, confidence, and autonomy. Their temperament is pacifying and they try to avoid conflict. They acquiesce to maintain nurturance, affection, protection, and security. They can be expected to be obliging, docile, and placating, and they seek relationships in which they can lean on others for emotional support. They have excessive needs both for attachment and to be taken care of, and they feel helpless when alone. They willingly submit to the wishes of others to maintain this security, and this behavior tends to elicit helping and nurturing behaviors in those around them. When threatened with a loss of security, they seek out other relationships or institutions to take care of them. Their basic conflict is a fear of abandonment. This fear leads them to be overly compliant to ensure themselves of enduring protection. Their need for support is overwhelming. They prefer the dependent state and are genuinely docile. They have a self-image as a weak and fragile person, avoiding responsibilities and thereby precluding any chance of autonomy. When stressed (with a disruption of security), they are prone to develop anxiety and depressive disorders and substance abuse problems.

Millon has subdivided the dependent personality disorder into five types. Patients with a 32A code closely resemble the disquieted dependent subtype. They retain the essential features of the dependent personality and have features of the avoidant personality. The cardinal features of these patients are a combination of dependent traits plus a pervasive sense of apprehension, tension, and a constant fear of rejection and abandonment. They cling to supportive authority or to institutions, lest they be totally abandoned. Hostility toward those on whom they depend is suppressed lest they experience rejection or loss of support. The intrapsychic struggle to suppress hostility and cling to supportive structures in the face of a desire for independence and yet a fear of rejection should they demonstrate assertive behaviors accounts for their restless demeanor. It can be expected, though, that their social anxiety will be sufficiently controlled so they will lean on institutions or others to take care of them.

The core motivation for the dependent personality is to obtain and maintain nurturing and supportive relationships. It is quite possible that these patients can act both passively and assertively to accomplish this central goal.

It has been theorized that some form of overprotection during childhood produces this style, in that these patients were not given the opportunity to learn autonomous behaviors.

Diagnosis: dependent personality disorder

3′

Patients with a 3′ code tend to lean on other people for security, support, guidance, and direction. Such patients are passive, submissive, dependent, and self-conscious and lack initiative, confidence, and autonomy. Their temperament is pacifying and they try to avoid conflict. They acquiesce to maintain nurturance, affection, protection, and security. They can be expected to be obliging, docile, and placating, and they seek relationships in which they can lean on others for emotional support. They have excessive needs both for attachment and to be taken care of, and they feel helpless when alone. They willingly submit to the wishes of others to maintain this security, and this behavior tends to elicit helping and nurturing behaviors in those around them. When threatened with a loss of security, they seek out other relationships or institutions to take care of them. Their basic conflict is a fear of abandonment. This fear leads them to be overly compliant to ensure themselves enduring protection. Their need for support is overwhelming. They prefer the dependent state and are genuinely docile. They have a self-image as a weak and fragile person, avoiding responsibilities and thereby precluding any chance of autonomy. When stressed (with a disruption of security), they are prone to develop anxiety and depressive disorders and substance abuse problems.

Millon has subdivided the dependent personality disorder into five types. Patients with a 3' code closely resemble the accommodating dependent subtype. They retain the essential features of the dependent personality and have features of the histrionic personality. Cardinal features of these patients are their accommodating, placating, obliging, and conciliatory behaviors exhibited to avoid conflict, rejection, loss, and abandonment. They subsume their own personal identity under that of those who meet their dependency needs. They act in an inferior manner so others may dominate them and provide them with security, but at the price of their own autonomy. They tend to focus on and cater to the wishes and needs of others, suppressing their felt resentments or disillusionment to maintain their support and approval.

The core motivation for the dependent personality is to obtain and maintain nurturing and supportive relationships. It is quite possible that these patients can act both passively and assertively to accomplish this central goal.

It has been theorized that some form of overprotection during childhood produces this style, in that these patients were not given the opportunity to learn autonomous behaviors.

Diagnosis: dependent personality

38B

Patients with a 38B code tend to lean on other people for security, support, guidance, and direction. Such patients are passive, submissive, dependent, and self-conscious and lack initiative, confidence, and autonomy. Their temperament is pacifying and they try to avoid conflict. They acquiesce to maintain nurturance, affection, protection, and security. They can be expected to be obliging, docile, and placating, and they seek relationships in which they can lean on others for emotional support. They have excessive needs for both attachment and to be taken care of, and they feel helpless when alone. They willingly submit to the wishes of others to maintain this security, and this behavior tends to elicit helping and nurturing behaviors in those around them. When threatened with a loss of security, they seek out other relationships or institutions to take care of them. Their basic conflict is a fear of abandonment. This fear leads them to be overly compliant to ensure themselves enduring protection. Their need for support is overwhelming. They prefer the dependent state and are genuinely docile. They have a self-image as a weak and fragile person, avoiding responsibilities and thereby precluding any chance of autonomy. When stressed (with a disruption of security), they are prone to develop anxiety and depressive disorders and substance abuse problems.

Millon has subdivided the dependent personality disorder into five types. Patients with a 38B code closely resemble the selfless dependent subtype. They retain the essential features of the dependent personality and have features of the self-defeating personality. The cardinal feature of these patients is their willingness to submerge their own identity so that it appears as fused with the accomplishments of a significant other. Their own sense of self comes from values and deeds of the cathected object. This provides them with a sense of self-esteem, security, and stability.

The core motivation for the dependent personality is to obtain and maintain nurturing and supportive relationships. It is quite possible that these patients can act both passively and assertively to accomplish this central goal.

It has been theorized that some form of overprotection during childhood produces this style, in that these patients were not given the opportunity to learn autonomous behaviors.

Diagnosis: dependent personality disorder

43

Expect patients with a 43 code to be overly dramatic, with strong needs to be the center of attention. Such patients are seductive, through speech, style, dress, or manner, and seek constant stimulation and excitement in an exhibitionistic atmosphere; they require praise and attention. They are emotionally labile, are easily excited, and have frequent emotional outbursts. They are very gregarious, assertive, and socially outgoing, but they manipulate people to draw their approval and affection. They have strong needs for constant social acceptance. They are socially facile and seductively engaging, such that others are drawn to their enchanting manner. Relationships are often shallow and strained, however, as a result of their repeatedly dramatic and emotional outbursts and their self-centeredness. Denial and repression are their main defenses. They court the favor of others, but beneath this confident and self-assured persona is a fear of autonomy and independence that requires constant acceptance and approval to keep it in abeyance. They tend to displace anxieties when stressed. They are at risk for somatoform disorders and marital problems.

Millon has subdivided the histrionic personality disorder into six subtypes. Patients with a 43 code closely resemble the appeasing histrionic subtype. They retain the essential features of the histrionic personality and have features of the dependent personality. The cardinal feature of these patients is their unrelenting desire to please other people. Their main goal is not to seek attention but rather approval. They would do almost anything to placate valued others, largely because of a self-image that they are inadequate and unlovable. This latter aspect is largely unconscious. Millon has theorized that this subtype represents a transferential pattern whereby repressed hostility felt toward an unpleasant childhood caretaker (usually a parent) is projected yet denied on to a symbolic object. Through reaction formation, these patients believe using an excessively conciliatory manner is necessary to gain approval.

Caution: Empirical research has shown that Scale 4 (1) correlates positively with measures of mental health and negatively with measures of mental disorders; (2) infrequently appears in MCMI code types in psychiatric patients, except for substance abuse; and (3) is frequently the scale with the most elevated scores among nonclinical patients who have taken this test, particularly among women. These people would have a gregarious, extroverted, and socially engaging personality style but not a histrionic disorder. The clinician needs to evaluate which of these two possibilities is applicable to the particular patient.

Diagnosis: histrionic personality disorder

45

Expect patients with a 45 code to be overly dramatic and have strong needs to be the center of attention. Such patients are seductive, through speech, style, dress, or manner, and seek constant stimulation and excitement in an exhibitionistic atmosphere; they require praise and attention. They are emotionally labile, are easily excited, and have frequent emotional outbursts. They are very gregarious, assertive, and socially outgoing, but they manipulate people to draw their approval and affection. They have strong needs for constant social acceptance. They are socially facile and seductively engaging, such that others are drawn to their enchanting manner. Relationships are often shallow and strained, however, as a result of their repeatedly dramatic and emotional outbursts and their self-centeredness. Denial and repression are their main defenses. They court the favor of others, but beneath this confident and self-assured persona is a fear of autonomy and independence that requires constant acceptance and approval to keep it in abeyance. They tend to displace anxieties when stressed. They are at risk for somatoform disorders and marital problems.

Millon has subdivided the histrionic personality disorder into six subtypes. Patients with a 45 code closely resemble the vivacious histrionic subtype. They retain the essential features of the histrionic personality and have features of the narcissistic personality. The cardinal features of this subtype are a hypomanic-like level of energy, enthusiasm, buoyancy, and flamboyance, combined with easy excitability, impulsiveness, and vivacious playfulness. They show many narcissistic traits and are quite animated. However, they retain the excessive need for attention and approval that is characteristic of the histrionic style and remain superficial and unaware of the effect of their behaviors on others.

Caution: Empirical research has shown that Scale 4 (1) correlates positively with measures of mental health and negatively with measures of mental disorders; (2) infrequently appears in MCMI code types in psychiatric patients, except for substance abuse; and (3) is frequently the scale with the most elevated scores among nonclinical patients who have taken this test, particularly among women. These people would have a gregarious, extroverted, and socially engaging personality style but not a histrionic disorder. The clinician needs to evaluate which of these two possibilities is applicable to the particular patient.

Diagnosis: histrionic personality disorder

46A

Expect patients with a 46A code to be overly dramatic, with strong needs to be the center of attention. Such patients are seductive, through speech, style, dress, or manner, and seek constant stimulation and excitement in an exhibitionistic atmosphere; they require praise and attention. They are emotionally labile, are easily excited, and have frequent emotional outbursts. They are very gregarious, assertive, and socially outgoing, but they manipulate people to draw their approval and affection. They have strong needs for constant social acceptance. They are socially facile and seductively engaging, such that others are drawn to their enchanting manner. Relationships are often shallow and strained, however, as a result of their repeatedly dramatic and emotional outbursts and their self-centeredness. Denial and repression are their main defenses. They court the favor of others, but beneath this confident and self-assured persona is a fear of autonomy and independence that requires constant acceptance and approval to keep it in abeyance. They tend to displace anxieties when stressed. They are at risk for somatoform disorders and marital problems.

Millon has subdivided the histrionic personality disorder into six subtypes. Patients with a 46A code closely resemble the disingenuous histrionic subtype. They retain the essential features of the histrionic personality and have features of the antisocial personality. The cardinal feature of these patients is their shallow, superficial interpersonal relationships. They are insincere, unreliable, calculating, and deceitful, despite their superficial charm and overt friendliness. Their basic defenses are denial, repression, rationalization, and externalization. They are quite egocentric and hedonistic and basically insincere in their relationships. Unconsciously, they believe they are unlovable, so they act in ways to force others to love them. These patients are easily provoked and may react vindictively.

Caution: Empirical research has shown that Scale 4 (1) correlates positively with measures of mental health and negatively with measures of mental disorders; (2) infrequently appears in MCMI code types in psychiatric patients, except for substance abuse; and (3) is frequently the scale with the most elevated scores among nonclinical patients who have taken this test, particularly among women. These people would have a gregarious, extroverted, and socially engaging personality style but not a histrionic disorder. The clinician needs to evaluate which of these two possibilities is applicable to the particular patient.

Diagnosis: histrionic personality disorder

48A

Expect patients with a 48A code to be overly dramatic, with strong needs to be the center of attention. Such patients are seductive, through speech, style, dress, or manner, and seek constant stimulation and excitement in an exhibitionistic atmosphere; they require praise and attention. They are emotionally labile, are easily excited, and have frequent emotional outbursts. They are very gregarious, assertive, and socially outgoing, but they manipulate people to draw their approval and affection. They have strong needs for constant social acceptance. They are socially facile and seductively engaging, such that others are drawn to their enchanting manner. Relationships are often shallow and strained, however, as a result of their repeatedly dramatic and emotional outbursts and their self-centeredness. Denial and repression are their main defenses. They court the favor of others, but beneath this confident and self-assured persona is a fear of autonomy and independence that requires constant acceptance and approval to keep it in abeyance. They tend to displace anxieties when stressed. They are at risk for somatoform disorders and marital problems.

Millon has subdivided the histrionic personality disorder into six subtypes. Patients with a 48A code closely resemble the tempestuous histrionic subtype. They retain the essential features of the histrionic personality and have features of the passive-aggressive (negativistic) personality. The cardinal features of these patients is their turbulent emotional expressiveness, which is reactive to minor provocations. This emotional lability and their impulsive acting-out behaviors comingle with a petulant, moody, querulous, and brooding demeanor that results in ephemeral displays of anger followed by a return to their basic histrionic style.

Caution: Empirical research has shown that Scale 4 (1) correlates positively with measures of mental health and negatively with measures of mental disorders; (2) infrequently appears in MCMI code types in psychiatric patients, except for substance abuse; and (3) is frequently the scale with the most elevated scores among nonclinical patients who have taken this test, particularly among women. These people would have a gregarious, extroverted, and socially engaging personality style but not a histrionic disorder. The clinician needs to evaluate which of these two possibilities is applicable to the particular patient.

Diagnosis: histrionic personality disorder

4C

Expect patients with a 4C code to be overly dramatic, with strong needs to be the center of attention. Such patients are seductive, through speech, style, dress, or manner, and seek constant stimulation and excitement in an exhibitionistic atmosphere; they require praise and attention. They are emotionally labile, are easily excited, and have frequent emotional outbursts. They are very gregarious, assertive, and socially outgoing, but they manipulate people to draw their approval and affection. They have strong needs for constant social acceptance. They are socially facile and seductively engaging, such that others are drawn to their enchanting manner. Relationships are often shallow and strained, however, as a result of their repeatedly dramatic and emotional outbursts and their self-centeredness. Denial and repression are their main defenses. They court the favor of others, but beneath this confident and self-assured persona is a fear of autonomy and independence that requires constant acceptance and approval to keep it in abeyance. They tend to displace anxieties when stressed. They are at risk for somatoform disorders and marital problems.

Millon has subdivided the histrionic personality disorder into six subtypes. Patients with a 4C code closely resemble the infantile histrionic subtype. They retain the essential features of the histrionic personality and have features of the borderline personality style. The cardinal feature of these patients is their erratic emotionality, characterized by labile and volatile emotional expression. They behave in very childlike ways (e.g., pouting, clinging, demanding) and they are overly attached to a strong figure.

Caution: Empirical research has shown that Scale 4 (1) correlates positively with measures of mental health and negatively with measures of mental disorders; (2) infrequently appears in MCMI code types in psychiatric patients, except for substance abuse; and (3) is frequently the code with the most elevated scores among nonclinical patients who have taken this test, particularly among women. These people would have a gregarious, extroverted, and socially engaging personality style but not a histrionic disorder. The clinician needs to evaluate which of these two possibilities is applicable with the particular patient.

Diagnosis: histrionic personality disorder

54

Patients with a 54 code are quite self-centered and expect people to recognize their special qualities, and they require constant praise and recognition. They have excessive entitlement expectations and demand special favors. Grandiose statements of self-importance are readily elicited, and they consider themselves particularly attractive. They appear egocentric, arrogant, haughty, conceited, boastful, snobbish, pretentious, and supercilious. They exploit people and manipulate them with an air of superiority. Although they can be momentarily charming, they have a deficient social conscience and think only of themselves. They show a social imperturbability and are likely to disregard social constraints. They exploit social relationships, are indifferent to the rights of others, relate in an autocratic manner, and expect others to focus on them. Although this basic style often alienates other people, they respond with a sense of contempt and indifference because their inflated sense of self needs no confirmation from other people. They are quite grandiose and arrogant and rarely show signs of self-doubt. If they are humiliated or experience a narcissistic injury, they are prone to develop an affective disorder and perhaps a paranoid disorder. Many substance abusers also have a narcissistic personality style.

Millon has subdivided the narcissistic personality disorder into four subtypes. Patients with a 54 code closely resemble the amorous narcissistic subtype. They retain the essential features of the narcissistic personality and have features of the histrionic personality. The cardinal features of these patients are their sexual seductiveness and desire for sexual conquest to demonstrate their self-worth. These patients resort to lying, sexual bantering, sexual excesses, and fraud and use any means to attain sexual dominance. Their self-worth seems to emanate from their ability to beguile others with their clever charm, air of superiority, self-confidence, and boastful exploits. Their relationships tend to be brief, as they need to begin the process over and over again. Unconsciously, the amorous narcissist probably has feelings of inadequacy and low self-worth.

Caution: Empirical research has shown that Scale 5 (1) correlates positively with measures of mental health and negatively with measures of mental disorders; (2) infrequently appears in MCMI code types in psychiatric patients, except for substance abuse; and (3) is frequently the scale with the most elevated scores among nonclinical patients who have taken this test, particularly among women. These people would have a confident demeanor with high self-regard and seem socially charming and perhaps even attention seeking as a personality style but do not have a narcissistic personality disorder. The clinician needs to evaluate which of these two possibilities is applicable to the particular patient.

Diagnosis: *narcissistic personality disorder*

56A

Patients with a 56A code are quite self-centered, expect people to recognize their special qualities, and require constant praise and recognition. They have excessive entitlement expectations and demand special favors. Grandiose statements of self-importance are readily elicited, and they consider themselves particularly attractive. They appear egocentric, arrogant, haughty, conceited, boastful, snobbish, pretentious, and supercilious. They exploit people and manipulate them with an air of superiority. Although they can be momentarily charming, they have a deficient social conscience and think only of themselves. They show a social imperturbability and are likely to disregard social constraints. They exploit social relationships, are indifferent to the rights of others, relate in an autocratic manner, and expect others to focus on them. Even though this basic style often alienates other people, they respond with a sense of contempt and indifference because their inflated sense of self needs no confirmation from other people. They are quite grandiose and arrogant and rarely show signs of self-doubt. If they are humiliated or experience a narcissistic injury, they are prone to develop an affective disorder and perhaps a paranoid disorder. Many substance abusers also have a narcissistic personality style.

Millon has subdivided the narcissistic personality disorder into four subtypes. Patients with a 56A code closely resemble the unprincipled narcissistic subtype. They retain the essential features of the narcissistic personality and have features of the antisocial personality. The cardinal features of these patients is their defective superego, demonstrated as antisocial behaviors and traits. They maintain relationships only when it is to their benefit. They have no sense of loyalty and no social conscience, so they are indifferent to the welfare of others and willingly exploit them. They tend to react impulsively when provoked. They may live on the edge of the law or flaunt the law, believing they are above it. They are replete with deceit, vindictiveness, and malice projected onto those they hold responsible for their annoyances. Their demeanor is one of arrogant disregard and they project an air of intimidation. They maintain a cool appearance and seem defiant in the face of threats or punishment. They are at extreme risk for legal problems, vocational problems, substance abuse, and marital disruptions.

Caution: Empirical research has shown that Scale 5 (1) correlates positively with measures of mental health and negatively with measures of mental disorders; (2) infrequently appears in MCMI code types in psychiatric patients, except for substance abuse; and (3) is frequently the scale with the most elevated scores among nonclinical patients who have taken this test, particularly among men. These people would have a confident demeanor with high self-regard and seem socially charming and perhaps even attention seeking as a personality style but they do not have a narcissistic personality disorder. The clinician needs to evaluate which of these two possibilities is applicable to the particular patient.

Diagnosis: narcissistic personality disorder, antisocial personality disorder, or both

58A or 52A

Patients with a 58A or 52A code are quite self-centered, expect people to recognize their special qualities, and require constant praise and recognition. They have excessive entitlement expectations and demand special favors. Grandiose statements of self-importance are readily elicited, and they consider themselves particularly attractive. They appear egocentric, arrogant, haughty, conceited, boastful, snobbish, pretentious, and supercilious. They exploit people and manipulate them with an air of superiority. Although they can be momentarily charming, they have a deficient social conscience and think only of themselves. They show a social imperturbability and are likely to disregard social constraints. They exploit social relationships, are indifferent to the rights of others, relate in an autocratic manner, and expect others to focus on them. Even though this basic style often alienates other people, they respond with a sense of contempt and indifference because their inflated sense of self needs no confirmation from other people. They are quite grandiose and arrogant and rarely show signs of self-doubt. If they are humiliated or experience a narcissistic injury, they are prone to develop an affective disorder and perhaps a paranoid disorder. Many substance abusers also have a narcissistic personality style.

Millon has subdivided the narcissistic personality disorder into four subtypes. Patients with a 58A or 52A code closely resemble the compensating narcissistic subtype. They retain the essential features of the narcissistic personality and have features of the passive-aggressive (negativistic) or avoidant personality styles. The cardinal feature of these patients is their strong desire to be seen as confident, superior, and worthy of worship, which derives from an underlying sense of insecurity and lack of self-esteem. They are attempting to compensate for early-life psychological deprivations by striving for prestige and enhancing their fragile sense of self. They live in fear that others will discover they are a fraud.

Caution: Empirical research has shown that Scale 5 (1) correlates positively with measures of mental health and negatively with measures of mental disorders; (2) infrequently appears in MCMI code types in psychiatric patients, except for substance abuse; and (3) is frequently the scale with the most elevated scores among nonclinical patients who have taken this test, particularly among men. These people would have a confident demeanor with high self-regard and seem socially charming and perhaps even attention seeking as a personality style, but they do not have a narcissistic personality disorder. The clinician needs to evaluate which of these two possibilities is applicable to the particular patient.

Diagnosis: narcissistic personality disorder

6A1 or 6A2A

Patients with a 6A1 or 6A2A code are quite narcissistic, fearless, pugnacious, daring, blunt, aggressive and assertive, irresponsible, impulsive, ruthless, victimizing, intimidating, and dominating; often are energetic and competitive; and are quite determined and independent. They are argumentative, self-reliant, revengeful, and vindictive. They are chronically dissatisfied and harbor resentments toward people who challenge, criticize, or express disapproval of their behavior. They are characteristically touchy and jealous, brood over perceived slights and wrongs, and provoke fear in those around them through their intimidating social demeanor. They tend to present with an angry, hostile affect. They are suspicious and skeptical of the motives of other people, plan revenge for past grievances, and view others as untrustworthy. They avoid expressions of warmth, gentleness, closeness, and intimacy, viewing such involvements as a sign of weakness. They often ascribe their own malicious tendencies onto the motives of others. They feel comfortable only when they have power and control over others. They are continually on guard against anticipated ridicule and act out in a socially intimidating manner, desiring to provoke fear in others and to exploit others for self-gain. These patients are driven by power, by malevolent projections, and by an expectation of suffering at the hands of others, so they react to maintain their autonomy and independence. Millon believes that their behavior is motivated by an expectancy that people will be rejecting and that other people are malicious, devious, and vengeful, thus justifying a forceful counteraction to maintain their own autonomy. They are alert for signs of ridicule and contempt, and they react with impulsive hostility in response to felt resentments. They are prone to substance abuse, relationship difficulties, vocational deficits, and legal problems.

Millon has subdivided the antisocial personality disorder into five types. Patients with a 6A1 or 6A2A code closely resemble the nomadic antisocial subtype. They have the features of the antisocial personality with those of the schizoid or avoidant personality styles. These patients are generally indifferent and disengaged from social responsibilities. They go through life remaining on the periphery of social roles, and they socially withdraw to mask their intense feelings of anger and resentment. In a psychoanalytic sense, their nomadic existence may symbolically represent a search for a home and for parental love and acceptance, which they feel have been missing in their lives. They feel that society has been unjust to them and they therefore distance themselves from the possibilities of continued further disappointments. These patients are comparatively more benign than other antisocial subtypes but remain asocial and angry over their "abandoned" status. Other people would describe them as loners.

Many drug addicts have tested as having this pattern on the MCMI-III. In those instances in which patients have not had a nomadic pattern, their Scale 1 spike may suggest an emotionally detached personality with a self-imposed withdrawal and isolating behavior to bind anxiety. However, when stressed, they are prone to erupt in antisocial behavior.

Note: It is possible to have an antisocial character style without engaging in antisocial (criminal) behavior.

Diagnosis: antisocial personality disorder

6A4

Patients with a 6A4 code are quite narcissistic, fearless, pugnacious, daring, blunt, aggressive and assertive, irresponsible, impulsive, ruthless, victimizing, intimidating, and dominating; are often energetic and competitive; and are quite determined and independent. They are argumentative, self-reliant, revengeful, and vindictive. They are chronically dissatisfied and harbor resentments against people who challenge, criticize, or express disapproval of their behavior. They are characteristically touchy and jealous, brood over perceived slights and wrongs, and provoke fear in those around them through their intimidating social demeanor. They tend to present with an angry and hostile affect. They are suspicious and skeptical of the motives of other people, plan revenge for past grievances, and view others as untrustworthy. They avoid expressions of warmth, gentleness, closeness, and intimacy, viewing such involvements as a sign of weakness. They often ascribe their own malicious tendencies onto the motives of others. They feel comfortable only when they have power and control over others. They are continually on guard against anticipated ridicule and act out in a socially intimidating manner, desiring to provoke fear in others and to exploit others for self-gain. These patients are driven by power, by malevolent projections, and by an expectation of suffering at the hands of others, so they react to maintain their autonomy and independence. Millon believes that their behavior is motivated by an expectancy that people will be rejecting and that other people are malicious, devious, and vengeful, thus justifying a forceful counteraction to maintain their own autonomy. They are alert for signs of ridicule and contempt, and they react with impulsive hostility in response to felt resentments. They are prone to substance abuse, relationship difficulties, vocational deficits, and legal problems.

Millon has subdivided the antisocial personality disorder into five types. Patients with a 6A4 code closely resemble the risk-taking antisocial type. They retain the essential features of the antisocial personality and have features of the histrionic personality. The cardinal feature of these patients is their desire for adventure, stimulation, danger, and perilous activity. This desire is motivated by a feeling of being trapped by routinized tasks and by daily responsibilities. These patients are sensation seekers who appear fun loving but are quite unreliable and undependable and possess essentially antisocial personality traits.

Note: It is possible to have an antisocial character style without engaging in antisocial (criminal) behavior.

Diagnosis: antisocial personality disorder

6A5

Patients with a 6A5 code are quite narcissistic, fearless, pugnacious, daring, blunt, aggressive and assertive, irresponsible, impulsive, ruthless, victimizing, intimidating, and dominating; are often energetic and competitive; and are quite determined and independent. They are argumentative, self-reliant, revengeful, and vindictive. They are chronically dissatisfied and harbor resentments against people who challenge, criticize, or express disapproval over their behavior. They are characteristically touchy and jealous, brood over perceived slights and wrongs, and provoke fear in those around them through their intimidating social demeanor. They tend to present with an angry, hostile affect. They are suspicious and skeptical of the motives of other people, plan revenge for past grievances, and view others as untrustworthy. They avoid expressions of warmth, gentleness, closeness, and intimacy, viewing such involvements as a sign of weakness. They often ascribe their own malicious tendencies onto the motives of others. They feel comfortable only when they have power and control over others. They are continually on guard against antici-pated ridicule and act out in a socially intimidating manner, desiring to provoke fear in others and to exploit others for self-gain. These patients are driven by power, by malevolent projections, and by an expectation of suffering at the hands of others, so they react to main-tain their autonomy and independence. Millon believes that their behavior is motivated by an expectancy that people will be rejecting and that other people are malicious, devious, and vengeful, thus jus-tifying a forceful counteraction to maintain their own autonomy. They are alert for signs of ridicule and contempt, and they react with impulsive hostility in response to felt resentments. They are prone to substance abuse, relationship difficulties, vocational deficits, and legal problems.

Millon has subdivided the antisocial personality disorder into five types. Patients with a 6A5 code closely resemble the reputation-defending antisocial type. They retain the essential features of the antisocial personality and have features of the narcissistic personality. The cardinal feature of these patients is their desire to maintain an image and reputation as a tough, aggressive, and mean-spirited person. Their personality style provides them with group status and usually a position of authority and leadership within a deviant subgroup. They are quick to attack and assail anyone or anything that threatens their status. They need to be seen as strong and as a person not to be "messed with."

Note: It is possible to have an antisocial character style without engaging in antisocial (criminal) behavior.

Diagnosis: antisocial personality disorder

6A6B or 6AP

Patients with a 6A6B or 6AP code are quite narcissistic, fearless, pugnacious, daring, blunt, aggressive and assertive, irresponsible, impulsive, ruthless, victimizing, intimidating, and dominating; are often energetic and competitive; and are quite determined and independent. They are argumentative, self-reliant, revengeful, and vindictive. They are chronically dissatisfied and harbor resentments against people that challenge, criticize, or express disapproval of their behavior. They are characteristically touchy and jealous, brood over perceived slights and wrongs, and provoke fear in those around them through their intimidating social demeanor. They tend to present with an angry, hostile affect. They are suspicious and skeptical of the motives of other people, plan revenge for past grievances, and view others as untrustworthy. They avoid expressions of warmth, gentleness, closeness, and intimacy, viewing such involvements as a sign of weakness. They often ascribe their own malicious tendencies onto the motives of others. They feel comfortable only when they have power and control over others. They are continually on guard against anticipated ridicule and act out in a socially intimidating manner, desiring to provoke fear in others and to exploit others for self-gain. These patients are driven by power, by malevolent projections, and by an expectation of suffering at the hands of others, so they react to maintain their autonomy and independence. Millon believes that their behavior is motivated by an expectancy that people will be rejecting and that other people are malicious, devious, and vengeful, thus justifying a forceful counteraction to maintain their own autonomy. They are alert for signs of ridicule and contempt, and they react with impulsive hostility in response to felt resentments. They are prone to substance abuse, relationship difficulties, vocational deficits, and legal problems.

Millon has subdivided the antisocial personality disorder into five types. Patients with a 6A6B or 6AP code closely resemble the malevolent antisocial type. They retain the essential features of the antisocial personality and have features of the aggressive/sadistic or paranoid personality styles. The cardinal features of these patients are their particularly evil intentions and behavior. These patients are especially hostile, vindictive, belligerent, aggressive, brutal, and resentful. They distrust others, anticipate punishment from them, and react with cold retaliation. They show or feel little guilt or remorse for any of their actions. They maintain an image of strength, power, and dominance.

    Diagnosis: antisocial personality disorder

6B2A

Patients with a 6B2A code may not be publicly antisocial, but their clinical features are quite similar to those of the antisocial personality and the style may be considered as a more pathological variant of the antisocial style. They engage in behaviors that are abusive and humiliating and may violate the rights and feelings of others. They are aggressive, forceful, commanding, militant, domineering, hardheaded, hostile, dominating, intimidating, pervasively destructive, and brutal. They become combative when provoked, and they are antagonistic and disagreeable people. They tend to be touchy, excitable, and irritable and react angrily when confronted. In psychoanalytic terms, they are sadistic personalities. Some are able to sublimate these traits into socially approved vocations. When their autonomy is threatened, they are prone to spouse abuse and explosive outbursts that may result in legal problems.

    Millon has subdivided the aggressive/sadistic personality disorder into four subtypes. Patients with a 6B2A code closely resemble the spineless sadist subtype. They retain the essential features of the aggressive/sadistic personality and have features of the avoidant personality. These patients show the essential prototype features of the aggressive/sadistic personality, but they do so to hide their feelings of inadequacy and fearfulness. Their aggressive behavior is counterphobic and is a reaction formation designed to hide their insecurities. They rely on group support to help them hide their weakness and they tend to pick on weaker scapegoats.

    Diagnosis: personality disorder not otherwise specified (NOS), aggressive personality traits

6B7

Patients with a 6B7 code may not be publicly antisocial, but their clinical features are quite similar to those of the antisocial personality and the style may be considered as a more pathological variant of the antisocial style. They engage in behaviors that are abusive and humiliating and may violate the rights and feelings of others. They are aggressive, forceful, commanding, militant, domineering, hardheaded, hostile, dominating, intimidating, pervasively destructive, and brutal. They become combative when provoked, and they are antagonistic and disagreeable people. They tend to be touchy, excitable, and irritable and react angrily when confronted. In psychoanalytic terms, they are sadistic personalities. Some are able to sublimate these traits into socially approved vocations. When their autonomy is threatened, they are prone to spouse abuse and explosive outbursts that may result in legal problems.

Millon has subdivided the aggressive/sadistic personality disorder into four subtypes. These patients closely resemble the enforcing sadist subtype. They retain the essential features of the aggressive/sadistic personality and have features of the compulsive personality. The cardinal feature of these patients is their abuse of social power. They are often in positions of socially sanctioned roles where their responsibilities include meting out punishment. They have lost their sense of balance and rigidly apply punishment in an inhumane and self-righteous manner. They may occupy legitimate social roles (e.g., police officer) or may be engaged in illicit social roles (e.g., mob hit man).

Diagnosis: personality disorder not otherwise specified (NOS), aggressive personality traits

6B8A *or* 6BP

Patients with a 6B8A or 6BP code may not be publicly antisocial, but their clinical features are quite similar to those of the antisocial personality and the style may be considered as a more pathological variant of the antisocial style. They engage in behaviors that are abusive and humiliating and may violate the rights and feelings of others.

They are aggressive, forceful, commanding, militant, domineering, hardheaded, hostile, dominating, intimidating, pervasively destructive, and brutal. They become combative when provoked, and they are antagonistic and disagreeable people. They tend to be touchy, excitable, and irritable and react angrily when confronted. In psychoanalytic terms, they are sadistic personalities. Some are able to sublimate these traits into socially approved vocations. When their autonomy is threatened, they are prone to spouse abuse and explosive outbursts that may result in legal problems.

Millon has subdivided the aggressive/sadistic personality disorder into four subtypes. Patients with a 6B8A or 6BP code closely resemble the tyrannical sadist subtype. They retain the essential features of the aggressive/sadistic personality and have features of the passive-aggressive (negativistic) or paranoid personality styles. The cardinal feature of these patients is their use of violence to intimidate, terrorize, and subjugate weaker people, forcing them to cooperate and obey. These patients act in a menacing, threatening, abusing, and demeaning manner and feel satisfied with the violence they perpetrate. If these patients do not have an actual history of physical violence, then they use threats of cruelty, verbal abuse, and threats of violence to keep people in line. Millon considers this type to be one of the most frightening and cruel types of any personality disorder.

Diagnosis: personality disorder not otherwise specified (NOS), aggressive personality traits

71

Patients with a 71 code are behaviorally rigid, constricted, conscientious, polite, organized, meticulous, punctual, respectful, often perfectionistic, formal, prudent, overconforming, cooperative, compliant with rules, serious, moralistic, self-righteous and self-disciplined, efficient, and relatively inflexible. They place high demands on themselves. They are emotionally restrained, suppressing strong resentments and anger, and they appear tense and grim but emotionally controlled. They are socially conforming and prone to a repetitive lifestyle, as a result of engaging in a series of patterned behaviors

..

and rules that must be followed. They have fears of social disapproval and are models of propriety and restraint. They show excessive respect for authority but may treat subordinates in an autocratic manner. They operate from a sense of duty that compels them to not let others down, thus risking the condemnation of authority figures. They show an anxious conformity. They strive to avoid criticism but expect it because of what they perceive to be their personal short-comings. They fear making mistakes because of expected disapproval. Their behavior stems from a conflict between a felt hostility that they wish to express and a fear of social disapproval should they expose this underlying oppositional resentment. This circumstance forces them to become overconforming, thus placing high demands on themselves that serve to control this intense anger, which occasionally breaks through into their behavior. Obsessive thinking may or may not be present.

Millon has subdivided the compulsive personality disorder into five subtypes. Patients with a 71 code closely resemble the parsimonious compulsive. They retain the essential features of the compulsive personality and have features of the schizoid personality. The cardinal feature of these patients is intensely tight-fisted, penny-pinching, hoarding behavior. These patients have been deprived at some point in their life and doggedly protect their possessions. They are unwilling to share. They maintain an emotional distance from people, focusing on external signs of self-worth to hide their inner sense of personal emptiness.

Caution: Empirical research has shown that (1) Scale 7 correlates positively with measures of mental health and negatively with measures of mental disorders; (2) Scale 7 infrequently appears in MCMI code types in psychiatric patients; (3) Scale 7 is frequently the scale with the most elevated scores among nonclinical patients who have taken this test, particularly among men; and (4) the only study that has used the MCMI with patients with an obsessive-compulsive disorder did not have elevated score on Scale 7. Thus, patients with elevated scores on Scale 7 would be conscientious, rule bound, and orderly, suggesting a compulsive personality style but not a compulsive disorder. The clinician needs to evaluate which of these two possibilities is applicable to the particular patient.

Diagnosis: compulsive personality disorder

75

Patients with a 75 code are behaviorally rigid, constricted, conscientious, polite, organized, meticulous, punctual, respectful, often perfectionistic, formal, prudent, overconforming, cooperative, compliant with rules, serious, moralistic, self-righteous and self-disciplined, efficient, and relatively inflexible. They place high demands on themselves. They are emotionally restrained, suppressing strong resentments and anger, and they appear tense and grim but emotionally controlled. They are socially conforming and prone to a repetitive lifestyle as a result of engaging in a series of patterned behaviors and rules that must be followed. They have fears of social disapproval and are models of propriety and restraint. They show excessive respect for authority but may treat subordinates in an autocratic manner. They operate from a sense of duty that compels them to not let others down, thus risking the condemnation of authority figures. They show an anxious conformity. They strive to avoid criticism but expect it because of what they perceive to be their personal shortcomings. They fear making mistakes because of expected disapproval. Their behavior stems from a conflict between a felt hostility that they wish to express and a fear of social disapproval should they expose this underlying oppositional resentment. This circumstance forces them to become overconforming, thus placing high demands on themselves that serve to control this intense anger, which occasionally breaks through into their behavior. Obsessive thinking may or may nor be present.

Millon has subdivided the compulsive personality disorder into five subtypes. Patients with a 75 code closely resemble the bureaucratic compulsive. They retain the essential features of the compulsive personality and have features of the narcissistic personality. The cardinal feature of these patients is their blind obedience to values, rules, and structure of an external authority. Adherence to rules, regulations, procedures, and instructions gives these patients a sense of security, absolves them from personal responsibility, and reduces opportunities for disapproval from authority figures. Although extremely loyal, dependable, conventional, and dedicated, they may also appear to be excessively rigid, closed-minded, and dogmatic. This style might be a transference and an effective sublimation from a rigid authority figure (parent) experienced early in life, or it could be the result of learned behavior from functioning in an extremely structured environment where roles are constantly threatened for minor mistakes.

Caution: Empirical research has shown that (1) Scale 7 correlates positively with measures of mental health and negatively with measures of mental disorders; (2) Scale 7 infrequently appears in MCMI code types in psychiatric patients; (3) Scale 7 is frequently the scale with the most elevated scores among nonclinical patients who have taken this test, particularly among men; and (4) the only study that has used the MCMI with patients with an obsessive-compulsive disorder did not have elevated scores on Scale 7. Thus, patients with elevated scores on Scale 7 would be conscientious, rule bound, and orderly, suggesting a compulsive personality style but not a compulsive disorder. The clinician needs to evaluate which of these two possibilities is applicable to the particular patient.

Diagnosis: compulsive personality disorder

78A

Patients with a 78A code are behaviorally rigid, constricted, conscientious, polite, organized, meticulous, punctual, respectful, often perfectionistic, formal, prudent, overconforming, cooperative, compliant with rules, serious, moralistic, self-righteous and self-disciplined, efficient, and relatively inflexible. They place high demands on themselves. They are emotionally restrained, suppressing strong resentments and anger, and they appear tense and grim but emotionally controlled. They are socially conforming and prone to a repetitive lifestyle as a result of engaging in a series of patterned behaviors and rules that must be followed. They have fears of social disapproval and are a model of propriety and restraint. They show excessive respect for authority but may treat subordinates in an autocratic manner. They operate from a sense of duty that compels them to not let others down, thus risking the condemnation of authority figures. They show an anxious conformity. They strive to avoid criticism but expect it because of what they perceive to be their personal short-comings. They fear making mistakes because of expected disapproval. Their behavior stems from a conflict between a felt hostility that they wish to express and a fear of social disapproval should they expose this underlying oppositional resentment. This circumstance forces them to become overconforming; thus they place high demands on themselves that serve to control this intense anger, which occasionally breaks through into their behavior. Obsessive thinking may or may not be present.

Millon has subdivided the compulsive personality disorder into five subtypes. Patients with a 78A code closely resemble the bedeviled compulsive. They retain the essential features of the compulsive personality and have features of the passive-aggressive (negativistic) personality. The cardinal feature of this subtype is a strong conflict between expressing oppositional tendencies and satisfying the wishes of others. This results in traits of discontentment, indecisiveness, confusion, and irritability and in a troubled inner mental life, although they may actually appear to be a paragon of rationality.

Caution: Empirical research has shown that (1) Scale 7 correlates positively with measures of mental health and negatively with measures of mental disorders; (2) Scale 7 infrequently appears in MCMI code types in psychiatric patients; (3) Scale 7 is frequently the scale with the most elevated scores among nonclinical patients who have taken this test, particularly among men; and (4) the only study that has used the MCMI with patients with an obsessive-compulsive disorder did not have elevated scores on Scale 7. Thus, patients with elevated scores on Scale 7 would be conscientious, rule bound, and orderly, suggesting a compulsive personality style but not a compulsive disorder. The clinician needs to evaluate which of these two possibilities is applicable to the particular patient.

Diagnosis: compulsive personality disorder

7P

Patients with a 7P code are behaviorally rigid, constricted, conscientious, polite, organized, meticulous, punctual, respectful, often perfectionistic, formal, prudent, overconforming, cooperative, compliant with rules, serious, moralistic, self-righteous and self-disciplined, efficient, and relatively inflexible. They place high demands on themselves. They are emotionally restrained, suppressing strong resentments and anger, and they appear tense, grim, but emotionally controlled. They are socially conforming and prone to a repetitive lifestyle as a result of engaging in a series of patterned behaviors and rules that must be followed. They have fears of social disapproval and are a model of propriety and restraint. They show excessive respect for authority but may treat subordinates in an autocratic manner. They operate from a sense of duty that compels them to not let others down, thus risking the condemnation of authority figures. They show an anxious conformity. They strive to avoid criticism but expect it because of what they perceive to be their personal shortcomings. They fear making mistakes because of expected disapproval. Their behavior stems from a conflict between a felt hostility that they wish to express and a fear of social disapproval should they expose this underlying oppositional resentment. This circumstance forces them to become overconforming; thus they place high demands on themselves that serve to control this intense anger, which occasionally breaks through into their behavior. Obsessive thinking may or may not be present.

Millon has subdivided the compulsive personality disorder into five subtypes. Patients with a 78A code closely resemble the puritanical compulsive. They retain the essential features of the compulsive personality and have features of the paranoid personality. The cardinal feature of these patients is a self-righteous distribution of morality. These patients are quite harsh, judgmental, prudish, controlled, and grim. They are anxious about making mistakes and fear humiliation. They behave as if they are responsible for redressing the sins of the world. Although not paranoid in the clinical sense, they have paranoid-like traits (e.g., being suspicious, overly judgmental, argumentative, resentful, opinionated, fault-finding, critical, and uncompromising).

Caution: Empirical research has shown that (1) Scale 7 correlates positively with measures of mental health and negatively with measures of mental disorders; (2) Scale 7 infrequently appears in MCMI code types in psychiatric patients; (3) Scale 7 is frequently the scale with the most elevated scores among nonclinical patients who have taken this test, particular among men; and (4) the only study that has used the MCMI with patients with an obsessive-compulsive disorder did not have elevated scores on Scale 7. Thus, patients with elevated scores on Scale 7 would be conscientious, rule bound, and orderly, suggesting a compulsive personality style but not a compulsive disorder. The clinician needs to evaluate which of these two possibilities is applicable to the particular patient.

Diagnosis: compulsive personality disorder

8A2B

Patients with an 8A2B code display a mixture of passive compliance and obedience at one time and oppositional and negativistic behavior at the next time. They are moody, irritable, and hostile; manifest a grumbling and pessimistic demeanor; and are erratically and explosively angry and stubborn at one moment and feel guilty and contrite at the next moment. Disillusionment seems to permeate their lives. They feel misunderstood, so they vacillate between passive dependency and stubborn contrariness, which provokes discomfort and exasperation in those around them. They expect disappointment and maintain an unstable and conflictual role in relations with others. They sulk, feel unappreciated and/or that they are being treated unfairly, constantly complain, and are persistently petulant and discontented. They often have problems with authority and, if employed, have job difficulties.

Millon has subdivided the passive-aggressive (negativistic) personality disorder into four subtypes. Patients with an 8A2B code closely resemble the discontented negativistic subtype. They retain the essential features of the passive-aggressive (negativistic) personality and have features of the depressive personality. The cardinal feature of these patients is their malcontentedness. They are negativistic in the true sense of the word and are intentionally complaining, grumbling, dissatisfied, discontented, testy, moody, and disgruntled. They tend to not openly confront those who have aggrieved them; rather, they tend to try to embarrass or undercut those who have wronged them while making themselves appear righteous.

Commentary: An elevation on Scale 8A is a good indicator of problems with authority and with criminal behaviors or potential criminal behavior. Also, clinical elevations on this scale appear in a number of profile codes involving psychiatric patients. Patients with elevations on Scale 8A warrant close clinical evaluation.

Diagnosis: personality disorder not otherwise specified (NOS), passive-aggressive (negativistic) traits

8A3

Patients with an 8A3 code display a mixture of passive compliance and obedience at one time and oppositional and negativistic behavior the next time. They are moody, irritable, and hostile; manifest a grumbling and pessimistic demeanor; and are erratically and explosively angry and stubborn at one moment and feel guilty and contrite at the next moment. Disillusionment seems to permeate their lives. They feel misunderstood, so they vacillate between passive dependency and stubborn contrariness, which provokes discomfort and exasperation in those around them. They expect disappointment and maintain an unstable and conflictual role in relations with others. They sulk, feel unappreciated and/or that they are being treated unfairly, constantly complain, and are persistently petulant and discontented. They often have problems with authority and, if employed, have job difficulties.

Millon has subdivided the passive-aggressive (negativistic) personality disorder into four subtypes. Patients with an 8A3 code closely resemble the circuitous negativistic subtype. They retain the essential features of the passive-aggressive (negativistic) personality and have features of the dependent personality. This subtype closely corresponds to the original meaning of the passive-aggressive personality in that these patients express their oppositional behavior indirectly and in a circuitous manner. They tend to be stubborn, "forgetful," procrastinating, neglectful, dawdling, and dependent. These behaviors are usually unconscious and these patients remain disagreeable and relatively impervious to insight and pressure.

Commentary: An elevation on Scale 8A is a good indicator of problems with authority and with criminal behaviors or potential criminal behavior. Also, clinical elevations on this scale appear in a number of profile codes involving psychiatric patients. Patients with elevations on Scale 8A warrant close clinical evaluation.

Diagnosis: personality disorder not otherwise specified (NOS), passive-aggressive (negativistic) traits

8A6B

Patients with an 8A6B code display a mixture of passive compliance and obedience at one time and oppositional and negativistic behavior at the next time. They are moody, irritable, and hostile; manifest a grumbling and pessimistic demeanor; and are erratically and explosively angry and stubborn at one moment and feel guilty and contrite at the next moment. Disillusionment seems to permeate their lives. They feel misunderstood, so they vacillate between passive dependency and stubborn contrariness, which provokes discomfort and exasperation in those around them. They expect disappointment and maintain an unstable and conflictual role in relations with others. They sulk, feel unappreciated and/or that they are being treated unfairly, constantly complain, and are persistently petulant and discontented. They often have problems with authority and, if employed, have job difficulties.

Millon has subdivided the passive-aggressive (negativistic) personality disorder into four subtypes. Patients with an 8A6B code closely resemble the abrasive negativistic subtype. They retain the essential features of the passive-aggressive (negativistic) personality and have features of the aggressive/sadistic personality. The cardinal feature of these patients is their contentious, quarrelsome, irritable, caustic, and abrasive manner that challenges their behavior. They are fault finding in a quite derogatory manner and they seem to delight in debasing others. They are quite angry people who distance others with their negativism.

Commentary: An elevation on Scale 8A is a good indicator of problems with authority and with criminal behaviors or potential criminal behaviors. Also, clinical elevations on this scale appear in a number of profile codes involving psychiatric patients. Patients with elevations on Scale 8A warrant close clinical evaluation.

Diagnosis: personality disorder not otherwise specified (NOS), passive-aggressive (negativistic) traits

8AC

Patients with an 8AC code display a mixture of passive compliance and obedience at one time and oppositional and negativistic behavior the next time. They are moody, irritable, and hostile; manifest a grumbling and pessimistic demeanor; and are erratically and explosively angry and stubborn at one moment and feel guilty and contrite at the next moment. Disillusionment seems to permeate their lives. They feel misunderstood, so they vacillate between passive dependency and stubborn contrariness, which provokes discomfort and exasperation in those around them. They expect disappointment and maintain an unstable and conflictual role in relations with others. They sulk, feel unappreciated and/or that they are being treated unfairly, constantly complain, and are persistently petulant and discontented. They often have problems with authority and, if employed, have job difficulties.

Millon has subdivided the passive-aggressive (negativistic) personality disorder into four subtypes. Patient with an 8AC code closely resemble the vacillating negativistic subtype. They retain the essential features of the passive-aggressive (negativistic) personality and have features of the borderline personality, particularly its erratic emotionality. The cardinal feature of these patients is the rapid fluctuation of their moods and behaviors. They can be aggressive and argumentative at one moment and submissive and dependent at the next; they can appear to be self-assured and decisive yet suddenly bewildered and helpless. These behaviors are quite public and keep significant others on edge.

Commentary: An elevation on Scale 8A is a good indicator of problems with authority and with criminal behaviors or potential criminal behavior. Also, clinical elevations on this scale appear in a number of profile codes involving psychiatric patients. Patients with elevations on Scale 8A warrant close clinical evaluation.

Diagnosis: personality disorder not otherwise specified (NOS), passive-aggressive (negativistic) traits

8B2B

Patients with an 8B2B code relate in a self-sacrificing, martyrlike manner, allowing others to take advantage of them. They seem to search for relationships in which they can lean on others for security and affection. Typically, they act in an unassuming manner, denigrating themselves into believing they deserve their fate. Thus, this pattern is repeated in most relationships, making them prone to being abused. The pattern is conceptually similar to the analytic concept of masochism.

Millon has subdivided the self-defeating personality disorder into four subtypes. Patients with an 8B2B code closely resemble the oppressed masochist subtype. They retain the essential features of the self-defeating personality and have features of the depressive personality. The cardinal feature of these patients is their use of physical and psychological symptoms to elicit sympathy and to induce guilt. These patients tend to feel quite miserable, but they use these circumstances to gain love, perpetuate dependence, and avoid adult responsibilities. They displace anger and resentment toward significant others onto their physical and psychological functioning. Because these patients act helpless, others reduce their demands on them.

Diagnosis: personality disorder not otherwise specified (NOS), self-defeating (masochistic) traits

8B3

Patients with an 8B3 code relate in a self-sacrificing, martyrlike manner, allowing others to take advantage of them. They seem to search for relationships in which they can lean on others for security and affection. Typically, they act in an unassuming manner, denigrating themselves into believing they deserve their fate. Thus, this pattern is repeated in most relationships, making them prone to being abused. The pattern is conceptually similar to the analytic concept of masochism.

Millon has subdivided the self-defeating personality disorder into four subtypes. Patients with an 8B3 code closely resemble the self-undoing masochist subtype. They retain the essential features of the self-defeating personality and have features of the dependent personality. The cardinal feature of these patients is their unconsciously acting in ways that draw victimization, humiliation, disgrace, punishment, and abuse. They seem to undo any successes and provoke others into demeaning them. This pattern is quite similar to the analytic concept of the masochistic personality.

Diagnosis: personality disorder not otherwise specified (NOS), self-defeating (masochistic) traits

8B4

Patients with an 8B4 code relate in a self-sacrificing, martyrlike manner, allowing others to take advantage of them. They seem to search for relationships in which they can lean on others for security and affection. Typically, they act in an unassuming manner, denigrating themselves into believing they deserve their fate. Thus, this pattern is repeated in most relationships, making them prone to being abused. The pattern is conceptually similar to the analytic concept of masochism.

Millon has subdivided the self-defeating personality disorder into four subtypes. Patients with an 8B4 code closely resemble the virtuous masochist subtype. They retain the essential features of the self-defeating personality and have features of the histrionic personality. The cardinal feature of these patients is acting in an unselfish, self-sacrificing manner. Their sometimes saintly demeanor brings with it their expectation of gratitude and attention. However, unconsciously, they have low self-esteem and feel that the love and attention they receive have been attained through manipulation rather than through legitimate means.

Diagnosis: personality disorder not otherwise specified (NOS), self-defeating (masochistic) traits

8B8A

Patients with an 8B8A code relate in a self-sacrificing, martyrlike manner, allowing others to take advantage of them. They seem to search for relationships in which they can lean on others for security and affection. Typically, they act in an unassuming manner, denigrating themselves into believing they deserve their fate. Thus, this pattern is repeated in most relationships, making them prone to being abused. It is conceptually similar to the analytic concept of masochism.

Millon has subdivided the self-defeating personality disorder into four subtypes. Patients with an 8B8A code closely resemble the possessive masochist subtype. They retain the essential features of the self-defeating personality and have features of the passive-aggressive (negativistic) personality. The cardinal feature of these patients is a controlling, dominating, and jealous overprotectiveness that intrudes into the lives of others. They make themselves feel indispensable by being extremely self-sacrificing. Millon has described their tendency to control others in terms of "obligatory dependence." Because these patients seem to give their all to others, they feel indispensable, but others see them as too possessive and too meddling.

Diagnosis: personality disorder not otherwise spcecified (NOS), self-defeating (masochistic) traits

S1, S12B, or S13

The profile pattern of patients with an S1, S12B, or S13 code represents a more severe dysfunctional variant of the schizoid or the avoidant personality disorder. Millon has subdivided this disorder into two types. The active variant is characteristically anxious, wary, and apprehensive, whereas the passive type is characteristically emotionally bland.

These patients have behavioral peculiarities and eccentricities and seem detached from the world around them, appearing strange and different. They tend to lean meaningless lives, drifting aimlessly from one activity to the next, remaining on the periphery of society. They are emotionally bland and tend to have flat affect, or perhaps they display an anxious wariness. They are socially detached and isolated and show a pervasive discomfort with others. They have few, if any, personal attachments and rarely develop any intimate relationships. Their thinking is irrelevant, tangential, disorganized, or autistic, and they suspiciously mistrust others. Cognitive confusion and perceptual distortions are the rule. They are self-absorbed and ruminative with feelings of derealization. They are prone to decompensate into schizophrenia if sufficiently stressed. If BR > 84, then, because of the severity of the disorder, a clinical evaluation is needed to determine if the patient is able to function on a daily basis.

Millon has further divided the schizotypal personality disorder into two subtypes. Patients with an S1, S12B, or S13 code closely resemble the insipid schizotype. They retain the essential features of the schizotypal personality and have features of the schizoid, depressive, or dependent personality styles. The cardinal features of these patients are their deficit in affective expression and their sense of depersonalization. They seem insensitive to feelings and indifferent to interpersonal stimulation. They appear bland, sluggish, and unmotivated, with vague, tangential, and confused thinking. They feel almost unreal. They cope poorly with stimulation, demands, and responsibilities and are at risk for psychotic disorders.

Diagnosis: schizotypal personality disorder

S2A or S8A

The profile pattern of patients with an S2A or S8A code represents a more severe dysfunctional variant of the schizoid or the avoidant personality disorder. Millon has subdivided this disorder into two types. The active variant is characteristically anxious, wary, and apprehensive, whereas the passive type is characteristically emotionally bland.

These patients have behavioral peculiarities and eccentricities and seem detached from the world around them, appearing strange and different. They tend to lean meaningless lives, drifting aimlessly from one activity to the next and remaining on the periphery of society. They are emotionally bland and tend to have flat affect, or perhaps they display an anxious wariness. They are socially detached and isolated and show a pervasive discomfort with others. They have few, if any, personal attachments and rarely develop any intimate relationships. Their thinking is irrelevant, tangential, disorganized or autistic, and they suspiciously mistrust others. Cognitive confusion and perceptual distortions are the rule. They are self-absorbed and ruminative and have feelings of derealization. They are prone to decompensate into schizophrenia if sufficiently stressed. If BR > 84, then, because of the severity of the disorder, a clinical evaluation is needed to determine if the patient is able to function on a daily basis.

Millon has further divided the schizotypal personality disorder into two subtypes. Patients with an S2A or S8A code closely resemble the timorous schizotype. They retain the essential features of the schizotypal personality and have features of the avoidant or passive-aggressive (negativistic) personality styles. The cardinal feature of these patients is their sense of depersonalization and derealization. They are apprehensive, suspicious, guarded, and socially introverted. They feel quite alienated, lack a sense of self worth, and suppress their feelings. They may appear eccentric and peculiar, and they engage in bizarre behavior. Hallucinations may be present.

Diagnosis: schizotypal personality disorder

C2A, C2B, or C3

Patients with a C2A, C2B, or C3 code have conflicting and ambivalent feelings, intensely resenting those on whom they depend yet being preoccupied with maintaining their emotional support. They show persistent attachment disorders with patterns of intense but unstable relationships. They tend to experience intense but labile emotions and frequent mood swings with recurring periods of depression, anxiety, or anger followed by dejection and apathy. They often present with intense affect and with a history of impulsive behaviors. Manifestations of cheerfulness are often temporary coverups that mask deep fears of insecurity and fears of abandonment. They have strong dependency needs and are preoccupied with seeking attention and emotional support and need considerable reassurance. These people are particularly vulnerable to separation from those who emotionally support them. Feelings of idealization are usually followed by feelings of devaluation, and there is considerable interpersonal ambivalence. They lack a clear sense of their own identity, and this uncertainty leads them to constantly seek approval, attention, and reaffirmation. Splitting and projective identification are their major defenses. They often have a punishing conscience and are prone to acts of self-mutilation and suicidal gestures. They are also prone to brief psychotic episodes and substance abuse.

Millon has subdivided the borderline personality disorder into four subtypes. Patients with a C2A, C2B, or C3 code closely resemble the discouraged borderline subtype. They retain the essential features of the borderline personality and have features of the avoidant, depressive, or dependent personality styles. The cardinal features of these patients are their excessive compliance, acquiescence, and submissiveness to a person on whom they depend for security. However, they feel quite insecure and periodically erupt in angry outbursts of resentment. They tend to be chronically depressed, feel helpless and hopeless, and may be at risk for suicidal gestures, self-mutilation, or other acts of self-punishment.

Diagnosis: borderline personality disorder

C2B *or* C8B

Patients with a C2B or C8B code have conflicting and ambivalent feelings, intensely resenting those on whom they depend yet being preoccupied with maintaining their emotional support. They show persistent attachment disorders with patterns of intense but unstable relationships. They tend to experience intense but labile emotions and frequent mood swings with recurring periods of depression, anxiety, or anger followed by dejection and apathy. They often present with intense affect and with a history of impulsive behaviors. Manifestations of cheerfulness are often temporary coverups that mask deep fears of insecurity and fears of abandonment. They have strong dependency needs and are preoccupied with seeking attention and emotional support and need considerable reassurance. These people are particularly vulnerable to separation from those who emotionally support them. Feelings of idealization are usually followed by feelings of devaluation, and there is considerable interpersonal ambivalence. They lack a clear sense of their own identity, and this uncertainty leads them to constantly seek approval, attention, and reaffirmation. Splitting and projective identification are their major defenses. They often have a punishing conscience and are prone to acts of self-mutilation and suicidal gestures. They are also prone to brief psychotic episodes and substance abuse.

Millon has subdivided the borderline personality disorder into four subtypes. Patients with a C2B or C8B code closely resemble the self-destructive borderline subtype. They retain the essential features of the borderline personality and have features of the depressive or self-defeating personalities. The cardinal feature of these patients is the conflict between their fear of autonomy and their need to be dependent and submissive to maintain a sense of security. They require constant emotional support and become dejected and depressed when they perceive this to be lacking. Then they become contrary and over-emotional. At others times, they may appear self-sacrificing, suppressing their resentment and hostility. However, this form of behavior is self-defeating in the long run and prevents the acquisition of independent behaviors.

Diagnosis: borderline personality disorder

C4 *or* C6A

Patients with a C4 or C6A code have conflicting and ambivalent feelings, intensely resenting those on whom they depend yet being preoccupied with maintaining their emotional support. They show persistent attachment disorders with patterns of intense but unstable relationships. They tend to experience intense but labile emotions and frequent mood swings with recurring periods of depression, anxiety, or anger followed by dejection and apathy. They often present with intense affect and with a history of impulsive behaviors. Manifestations of cheerfulness are often temporary coverups that mask deep fears of insecurity and fears of abandonment. They have strong dependency needs, are preoccupied with seeking attention and emotional support, and need considerable reassurance. These people are particularly vulnerable to separation from those who emotionally support them. Feelings of idealization are usually followed by feelings of devaluation, and there is considerable interpersonal ambivalence. They lack a clear sense of their own identity, and this uncertainty leads them to constantly seek approval, attention, and reaffirmation. Splitting and projective identification are their major defenses. They often have a punishing conscience and are prone to acts of self-mutilation and suicidal gestures. They are also prone to brief psychotic episodes and substance abuse.

Millon has subdivided the borderline personality disorder into four subtypes. Patients with a C4 or C6A code closely resemble the impulsive borderline subtype. They retain the essential features of the borderline personality and have features of the histrionic and antisocial personality styles. The cardinal features of these patients are their superficiality, seductiveness, and constant need for attention combined with irresponsibility and flighty and impulsive behaviors. They tend to be restless, live for the moment, and resent the confinements of social rules and regulations. Fear of abandonment may underlie much of their behavior.

Diagnosis: borderline personality disorder

C8A

Patients with a C8A code have conflicting and ambivalent feelings, intensely resenting those on whom they depend yet being preoccupied with maintaining their emotional support. They show persistent attachment disorders with patterns of intense but unstable relationships. They tend to experience intense but labile emotions and frequent mood swings with recurring periods of depression, anxiety, or anger followed by dejection and apathy. They often present with intense affect and with a history of impulsive behaviors. Manifestations of cheerfulness are often temporary coverups that mask deep fears of insecurity and fears of abandonment. They have strong dependency needs, are preoccupied with seeking attention and emotional support, and need considerable reassurance. These people are particularly vulnerable to separation from those who emotionally support them. Feelings of idealization are usually followed by feelings of devaluation, and there is considerable interpersonal ambivalence. They lack a clear sense of their own identity, and this uncertainty leads them to constantly seek approval, attention, and reaffirmation. Splitting is their main defense mechanism.

Millon has subdivided the borderline personality disorder into four subtypes. Patients with a C8A code closely resemble the petulant borderline subtype. They retain the essential features of the borderline personality and have features of the passive-aggressive (negativistic) personality, particularly traits of anger, resentment, restlessness, and complaining tendencies, along with unpredictability. They fear abandonment and isolation but also resent their dependence on others, so they vacillate between being apologetic and overtly irritable. Their chronic negativism may result in self-punishing acts or angry tirades that are out of control. These behaviors may be the result of internal conflicts with issues of separation and individuation.

Diagnosis: borderline personality disorder

P2A

Millon believes that patients with a P2A code are conflicted between issues of control and of affiliation. They vigilantly mistrust others and have an abrasive, hostile, irritable, touchy, and irascible demeanor; they readily attack and humiliate anyone whom they perceive as trying to control them. They may become belligerent, with such behavior stemming from distorted cognitions or actual delusions. They tend to magnify interpersonal slights, are prone to distort events to support their own suspicions, and strongly resist external influence. They are fiercely independent and tend to be provocative in interpersonal relationships, precipitating fear and exasperation in those around them. Their thinking is rigid and they often become argumentative. Projection is their main defense. They are particularly sensitive to perceived threats to their own sense of self-determination. Delusions of grandeur or persecution or ideas of reference may be present in the more extreme form of the disorder.

Millon has subdivided the paranoid personality disorder into five subtypes. Patients with a P2A code closely resemble the insular paranoid subtype. They retain the essential features of the paranoid personality and have features of the avoidant personality. These patients are fearful of being controlled, so they exhibit an avoidant personality style, characterized by a withdrawn, seclusive, and secretive (lack of) interpersonal style, to prevent others from controlling them. They are quite frightened and protectively withdrawn, fearing that people are trying to poison them or do them harm in other ways. They eventually withdraw into a world of unreality.

Diagnosis: paranoid personality disorder

P5

Millon believes that patients with a P5 code are conflicted between issues of control and of affiliation. They vigilantly mistrust others and have an abrasive, hostile, irritable, touchy, and irascible demeanor; they readily attack and humiliate anyone whom they perceive as trying to control them. They may become belligerent, such behavior stemming from distorted cognitions or actual delusions. They tend to magnify interpersonal slights, are prone to distort events to support their own suspicions, and strongly resist external influence. They are fiercely independent and tend to be provocative in interpersonal relationships, precipitating fear and exasperation in those around them. Their thinking is rigid and they often become argumentative. Projection is their main defense. They are particularly sensitive to perceived threats to their own sense of self-determination. Delusions of grandeur or persecution or ideas of reference may be present in the more extreme form of the disorder.

Millon has subdivided the paranoid personality disorder into five subtypes. Patients with a P5 code closely resemble the fanatic paranoid subtype. They retain the essential features of the paranoid personality and have features of the narcissistic personality. The cardinal features of these patients are grandiose ideas and expansive, delusional plans. These patients have suffered a perceived blow to their self-esteem and counteract this devastating narcissistic wound by developing grandiose delusions. Typically, they assert they are on some grand mission, often of a supernatural or extravagant nature. Obvious contradictions and objective facts hold no sway in convincing these patients of their erroneous beliefs.

Diagnosis: paranoid personality disorder

P6B

Millon believes that patients with a P6B code are conflicted between issues of control and of affiliation. They vigilantly mistrust others and have an abrasive, hostile, irritable, touchy, and irascible demeanor; they readily attack and humiliate anyone whom they perceive as trying to control them. They may become belligerent, with such behavior stemming from distorted cognitions or actual delusions. They tend to magnify interpersonal slights, are prone to distort events to support their own suspicions, and strongly resist external influence. They are fiercely independent and tend to be provocative in interpersonal relationships, precipitating fear and exasperation in those around them. Their thinking is rigid and they often become argumentative. Projection is their main defense. They are particularly sensitive to perceived threats to their own sense of self-determination. Delusions of grandeur or persecution or ideas of reference may be present in the more extreme form of the disorder.

Millon has subdivided the paranoid personality disorder into five subtypes. Patients with a P6B code closely resemble the malignant paranoid subtype. They retain the essential features of the paranoid personality and have features of the aggressive/sadistic personality style. The cardinal feature of these patients is their persecutory and grandiose delusions. They tend to be belligerent, intimidating, argumentative, antagonistic, abrasive, tyrannical, hostile, and brutal. They imagine that people are constantly plotting against them and are easily provoked into aggressive behaviors, though some may limit their hostility to fantasy only.

Diagnosis: *paranoid personality disorder*

P7

Millon believes that patients with a P7 code are conflicted between issues of control and of affiliation. They vigilantly mistrust others and have an abrasive, hostile, irritable, touchy, and irascible demeanor; they readily attack and humiliate anyone whom they perceive as trying to control them. They may become belligerent, with such behavior stemming from distorted cognitions or actual delusions. They tend to magnify interpersonal slights, are prone to distort events to support their own suspicions, and strongly resist external influence. They are fiercely independent and tend to be provocative in interpersonal relationships, precipitating fear and exasperation in those around them. Their thinking is rigid and they often become argumentative. Projection is their main defense. They are particularly sensitive to perceived threats to their own sense of self-determination. Delusions of grandeur or persecution or ideas of reference may be present in the more extreme form of the disorder.

Millon has subdivided the paranoid personality disorder into five subtypes. Patients with a P7 code closely resemble the obdurate paranoid subtype. They retain the essential features of the paranoid personality and have features of the compulsive personality style. The cardinal feature of these patients is a well-entrenched and encapsulated delusional style. These patients may appear relatively normal until their delusional system is attacked. Then they become self-righteous and overly legalistic, use excessive intellectualization, and become increasingly hostile and irrational.

Diagnosis: *paranoid personality disorder*

P8A

Millon believes that patients with a P8A code are conflicted between issues of control and affiliation. They vigilantly mistrust others and have an abrasive, hostile, irritable, touchy, and irascible demeanor; they readily attack and humiliate anyone whom they perceive as trying to control them. They may become belligerent, with such behavior stemming from distorted cognitions or actual delusions. They tend to magnify interpersonal slights, are prone to distort events to support their own suspicions, and strongly resist external influence. They are fiercely independent and tend to be provocative in interpersonal relationships, precipitating fear and exasperation in those around them. Their thinking is rigid and they often become argumentative. Projection is their main defense. They are particularly sensitive to perceived threats to their own sense of self-determination. Delusions of grandeur or persecution or ideas of reference may be present in the more extreme form of the disorder.

Millon has subdivided the paranoid personality disorder into five subtypes. Patients with a P8A code closely resemble the querulous paranoid subtype. They retain the essential features of the paranoid personality and have features of the passive-aggressive (negativistic) personality style. The cardinal features of these patients are delusions and extreme hostility. These patients may be described as argumentative, petulant, jealous, fault finding, disdainful, stubborn, pessimistic, resentful, aggressive, and negativistic. Millon has reported that this subtype is prone to experience erotic delusions and to commit molestations.

Diagnosis: paranoid personality disorder

CLINICAL SYNDROMES

Anxiety (Scale A)

Patients with scores of BR > 84 on Scale A have reported many symptoms associated with anxiety. High scores on this scale are often seen in patients who are restless, anxious, apprehensive, edgy, and jittery. These patients tend to have a variety of somatic complaints associated with physiological overarousal, including insomnia, headaches, nausea, cold sweats, undue perspiration, clammy hands, and palpitations. The intensity of these symptoms appears to be experienced by the patient as quite severe and possibly disabling.

Diagnosis: generalized anxiety disorder, unless specific phobias or trauma explain the symptom picture

Somatoform Disorder (Scale H)

Patients with scores of BR > 84 on Scale H appear to be persistently preoccupied with perceptions of poor health and report symptoms that may not correspond to clearly defined organic disorders. Similar patients often express their psychological problems by developing symptoms that defy clear-cut medical diagnoses. Others may have a legitimate physical condition but do not cope well with it. In either case, these patients are often whining, demanding, and complaining and tend to deny psychological or emotional factors affecting the development or exacerbation of their physical disorder.

Diagnosis: rule out somatoform disorder and psychological factors affecting physical condition

Bipolar Disorder, Manic (Scale N)

Patients who score at the level of BR > 84 on Scale N often report symptoms primarily consisting of labile emotions, including both mania and depression. These symptoms may be the result of substance abuse or of a primary disorder that is being self-medicated by substance abuse (see Scales B, page 187, and T, page 188), or the two conditions may coexist independent of one another. A more thorough clinical evaluation for affective disorders and/or substance abuse is recommended.

Diagnosis: bipolar disorder, manic

Dysthymia (Scale D)

Patients with a score of BR > 84 on Scale D have many problems and symptoms associated with depression. These may include apathy, social withdrawal, guilt, pessimism, low self-esteem, feelings of inadequacy and worthlessness, self-doubts, and a diminished sense of pleasure. Generally, such patients can meet their day-to-day responsibilities but continue to experience chronic dysphoria.

Diagnosis: dysthymic disorder

Alcohol Dependence (Scale B)

Patients with a score of BR > 84 on Scale B have reported symptoms and traits commonly associated with alcohol abuse, alcohol dependence, or both. It is also possible that these patients have endorsed personality traits often seen in those who subsequently develop problematic drinking or that these patients have had problems with alcohol and are now in recovery. A more thorough evaluation should be conducted to determine the presence of any specific problems (e.g., medical, social, legal, psychological, psychiatric, vocational, spiritual) that may be associated with this condition. Scores at this level almost always reflect a diagnosis associated with alcohol.

Diagnosis: alcohol abuse dependence

Drug Dependence (Scale T)

Patients with scores of BR > 84 on Scale T have reported symptoms and traits commonly associated with drug abuse, drug dependence, or both. It is also possible that these patients have endorsed personality traits often seen in those who subsequently develop problems associated with drug abuse or that these patients have had problems with drugs and are now in recovery. A more thorough evaluation should be conducted to determine the presence of any specific problems (e.g., medical, social, legal, psychological, psychiatric, vocational, spiritual) that may be associated with this condition. Scores at this level almost always reflect a diagnosis associated with drug abuse.

Diagnosis: drug abuse or drug dependence

Posttraumatic Stress Disorder (Scale T)

Patients with scores of BR > 84 on Scale T have reported symptoms often associated with posttraumatic stress. These symptoms might include distressing and intrusive thoughts; flashbacks; startle responses; emotional numbing; problems in anger management; difficulties with sleep or concentration; and psychological distress on exposure to people, places, or events that symbolize or resemble some aspect of the traumatic event. A clinical evaluation is suggested to determine which symptoms are present and the degree of functional impairment. If there is no trauma in the patient's history, then scores at this level could suggest emotional turmoil of a nontraumatic nature.

    Diagnosis: posttraumatic stress disorder

Thought Disorder (Scale SS)

Patients with scores of BR > 84 on Scale SS have reported a number of symptoms associated with a possible thought disorder, ranging from confused, fragmented, and bizarre thinking to scattered hallucinations and unsystematized delusions. A more thorough clinical evaluation is highly recommended.

    Diagnoses: rule out brief reactive psychosis, schizophreniform disorder, and schizophrenia

Major Depression (Scale CC)

Patients with scores of BR > 84 on Scale CC have reported many problems and symptoms associated with depression, including feelings of inadequacy and worthlessness, a loss of energy, diminished desire for sex or engagement in formerly pleasurable activities, loss of appetite, reduced ability to think or concentrate, possible suicidal ideation, and a chronically depressed mood. These patients usually are unable to carry on their daily activities without treatment intervention. A more thorough clinical review is recommended.

    Diagnosis: major depression

Delusional Disorder (Scale PP)

Patients with high scores on Scale PP have reported many symptoms usually associated with paranoia. Their mood may be hostile and they may be hypervigilant to perceived threats. Ideas of reference, thought control, or thought influence may be present. A more thorough clinical evaluation is recommended to determine which specific symptoms are present and what kind of clinical intervention is necessary.

    Diagnosis: delusional disorder

SCALE INTERACTIONS OR COMBINATIONS

Elevations on some scales might change the interpretation of other scales. Below are some of the more common scale interactions and associated interpretations. Refer to the original scale to see what has been added changed.

Scale 3 with Another Scale

- Scale A, BR > 74: Because this patient is reporting many anxiety symptoms, it is recommended that the clinician determine if support systems have become unreliable, which may the source of this anxiety.
- Scale D, BR > 74: Because this patent is reporting many symptoms associated with depression, it is recommended that the clinician determine exactly which support systems have become unreliable, which may the source of this dysphoria.
- Scale A and D, BR > 74: Because this patient is reporting many symptoms associated with both anxiety and depression, it is recommended that the clinician determine if support systems have become unreliable, which may be the source of this psychological distress.
- Scale B or T, BR > 74: Because this patient is reporting many symptoms and behaviors associated with substance abuse, it

is recommended that the clinician determine whether the patient is a substance abuser with a dependent personality or has recently turned to abusing substances to cope with the anxiety associated with the loss of security in relationships.

- Scale D or CC, BR > 84: Because this patient may have a clinical depression, the personality profile described here may be a manifestation of depression and not the patient's basic personality style. If this is true, then these symptoms and behaviors should abate when the depression has been successfully treated and the patient may not look so dependent. However, Millon has argued that the clinical symptoms are an extension of personality style, so that although the intensity of expression may be reduced somewhat, the essential features of a dependent personality style may remain.

Scale N with Another Scale

- Scale B or T, BR > 74: Patients who score at this level of Scale N often have symptoms of labile emotions and frequent mood swings, including behaviors characterized by mania. These symptoms may be the result of substance abuse or of a primary manic disorder that is being self-medicated by substance abuse, or the two conditions may coexist independently of one another. A more thorough clinical evaluation is recommended.
- Scale PP, BR > 84: This patient is reporting symptoms of labile emotions, including both mania and depression, and of hallucinations, delusions, or both. A more thorough clinical evaluation is recommended.
- Scale PP, BR > 84; Scale B or T, BR > 74; and/or Scale D or CC > 74: This patient is reporting symptoms of labile emotions, including both mania and depression, and of hallucinations, delusions, or both. These symptoms may be due to a primary affective disorder with psychotic features, to a pri-

mary delusional disorder with affective features, to a substance abuse disorder (especially hallucinogenic use of PCP),
or to one or more of these disorders that co-exist independently of one another. A more thorough clinical evaluation
is recommended.

Scale D with Scale B or T, BR > 74

This depression may be secondary to substance abuse, particularly
alcoholism or alcohol abuse. A more thorough clinical evaluation is
recommended to determine if there are vegetative signs of depression
and to determine which disorder, depression, or substance abuse is
primary.

Scale SS with Scale B or T, BR > 74

Toxic or drug-induced psychosis should be ruled out as a cause of this
thought disorder.

Scale PP with Scale B or T, BR > 74

Given the apparent substance abuse of patients with scores of BR >
74 on Scales PP and B or T, a drug-induced paranoia may may also be
present. A more thorough clinical evaluation is recommended to
determine which specific symptoms are present, their cause, and
what kind of clinical intervention is necessary. On the other hand,
there is a high correlation between Scales PP, B, and T. Thus, it may
be the case that these patients' primary diagnosis is substance abuse
and the traits and behaviors, such as hypervigilance, defensive scan-
ning of the environment, and a feeling that people are out to get
them, are really associated with the drug abuser lifestyle rather than
with clinical paranoia. A clinical evaluation is necessary to determine which diagnosis is the case. A delusional paranoid disorder, a
paranoid disorder, or a drug-induced paranoid condition, such as
toxic psychosis, should be considered.

References

Choca, J. P., & VanDenburg, E. (1997). *Interpretive guide to the Millon Clinical Multiaxial Inventory* (2nd ed.). Washington, D.C.: American Psychological Association.

Craig, R. J. (Ed.) (1993a). *The Millon Clinical Multiaxial Inventory: A clinical and research information synthesis*. Hillsdale, NJ: Lawrence Erlbaum Associates.

Craig, R. J. (1993b). *Psychological assessment with the Millon Clinical Multiaxial Inventory (II): An interpretive guide*. Odessa, FL: Psychological Assessment Resources.

Craig, R. J. (1994). *MCMI II/III interpretive system*. Odessa, FL: Psychological Assessment Resources.

Millon, T. (1984). Interpretive guide to the Millon Clinical Multiaxial Inventory. In P. McReynolds & G. J. Chelune (Eds.), *Advances in personality assessment* (Vol. 6, pp. 1–41). San Francisco: Jossey-Bass.

Millon, T. (1995, August). Subtypes of personality disorders. Presentation given at the Conference on the Millon Inventories, Minneapolis.

Millon, T. (1997a) *Millon Clinical Multiaxial Inventory–III Manual* (2nd ed.). Minneapolis: National Computer Systems.

Millon, T. (Ed.) (1997b). *The Millon inventories: Clinical and personality assessment*. New York: Guilford Publishing.

Millon, T., & Davis, R. D. (1995). *Disorders of personality: DSM-IV and beyond*. New York: Wiley-Interscience.

Millon, T., & Davis, R. D. (1996). The Millon Clinical Multiaxial Inventory–III (MCMI-III) In C. S. Newmark (Ed.), *Major psychological assessment instruments* (2nd ed., pp. 108–147). Boston: Allyn & Bacon.

CHAPTER 3

California Psychological Inventory–Revised Interpretive Manual

General Overview

THE CALIFORNIA PSYCHOLOGICAL INVENTORY (CPI) was initially published in 1957 and last revised in 1996 as the CPI-R. Consisting of 434 items requiring a fifth-grade reading ability, the test was restandardized using 3,000 men and 3,000 women as test subjects. Although the test was designed for use with people aged 13 and above, it is really an adult personality test, though some scales have a substantial research base with high school students. A total of 158 items also appear in the Minnesota Multiphasic Personality Inventory–2 (MMPI-2). It has cross-cultural applications and has been translated into 29 foreign languages. Recent factor analysis studies reported five general factors labeled Ascendance (I), Dependability (II), Communality/Conventionality (III), Originality (IV), and Femininity/Masculinity (V).

Philosophical Basis of the CPI-R

Harrison Gough, the test's developer, decided to create a personality inventory that would be designed for use with nonclinical populations and would use concepts that are already part of everyday language to describe interpersonal behavior, behavior patterns, and personality traits. These same concepts would also be culturally universal. Gough called these terms folk concepts. The advantage of such an approach is that these concepts would be generally understood by a wide range of people from different cultures. Gough had earlier tried to develop similar trait scales from the MMPI item pool and had already developed the MMPI-derived scales of Social Status, Prejudice, Dominance, and Responsibility, but there were too many pathology-based items in the MMPI to create the kind of test he wanted to use with nonclinical populations; hence, he went on to develop the CPI.

In the latest CPI revision, Gough derived scale interpretations from five main data sources: correlations of CPI scales with (1) other scales, (2) the adjective checklists from observers, (3) the California Q-set descriptions by observers, (4) the Interpersonal Q-sort descriptions by observers, and (5) items in the interviewer's checklist.

Scale Interpretation

GENERAL CONSIDERATIONS

In interpreting scale scores, clinicians need to follow these steps:

1. Determine profile validity using validity scales described below.
2. Inspect patterns of elevations on different classes of scales. The CPI-R subdivides the 19 scales into four classes. *Class I* scales assess interpersonal adequacy and comprise scales for Dominance (Do), Capacity for Status (Cs), Sociability (Sy), Social Presence (Sp), Self-Acceptance (Sa), Independence (In), and Empathy (Em). *Class II* scales assess interpersonal controls, values, and beliefs and consist of scales for Responsibility (Re), Socialization (So), Self-Control (Sc), Good Impression (Gi), Communality (Cm), Well-Being (Wb), and Tolerance (To). *Class III* scales assess intellectual achieve-

ment and academic ability and consist of scales for Achievement via Conformance (Ac), Achievement via Independence (Ai), and Intellectual Efficiency (Ie). *Class IV* scales
assess measures of personal styles and consist of scales for Psychological Mindedness (Py), Flexibility (Fx), and Feminin-
ity/Masculininity (F/M). Differential areas of maladjustment
or healthy functioning can be assessed by inspecting these
clusters as separate groups. On most CPI scales, scores above
50 suggest psychological health and adjustment, whereas
scores below 50 suggest maladjustment and problem behaviors.

3. Interpret the individual scales and look for scale interactions
   that may alter the meaning on an individual scale.
4. Consider structural scale interpretation (see below).
5. Integrate test data with other sources of information.

VALIDITY SCALES

See Gi (page 211), Cm (page 212), and Wb (page 214) Scales.

STRUCTURAL INTERPRETATION

One advantage of such tests as the MMPI-2 and Millon Clinical Multiaxial Inventory–III (MCMI-III) is that one can look at the profile
and know immediately, on the basis of score elevations of the scales,
what diagnostic ballpark the patient is in. The MMPI-2 tells the
examiner rather quickly whether the profile is suggestive of neurotic,
character, or psychotic disorders or whether there is a general absence
of psychopathology. The MCMI-III profile provides rapid assessment
of personality disorders and major clinical syndromes through visual
profile inspection. The original version of the CPI gave the examiner
no such ability. Gough sought to provide a way to alert the examiner
as to the kind of personality type one is dealing with by creating a
structural interpretation to the CPI-R.

On the basis of factor analysis of the CPI-R, Gough developed what he called a cuboid model consisting of three vectors. The first dimension pertains to extroversion/introversion, which he called externality/internality. This vector addresses such things as extroversion, social poise, and self-assurance. The second vector represents the degree to which the respondent adheres to social norms, which Gough labeled norm-favoring/norm-questioning. The third vector assesses the degree to which the person has realized and/or integrated his or her basic type.

Gough called these basic types (e.g., vector 2) alphas, betas, gammas, and deltas and used a seven-point rating scale for vector 3 (1 = poor; 2 = well below average; 3 = below average; 4 = average; 5 = above average; 6 = well above average; and 7 = superior) to specify the relative strength of each type within the person. Thus, an alpha 7 is a fully realized alpha type. Gough determined that these four types were relatively evenly distributed within the general population.

Alphas

The alpha style combines adherence to norms with an external approach to relationships and is considered a very managerial style. Alphas are the doers in an organization and their style tends to be participative. They focus on tasks and are productive. They get things done and implement the polices and mandates of the larger organization. They are seen as forceful, dominant, ambitious, assertive, extroverted, and action oriented. As managers, they work toward fulfillment of organizational goals, emphasize accountability and deadlines, pay close attention to follow-up, and are seen as influential. At their best (V7), they are charismatic leaders; at their worst (V1), they are manipulative and self-serving; are intolerant of those who disagree with them; and tend to be authoritarian, punitive, and concerned only with achieving their own ends.

Betas

The beta style combines the acceptance of norms with an internal, introverted, detached cathexis toward the world. They are seen as being low keyed, nurturant, responsible, stable, steady, dependable, moderating, skillful, and predictable and as preserving the values and mores of a group. As managers, they also work toward fulfillment of organizational goals but in a low-key fashion. They tend to rely on managers to set direction and are good at staff roles. They prefer the role of a follower. At their best (V7), they are inspirational models of propriety and goodness and also quite nurturing; at their worst (V1), they are overly cautious, rigid, and fearful conformists.

Gammas

The gamma style combines norm doubting with an extroverted orientation. Gammas are visionaries—perhaps strategic leaders who can change the direction of an organization. They question the status quo. As managers, they question organization mission and goals, prefer to change organizational directives, and emphasize innovation. They are seen as innovative, clever, and adventurous. At their best (V7), they are creative, visionary, imaginative, perceptive, and innovative; at their worst (V1), they are rebellious, impulsive, intolerant, self-indulgent, and disruptive.

Deltas

The delta style combines norm doubting with a more detached internal style. Deltas are more reflective, detached, preoccupied, and perceptive and tend to be more scientifically and technically expert. As managers, they tend to work best in small groups and in small organizations where they can be somewhat independent. At their best (V7), they are idealistic, preoccupied, imaginative, artistic, and visionary; at their worst (V1), they are reserved, conflicted, withdrawn, aloof, and fragmented. At the low end of the scale, there is fragmentation and disorganization of personality. Chronic long-term psychiatric patients and prison inmates often score low on delta, suggesting a need for an external and structured environment to hold them together.

High versus Low Scores

In the descriptions reported below, the interpretations were recorded when a competent authority or when empirical research suggested an interpretation at a particular scale elevation. Often the source material merely referenced "high scores" or "low scores" when providing interpretive statements. It is suggested that when making a choice as to what should be considered high or low, the clinician use ±3 standard deviations (*SD*) above/below the mean. The CPI-R has a mean of 50 and an *SD* of 10. In some settings and with certain base rates, ±2 *SD* may be considered. For each scale, suggested interpretations of standard scores (SS) are given.

CLASS I SCALES: MEASURES OF POISE, SELF-ASSURANCE, AND INTERPERSONAL PROCLIVITIES

Dominance (Do; 36 Items)

The Do Scale was designed to measure leadership ability, dominance, and persistence to achieve a social good. It is a relatively pure measure of leadership or a willingness to take a leadership role. The method of scale construction was empirical. The scale has four main factors, labeled Leadership (I), Self-Mastery (II), Authority (III), and Obligations (IV).

Very High Scores. (Raw Scores > 32 [SS ≥ 72])   On the CPI-R, Do scores are curvilinear and high scores may indicate too much of a good thing. Scores at the level of SS ≥ 72 suggest people with a desire to seek power and control to the point of abrasiveness and a willingness to step on others to get their way. They are aggressive, ambitious, and have a great deal of initiative. Consult elevations on Scales Re (page 207), So (page 209) and To (page 215) to see whether such dominating behavior remains prosocial or perverted.

High Scores (SS 55 to 70)   High scores on the Do Scale suggest people who both have a strong affiliative component and are dominant in a prosocial sense. Scores at the level of SS between 55 and 70 suggest people who are influential and ascendant and who are helpful to the group and want them to succeed. They enjoy influencing others and have the ability to gain others' respect. They are willing to support group goals and even to take a subordinate role as long as it results in accomplishing a task. They are very enterprising people with strong leadership potential or skills; prefer to be in charge; are self-confident, secure, ambitious, task-oriented, energetic, talkative, and persuasive; and have a strong belief in communal participation and in doing the right thing.

Low Scores (SS 40 to 50) Moderately low scores on the Do Scale suggest people who feel uncomfortable in a leadership role and would prefer to be followers. Even if they are in positions of authority, they dislike it, are likely to have problems in planning, and are seen as nonasssertive.

Very Low Scores (SS < 40) Scores at the level of SS < 40 suggest a submissiveness, a lack assertiveness, and possibly maladjustment. These people appear socially withdrawn and insecure and therefore willingly yield to the influence of others and hesitate to take the initiative. They tend to worry, have many self-doubts, are passive, and lack ambition. They feel awkward in social situations and are described as quiet, retiring, unassuming, hesitating, inhibited, and cautious. They feel uncomfortable being responsible for the actions of others and taking leadership roles.

Scale Interactions Elevated scores on some scales may change the interpretation of scores on other scales. Below are some of the more common scale interactions and associated interpretations.

- High Do, Cs, and Sp: show leadership qualities, enjoy being the center of attention, may be persuasive and charismatic
- High Do, Sa, and Ac: have a high need for control, structure, and attention
- High Do, high Gi: work hard with upward communication to superiors but are hard on subordinates

- High Do, low Gi: do not that work hard at upward communication; may be critical, autocratic, and domineering; show little concern over maintaining harmonious group relations; are more task oriented
- High Do, high Cs: like to be sought after for opinions, expertise, and information
- High Do, low Re: could be anything from gang leaders to people who ignore details but get things done
- High Do, high Sy: show strong leadership qualities; like to direct the activities of others
- High Do, low Sy: are dominant but keep people at an emotionally comfortable distance, which allows these people to be critical and judgmental
- High Do, high Sa: are arrogant, cocky, egotistical, overvaluing their own skills and abilities
- High Do, high Gi: may have difficulty saying no to others; tend to be people pleasers
- High Do, low Gi: are argumentative, egotistical, and domineering; do not try to please people; want their own way; tend to have an autocratic style; are very blunt, showing little empathy or few nurturing behaviors toward people
- High Do, low F/M: are strongly assertive and strive for responsibility
- High Do, low To: want to get their own way to get results
- High Do and Re: are progressive leaders who are conscientious and ambitious
- High Do, low Re: are leaders who are likely to be dominant, rigid, and aggressive
- Low Do, high Gi: shyly seek approval from others; are seen as withdrawn and socially inept
- Low Do and Gi: are passive and withdrawn, perhaps socially inept; may spend too much time seeking the approval of others

Note: This scale is identical to the Do scale of the MMPI-2, though the research traditions associated with this scale diverge somewhat from those of the MMPI-2. The reader may consult the interpretation for the Do scale (page 52) in the MMPI-2 section of this manual.

Capacity for Status (Cs; 28 Items)

The Cs scale was originally developed to identify people who (1) view themselves as possessing high status; (2) are ambitious and self-assured, traits that often lead to the attainment of status; or (3) worship high status. It is not a measure of people who have high-status roles or positions. The method of scale construction was empirical. The scale has four factors, labeled (1) Poise and Self-Assurance, (2) Esthetic/Cultural Interests, (3) Optimism and Confidence, and (4) Recognizing the Advantage of Status and Success.

Raw Scores of 26 to 28 (SS 74 to 79) Patients with an SS between 74 an 79 have feelings of entitlement, are indifferent to conventions, feel justified in their behavior, are overbearing and self-satisfied, and feel superior to others.

High Raw Scores Patients with high raw scores are gregarious, talkative, independent, forward, witty, ambitious, self-confident, sophisticated, and socially poised; have many interests and high aspirations; value intellectual pursuits; are alert; try to make a good impression; are animated, verbally fluent, and optimistic; want to be successful; are self-directed and achievement-oriented; have high aspirations; and are willing to make the personal sacrifices necessary over the long haul to achieve success.

Low Raw Scores Patients with low raw scores have little goal direction. They are reserved, yielding, cautious, shy, timid, withdrawn, quiet, self-defeating, uncomfortable with ambiguity, awkward, and bumbling; have feelings of inadequacy and difficulty in coping with complex social situations; are likely to show poor verbal skills; have problems dealing with setbacks and adversity; and dislike competition. Although they may have strong achievement motivation, they are not willing to make personal sacrifices to get ahead. Also, they may lack the required drive, ambition, and focused motivation necessary to achieve recognition and success. They tend to give up easily when stressed or when faced with difficult situations and respond poorly to pressure.

Sociability (Sy; 32 Items)

The original purpose of the Sy Scale was to identify people who like to engage in social activities and are socially outgoing compared to those who avoid social visibility. The method of scale construction was empirical. The scale has four factors, labeled (1) Comfort and Assurance in Social Situations, (2) Enjoyment of Social Functions, (3) Self-Confidence, and (4) Enjoys Attention.

High Scores   Patients with high raw scores are outgoing; enjoy social activities; have a participative temperament; enjoy planning social activities; feel comfortable among strangers; readily enrich their life with social events; are enterprising, more mature, enthusiastic, talkative, confident, optimistic, gregarious, and animated; mix easily with others; and make a good impression in an interview.

Low Scores   Patients with low scores prefer to remain at home; are cautious, inhibited, reserved, silent, and shy; have limited interests and ambition; are ruminative, self-defeating, socially retiring, and reluctant to take stands; avoid close interpersonal relationships; are unsure of themselves and ill at ease in an interview; report many problems and worries; are awkward, bland, and easily embarrassed; may be neurotic; prefer to stay in the background in social situations, although they may be able to mix with others without disabling anxiety; dislike being the center of attention; and have a subdued social demeanor. Extremely low scores (< 35) suggest introversion.

Social Presence (Sp; 38 Items)

The Sp Scale was developed to assess feelings of personal worth, self-confidence, accomplishment, spontaneity and poise in social situations, and self-esteem. The method of scale construction was based on rational means of internal consistency. The scale has three factors, labeled (1) Self-Confidence and Self-Assurance, (2) Self-Assertion and Liking Attention, and (3) Pleasure Seeking and Zest for New Experiences.

Note: There is some similarity between the Social Presence Scale and the Sociability Scale. People who score high on the Sy Scale may be sociable but may not necessarily have social presence. High-scoring people on the Sp Scale have both sociability and social presence, as defined below.

High Scores Patients with high scores have the capacity for independent decision making; are willing to take stands that may be at variance with normative conventions; have interests in ideas and cognitive pursuits; enjoy festivities and take an active part in them; use their wit to overcome tensions; are clever; have broad interests; are spontaneous, versatile, expressive, and socially poised; have the capacity for imaginative play; are relatively free from neurotic concerns; are self-confident; make a good impression in interviews; are pleasure seeking; may manipulate others to attain social power and recognition; and have strong social skills.

Low Scores Patients with low scores avoid self-assertive activities; tend to be compliant; appear to be dull, inhibited, cautious, conservative, and meek; tend to withdraw from social encounters; are overcontrolled and submissive; use humor to attack and disparage others; report many worries and problems; lack self-assurance; have many self-doubts; appear nervous and ill at ease in interviews; are prone to feel guilt and self-blame; are hesitant to express their views; may be concerned with displaying proper etiquette; tend to believe that people should conform to a set of defined standards of behavior; show limited acceptance of behavior that differs substantially from their own set of standards for behavior; are more interested in cooperation than in manipulation; and need time to deal with change.

Note: People who fake poorly on the CPI-R attain their lowest score on the Sp Scale.

Self-Acceptance (Sa; 28 Items)

The Sa Scale was originally developed to measure people's sense of personal worth and self-acceptance. The method of scale construction was rational, using internal consistency. The scale has three factors, labeled (1) Comfortable and Confident in Dealing with Others, (2) Willing to Admit Self-Serving and Self-Centered Behavior, and (3) Positive Self-Evaluation.

Very High Scores (Raw Scores of 26 to 28 [SS 74 to 80])   Patients with very high scores are narcissistic, opportunistic, exploitative, and demanding; may engage in antisocial activity; and may be masking their insecurities with an inflated self-concept.

High Scores   Patients with high scores feel fulfilled in their work; seek a central and visible role; act to bring attention to themselves; will speak their mind in most situations; are outgoing, sociable, self-confident, self-assured, ambitious, aggressive, energetic, talkative, secure, reasonable, socially poised, and verbally fluent; think well of themselves; are optimistic about the future; enjoy social contacts; express themselves with clarity; and take initiative.

Low Scores   Patients with low scores are mild mannered, quiet, silent, shy, and easily dominated; lack perseverance and self-confidence; are reluctant to take a stand, taciturn, self-doubting, and inept; worry; avoid competition; are afraid to take risks; have difficulty expressing their ideas; may be prone to insecurity and depression; and are submissive, shy, withdrawn, retiring, and inhibited.

Scale Interactions
Elevated scores on some scales may change the interpretation of scores on other scales. Below are some of the more common scale interactions and associated interpretations.

- High Sa, low Wb: tend to rely on their own judgments and evaluations; feel a certain amount of distrust toward others

- Low Sa, high Wb: believe that others may have better judgment than they do, which tends to result in a high degree of acceptance of the decisions of others
- Low Sa, low Wb: have many self-doubts and perhaps excessive dependency; do not feel competent

Independence (In; 30 Items)

The In Scale was designed to measure the extent to which people strive for autonomy. The method of scale construction was empirical. There are four factors, labeled (1) Resoluteness, Perseverance, and feeling competent; (2) Self-Confident and Assurance under Scrutiny; and (3) Self-Sufficient, Relative Unconcern, and Willingness to Follow Own Judgment though others may disagree. There are two main themes to this scale: (1) self-assurance, resourcefulness, and competence; and (2) distance of self from others and from perfunctory or conventional demands (detachment).

Very High Scores (Raw Scores of 28 to 30 [SS 73 to 79])   Patients with very high scores have too much indifference to the opinions of others and an unwillingness to compromise or yield.

High Scores   The main traits of those with high scores are strength, resilience, and fortitude. These patients are distant from other people and stand apart from the group. They often need to go it alone and have the resolve to do so. They are confident, self-assured, resourceful, determined, enterprising, independent, individualistic, lone wolves, assertive, socially poised, forceful, and detached, and they tend to be dominant in interpersonal relations.

Low Scores   Patients with low score have many self-doubts; feel inadequate; are meek, weak, reticent, quiet, shy, silent, dissatisfied, distractible, unassuming, uncomfortable with ambiguity, and submissive; worry; are prone to have guilt feelings; are socially awkward, easily embarrassed, dependent, acquiescent, and cautious; try to avoid conflict; tend to rely on others for decision making; lack initiative and self-confidence; try to please others; and avoid social disapproval.

Empathy (Em; 38 items)

The Em Scale was designed as a relatively pure measure of the trait of empathy, the ability to perceive and feel the experiences of others. The method of scale construction was empirical. The scale has four main factors, labeled (1) Resolute, Persevering, and Competent; (2) Self-Confident and Self-Assured; (3) Self-Sufficient; and (4) Likes Positions of Authority and Decision Making.

Very High Sores (Raw Scores of 28 to 30 [SS 65 to 69])   Patients with very high scores are too indifferent to the opinions of others and are unwilling to compromise. Even with scores at this level, however, these people are effective and insightful and have an imaginative way of dealing with social situations and with interpersonal relations.

High Scores   People with high scores seem able to put themselves into the psychological frames of others and understand how they feel. They are self-assured, resourceful, competent, willing to go it alone when necessary (and have the resolve to do so), confident, determined, perceptive, intuitive, enterprising, individualistic, lone wolves, assertive, socially poised, and verbally fluent; have a wide range of interests; are forceful; have leadership skills; can deal with complex and demanding situations; and are sociable, outgoing, spontaneous, talkative, experience seeking, insightful, tactful, versatile, lively, clever, witty, and perceptive of social nuances.

Low Scores   People with low scores are slow to understand the feel feelings of others. They worry; feel inadequate, weak, reticent, uncomfortable with ambiguity, easily defeated, ill at ease in interviews, dependent, acquiescent, and inferior; have self-doubts; are cautious about doing anything that could result in withdrawal of security, unsociable, shy, quiet, reserved, inhibited, dispirited, gloomy, sad, and temperamental; dislike ambiguity; are vulnerable to perceived threat; describe their fathers as stern and authoritarian; and are skeptical about others' intentions.

Very Low Scores   People with very low scores have difficulty understanding the behavior of others. They may be insensitive and distant, may hold rigid and authoritarian views, and may have conservative values.

Scale Interactions   Elevated scores on some scales may change the interpretation of scores on other scales. Below are some of the more common scale interactions and associated interpretations.

- Average on Em, high on So: tend to be nonusers of drugs
- Low on Em, high on So: tend to be nonusers of drugs with a passion
- Low on Em and So: are at serious risk for drug abuse

CLASS II SCALES: MEASURES OF NORMATIVE ORIENTATION AND VALUES

Responsibility (Re; 36 Items)

The Re Scale was designed to assess social responsibility. The method of scale construction was empirical. The scale has four factors, labeled (1) Feelings of Responsibility, (2) Dependability, (3) Civic Responsibilities for Citizens, and (4) Positive Attitudes toward Education and Self-Improvement. However, the key theme to this scale is the acceptance of social rules because the person has a true understanding of the need for such rules.

High Scores   People who score high on the Re Scale are considered to be responsible, dependable, and trustworthy; to accept the consequences of their own behavior; and to have a sense of obligation to the group. They accept rules and order. They have a concern for civic, social, and moral obligations. They have a participative temperament, an awareness of ongoing political and social phenomena, and a sense of the responsibility of each citizen. They exhibit interpersonal maturity and relative freedom from neurotic symptoms and distress. They are responsible, self-disciplined, reliable, and attentive to others; may be involved in a religious group; observe schedules;

take note of political issues; are reliable, conscientious, organized, efficient, persevering, methodical, discreet, productive, and attentive to intellectual matters; have high levels of aspiration and of integrity; were reared with attention to conventional standards and to a sense of duty; are stable; tend to do well in school; tend toward ethical behavior; comply with rules; are courteous; and may be willing to sacrifice their own needs for the benefit of the larger group. They show strong commitment to social and moral values and have a strong sense of civic responsibility.

Low Scores   Low scores are usually associated with rebellious and antisocial attitudes and behavior. These people may dress provocatively; tend not to return others' lost articles; tend to let others pay drink or meal tabs; are impulsive, infantile, pleasure seeking, reckless, restless, flirtatious, erratic, uncontrolled, exploitative, immature, unpredictable, self-indulgent, and rule testing; have parental relations that are fraught with friction; and are underachievers, distrustful, crude, moody, dissatisfied, recalcitrant, and cynical. They do not feel concerned about the "general good." Groups characterized by antisocial behavior tend to score low on this scale.

   Note: This scale is identical to the Re scale of the MMPI-2, though the research traditions associated with this scale diverge somewhat from those of the MMPI-2. The reader may consult the interpretation for the Re scale (page 52) in the MMPI-2 section of this manual.

Scale Interactions   Elevated scores on some scales may change the interpretation of scores on other scales. Below are some of the more common scale interactions and associated interpretations.

   - Re high, So moderate to high: these people tend to do the right thing without thinking much about it
   - Re low, So moderate: these people may be creative, innovative, and willing to break rules when such rules need to be broken to produce something new

Socialization (So; 46 items)

The So Scale was originally designed as a measure of delinquency, with high scores reflecting adherence to social norms. The method of scale construction was empirical. Many consider this scale the most validated scale on the CPI-R because there has been extensive research with this scale, including regarding cross-cultural applications, and the scale demonstrates excellent concurrent and predictive validity. There are four factors on this scale, labeled (1) Self-Discipline and Rule-Observing Behavior; (2) Optimistic, Self-Confident, and Positive Emotionality; (3) Good Upbringing and Favorable Family Memories; and (4) Interpersonal Awareness and Reflective Temperament.

Above-average compliance with social norms is indicated in men by raw scores > 31 (SS > 50) and in women by raw scores > 32 (SS > 50). Ordinary compliance with social norms is indicated in men by raw scores of 30 or 31 (SS 50) and in women by raw scores of 30 to 32 (SS 48 to 51). Moderate waywardness is indicated in men by raw scores of 26 to 29 (SS 44 to 48) and in women by raw scores of 26 to 29 (SS 42 to 46). Severe problems with rule-following and norm-accepting behavior is indicated by raw scores ≤ 25 for both genders.

Very High Scores (Raw Scores > 37 [SS > 60])   Patients with very high scores exhibit too much conformity, readily accepting conventions that may not be in their own best interests. They can be harsh and punitive judges of weaknesses in others.

High Scores   Patients with high scores show social maturity and integrity; do what good citizens are expected to do; are conscientious, dependable, honest, reliable, cooperative, modest, tactful, sensitive to the feelings of others, conservative, and conventional; report that their fathers were benevolent and tolerant; had a happy home life; were socialized toward compliance and rule-respecting behavior; are well organized, adaptable, efficient, controlled, optimistic, productive, and emotionally stable; and accept social norms and standards.

Low Scores   Patients with low scores are unconventional, self-serving, careless, unempathic, self-indulgent, impulsive, and self-serving; tend to feel ashamed of at least one of their parents; felt unhappy at home and in school and rejected family ties; report a delinquent-like existence; tended to reject parental control; show rule-testing and rule-violating behavior; are restless, headstrong, moody, and likely to have many conflicts with society; get into trouble easily; are unlikely to sustain positive relationship; have serious problems with impulse control; and *are prone to substance abuse, crime, and violence.* Studies have repeatedly found that delinquents, both male and female, get low scores on the So Scale. Low scores on this scale are also predictive of a personality disorder.

Scale Interactions   Elevated scores on the Re and Sc Scales affect the interpretation of low scores on the So Scale. People with low So scores and high Re and Sc scores are very susceptible to situational stress, prone to explode, and are very guarded and defensive.

Self-Control (Sc; 38 Items)

The Sc Scale was originally intended to assess internalized social norms and values and to assess self-regulation, self-control, and freedom from impulsive behavior. The method of scale construction was rational using internal consistency. There are four factors on the scale, labeled (1) Self-Control, (2) Modest and Selfless, (3) Denying Rule-Breaking Propensities, and (4) Suppression of Hedonistic or Aggressive Feelings.

Very High Scores (Raw Scores > 31 [SS > 66])   Very high scores suggest overcontrolled and highly suppressed feelings and hence a potential for the volatile eruption and explosion of emotion, particularly destructive anger that has been bottled up and denied. Such people are prone to violent reactions. Such high scores also suggest overly judgmental behavior.

High Scores   Patients with high scores are aware of and understand the meaning of and nature of normative sanctions and that such rules are morally right; their compliance is based on rational and discretionary motives. They may also be controlled, patient, organized, conscientious, harsh, judgmental, dependable, moderate, conservative, considerate, precise, mild, fastidious, stubborn, patient, observant of personal standards, and able to bind tension. They seek to please others, want to be seen as admirable and upstanding, avoid blatant expressions of aggression or eroticism, and try to control emotions and temper.

Low Scores   Patients with low scores are impulsive (particularly with erotic impulses), uninhibited, adventurous, mischievous, pleasure seeking, reckless, careless, temperamental, changeable, unrealistic, superficial, restless, undercontrolled, rebellious, nonconforming, self-indulgent (particularly sexually), fretful when confronted with constraints or limits, headstrong, moody, narcissistic, and undercontrolled.

Scale Interactions   Low scores on the So and Re Scales affect the interpretation of high scores on the Sc Scale. People with high Sc scores and below-average So and Re scores show undue expression of impulses, a lack of insight concerning aggressive feelings, and a potential for explosive or uncontrolled, aggressive, and destructive behavior.

Good Impression (Gi; 40 Items)

The Gi Scale was designed to detect invalid or dissimulated profiles and to assess the degree to which respondents are attempting to make a favorable impression. The method of scale construction was empirical using internal consistency. There are four factors on this scale, labeled (1) Denying Self-Serving or Egotistic Motives, (2) Claiming Equanimity and Absence of Moodiness or Irritability, (3) Willingness to Accept Supervision and Work under Strictly Defined Rules, and (4) Expressing Faith in Ethicality and Goodwill.

Raw Scores > 29 (SS > 66 for men and > 71 for women)   Patients with raw scores > 29 are possibly placing themselves in an extremely favorable light; theirs is a faked-good response set.

Raw Scores of 18 to 29 (SS 50 to 66)   Patients with raw scores from 18 and 29 show increased concern about the reactions of others.

Raw Scores < 15 (SS < 45)   Respondents with raw scores < 15 are asserting a rejection of the idea that their actions and beliefs are guided by an attempt to win favor.

Raw Scores < 13 (SS < 42)   Respondents with raw scores < 13 have revealed a prickly, isolative demeanor.

Raw Scores < 8 (SS < 35)   Patients with raw scores < 8 are endorsing negative aspects of personality; such low scores may also suggest faking a bad response set or a cry for help.

High Scores   Patients with high scores want to make a good impression; are conscientious, dependable, moderate, thorough, quiet, fastidious, moralistic, conventional, considerate, cooperative, helpful, and opportunistic; often seek to ingratiate themselves with superiors but overlook or ignore feelings in their subordinates; exaggerate their positive qualities and minimize their negative traits; and present themselves as self-assured, competent, and behaving in socially approved ways.

Low Scores   Low scores suggest resistance to the demands of others and an insistence on having one's own way. These patients are argumentative, dissatisfied, complaining, temperamental, arrogant, sarcastic, rebellious, headstrong, mischievous, pleasure seeking, cynical, changeable, nonconforming, self-indulgent, and insensitive; tend to be aggressively indifferent to what others think and to judge their own behavior independently of what others think; lack nurturing behaviors; are quick to complain and criticize; and are skeptical, dissatisfied in many situations, easily annoyed, and irritated.

Communality (Cm; 38 Items)

The Cm Scale was developed to identify protocols that are invalid because of careless responding, random responding, or other unusual response patterns in the inventory. The method of scale construction was empirical using internal consistency. There are four factors in this scale, labeled (1) Disagreeing with Cynical or Antagonistic Views of Human Nature, (2) Optimism about Self and Society, (3) Recognizing Benefits That Accrue from Life Experiences, and (4) Admitting to Ordinary Emotionality and Affect.

Very High Scores (Raw Scores of 37 or 38 [SS 58 to 62])   Very high scores suggest an overly conventional attitude with undue conformity.

High Scores   Patients with high scores tend to practice conventional activities (arrive on time for meetings, go to religious services, send greeting cards, use humor to relieve tension). They are comfortable in their milieu and function effectively in it. These people are reasonable, dependable, and conscientious, efficient, organized, practical, ambitious, contented, mature, stable, dependable, and practical and they fit in easily.

Raw Scores of 30 to 34 (SS 38 to 50)   People with raw scores between 30 and 34 are independent, exhibit creative differences from the norm, and are assertive.

Low Scores   People with low scores practice unconventional activities (hang up on phone calls abruptly, mumble instead of talking clearly, do not make weekend plans, avoid eye contact). These people are seen as lazy, shiftless, moody, indifferent, careless, absentminded, forgetful, changeable, reckless, impulsive, moody, unconventional, and dissatisfied. They feel marginal and show poor interpersonal functioning.

Very Low Scores (Raw Scores < 30 for Men and < 25 for Women [SS < 25])   Very low scores indicate erratic or atypical responding, perhaps due to random or careless responding, faking bad scores, or reading difficulties. They can also indicate poor morale, self-doubts, feelings of alienation, and general instability.

Well-Being (Wb; 38 Items)

The Wb Scale is a derivative of the Gough's MMPI-based Dissimulation (Ds) Scale and was developed to identify people feigning emotional disturbance from those who responded more truthfully to the items. It is used as a scale to measure a faked bad response set. The method of scale construction was empirical using internal consistency. There are four factors in this scale, labeled (1) Feelings of Wholeness and Able to Withstand Stress, (2) Trust in Others and Feelings That Life Is Fair, (3) Good Relations with Others and Absence of Extreme Irritation, and (4) Happiness and Good Morale. (In fact, this scale could be thought of as a morale scale.)

Very High Scores (Raw Scores > 29 [SS > 45])   Raw scores > 29 suggest faking of a good response set.

Raw Scores 20 to 38 (SS 27 to 64)   People with raw scores between 20 and 38 like competition and are willing to try something new. They feel good, have both energy and stability, and can get things done.

High Scores   People with high scores are productive, satisfied with their life, cheerful, socially at ease, and self-confident; cope well with pressure; are energetic, contented, and enterprising; and have a good level of psychological adjustment. They have good interpersonal relationships and are stable and dependable people. They tend to minimize complaints and problems.

Low Scores   People with low scores have diminished vitality and are unable to meet the demands of everyday life. They have poor morale; feel victimized; are self-pitying, nervous, distractable, and anxious; worry; tend to emphasize or complain about problems; and feel a lack of support from others. They have low morale. Raw scores < 35 suggest symptom exaggeration, whereas raw scores < 20 (SS < 28) suggest serious personality problems, either an exaggerated emphasis on personal problems or faking bad, a brittle ego, and feeling beset by problems and being unsure as to how to deal with them.

Scale Interactions   Elevated scores on some scales may change the interpretation of scores on other scales. Below are some of the more common scale interactions and associated interpretations.

- High Wb, low Sa: are generally self-reliant but tend to rely on the judgment of others when making decisions; may be extremely loyal to authority figures
- Low Wb and Sc and high Cm: are prone to psychosomatic disorders
- Low Wb, high Sa: are self-reliant and self-assured
- Low Wb, high F/M: may have dependency and affiliative needs that are unsatisfied, along with feelings of alienation, which may result in gastrointestinal symptoms or headaches

Tolerance (To; 32 Items)

The To Scale was originally called the Prejudice Scale in the MMPI and was designed to detect anti-Semitic prejudice. It also measures nonjudgmental social beliefs and intolerant attitudes. The method of scale construction was empirical. Scale content pertains to pessimism, cynicism, distrust, suspicion, misanthropy, discontent with current status, a rigid and dogmatic thinking style, and feelings of estrangement. There are four factors on this scale, labeled (1) Integrity and Goodwill, (2) Feelings of Being Treated Fairly, (3) Concern for Others, and (4) Belief in the Ideas of Fairness and Equity

High Scores   People with high scores help promote the well-being of a group; feel an involvement with everyone's goodwill; are cooperative, fairminded, forgiving, nonjudgmental, reasonable, sincere, willing to accept and understand others (this comes from cognitive attitudes rather than from warmth or truly positive feelings); maintain realistic attitudes; are relatively free from serious conflicts or psychological problems, tolerant of others' beliefs and attitudes, and permissive.

Low Scores   The overall picture implied by low scores is one of harassed, tormented, resentful, peevish, querulous, judgmental, constricted, cold, authoritarian, dogmatic, defensive, outspoken, narrowminded, disillusioned, embittered, distrustful, rancorous, apprehensive, and somewhat bewildered people. These people tend to snub others; talk behind others' back; spend money on attention-getting, provocative clothing; tend to have divisive and disruptive interpersonal relations; are self-centered, unconcerned about the feelings of others, ready to criticize, distrustful, prejudiced, intolerant, and apt to verbally attack others or exploit them if possible; distrust the motives of others; and are fault finding. Low scores on this scale significantly correlate with spousal ratings of intolerant behavior.

Scale Interactions   Scores on other scales can affect the interpretation of scores on the To Scale. Very low To, low Sc, and low So scores indicate impulsivity and are and diagnostic of potential for interpersonal violence.

CLASS III SCALES: MEASURES OF COGNITIVE AND INTELLECTUAL FUNCTIONING

Achievement via Conformance (Ac; 38 Items)

The Ac Scale initially was developed to assess motivational and personality factors associated with predicting high school academic achievement (but was ineffective at predicting performance in college). The method of scale construction was empirical. There are four factors in this scale, labeled (1) Able to Concentrate and Think in Order to Persevere, (2) Acceptance of Rules and Conformity, (3) Expresses a Liking for School, and (4) Planfulness and Orientation towards the Future. There are essentially two components to this scale: a strong need for achievement and a strong need for structure.

High Scores   People with high scores show good organization and use of personal resources; are industrious, methodical, organized, mature, able to adapt to societal norms, clear thinking, persistent, industrious, ambitious with strong achievement motivation, responsible, fastidious, and productive; enjoy taking part in community affairs; have high aspirations; tend to have been honor students in high school; are optimistic about the future; have leadership potential; and maintain self-discipline in pursuit of goals.

Low Scores   People with low scores have isolative and self-protective tendencies; are rebellious and changeable; feel a lack of meaning in their life; report unhappy an childhood, nonconformist behavior in high school, and academic underachievement; are distrustful, poorly organized, and moody; tend to give up easily; value personal pleasure more than school accomplishments;are easily distracted and unsure of their abilities; has difficulty working in environments with strict rules and regulations; become disorganized when too many demands are placed on them; and probably are underachievers.

Scale Interactions   Elevated scores on some scales may change the interpretation of scores on other scales. Below are some of the more common scale interactions and associated interpretations.

- Low Ac, Re, and So: suggest delinquency and people with severe problems with rule breaking
- Low AC, high Ai (plus other signs of personal resourcefulness in the profile): suggest creativity
- High Ac, low Ai: These people are responsible and ambitious but also conservative, value intellectual effort, and enjoy working in highly structured settings with well-defined criteria for expectations and performance
- High Ac—higher than Ai by > 10: These people prefer occupations requiring external structure, such as middle-management positions

Achievement via Independence (Ai; 36 Items)

The Ai Scale was designed to predict achievement in college undergraduate courses, especially courses in psychology, but has evolved as a scale that predicts superior performance in settings requiring independent planning and effort. The method of scale construction was empirical. The scale has four factors, labeled (1) Iconoclastic and Independent Beliefs, (2) Confidence in Self and in the Future, (3) Breadth of Interests, and (4) Denying Common Fears.

High Scores   There is a touch of egoism or self-centeredness in high scorers. They are prudent, dependable, self-disciplined, independent, intuitive, and able to get the most out of circumstances; maximize achievement; can set goals and evolve effective means to attain them; take the initiative; are logical, rational, enterprising, creative, and foresighted; value intellectual matters; have high levels of aspiration; are very self-motivated; do not like a lot of structure; tend to have been superior achievers in high school; are perceptive and verbally fluent; may be indifferent to the feelings of others and may lack personal warmth; and like work environments where there is individual freedom.

Low Scores   Low scorers are poor risks for academic achievement at all educational levels. They may be dependent on others and concerned about others' opinions; lack clarity of thought; have narrow interests; are somewhat rattlebrained, distrustful, fussy, suspicious, prejudiced, and more conservative; tend to give up easily when faced with obstacles and adversity; do not do well in situations calling for independent effort and self-direction; are prone to make grammatical mistakes; are dull, unambitious, warm, uncomplicated, and uncomfortable with ambiguous situations; do not deal well with intellectual demands; do not trust their own abilities; seem simple; and do best in settings where little is expected of them.

Scale Interactions   Scores on the Ac Scale can affect the interpretation of scores on the Ai Scale. When high Ai scores are significantly higher (by > 10) than Ac scores, test takers prefer occupations requiring independence, such as authors and researchers. These people are highly motivated to achieve, trust their judgments, and act in unconventional ways. Structure is see as an inhibiting condition on their talent.

Intellectual Efficiency (Ie; 42 Items)

The Ie Scale was originally designed to assess a series of personality traits that would correlate with good measures of intelligence. The current version assesses intellectual resources and endurance. The method of scale construction was empirical. The scale has four main factors, labeled (1) Good Morale and Confident about the Future, (2) Denying Common Fears and Worries, (3) Participation in Intellectual Activity, and (4) Enjoys Science. **Note:** There is no high point at which respondents become too intellectual, too wrapped up in cognitive pursuits, too eager to succeed.

High Scores   High scorers are capable, self-confident, clever, clear thinking, resourceful, insightful, rational, civilized, idealistic, and reflective; value intellectual matters; are socially poised; express themselves well; have a good vocabulary; make a good impression; tend to have high levels of aspiration; tend to have been honor students in high school; have leadership potential and better psychological well-being; and are not easily discouraged.

Low Scores   Low scores are suggestive of moderate to below-average intellectual ability. People with low scores have low morale and poor adjustment; are gloomy, bitter, nervous, weak, apathetic, silent, simple, slow, awkward, dependent, shy, and temperamental; tend to withdraw when stymied; are self-pitying; have difficulty expressing ideas; make mistakes in language usage; are dull, lacking in and insecure over their intellectual ability, and moody; become anxious if required to deal with change; deal poorly with stress and trauma; feel victimized; are often self-defeating; may feel uncertain about their intellectual abilities; and are not interested in scholarly or intellectual pursuits.

CLASS IV SCALES: MEASURES OF ROLE AND PERSONAL STYLE

Psychological Mindedness (Py; 28 Items)

The Py Scale was designed to identify people who have a knack for figuring our how other people think and feel by being sensitive to their needs, motives, and experiences. It does not detect whether such people would be empathic (see Em Scale, page 206) or nurturing, nor does it imply warmth or sympathetic behavior. Accordingly, it detects those people both interested in and working in psychology and also relates to the quality of work done in psychology. The method of scale construction was empirical. The scale has four factors, labeled (1) Ability to Direct and Maintain Intellectual Functions, (2) Indifference to Minor Conventions and Personal Neatness, (3) Liking for Intellectual Endeavors, and (4) Nonjudgmental until One Has All the Facts.

High Scores   High scorers possess an analytic, rational conceptualizing kind of psychological mindedness and tend to be interested in psychological phenomena, including the field itself. In relations with others, they tend to be somewhat distant and not usually warm or supportive; in intimacy, they take more than they give. However, they do understand the feelings of others. They are perceptive, observant of subtleties in behavior, creative, verbally fluent, open-minded, interested in new ideas, independent, willing to help others on intellectual tasks, reflective, alert, foresighted, and confident; take the initiative; are tolerant, ingenious, socially ill at ease, and wedded to routine; and have wide interests and superior intellectual ability.

Low Scores   Low scorers show apologetic behaviors; are embarrassed when attention is drawn to them; avoid conflict with exploitative friends; are sensitive to beind-the-back remarks, apathetic, unambitious, weak, given to complaining, whiny, and uncomfortable dealing with complexity; lack perseverance; are frustrated with adversity, self-indulgent, and self-doubting; pursue gratification in nonintellectual pursuits; feel put upon by the vicissitudes of life; rely on devious methods rather than direct methods of coping; are not interested in scholarly pursuits; and generally take the motivation of other people at face value.

Flexibility (Fx; 28 Items)

The Fx Scale was designed to identify people who are both flexible and adaptable. Gough now says that the scale gets at the rigidity factor of the authoritarian personality. The method of scale construction was rational, using internal consistency. There are four factors, labeled (1) Tolerance for Ambiguity, (2) Noncompulsive, (3) Admitting Bias and Prejudgment, and (4) Absence of Severe or Punitive Superego.

Those with raw scores > 21 (SS > 67) are adaptive, receptive to change, and think creatively. Those with raw scores < 20 (SS < 64) are impatient and irritable. Those with raw scores < 8 (SS < 36) are rigid, moralistic, and judgmental and exhibit deliberate, slow-moving behavior.

High Scores   High scorers are spontaneous and lively; delight in new experiences; are impatient with routine, adventurous, changeable, pleasure seeking, uninhibited, clever, witty, imaginative, sharp witted, curious, innovative, rebellious, and volatile; enjoy sensual pleasures; are animated; have a zest for life, good ability to adapt to change, and an adventurous spirit; are somewhat loose and disorganized, and may be emotionally unstable.

Low Scores   Low scores suggest more deliberation and planning and more awareness of consequences. Low scorers are cautious, conservative, deliberate, industrious, fussy, prejudiced, prudish, and moralistic; have strong religious beliefs; report they had stern fathers; behave in an overcontrolled manner; and are serious, conscientious, inflexible, steady, rigid, organized, and conventional.

Femininity/Masculinity (F/M; 32 Items)

The F/M Scale attempts to array men and women along a dimension that is consonant with what it means to be masculine or feminine in most cultures, although its original purpose was to produce a scale that would differentiate men from women in terms of a psychological continuum as well as homosexual men and women from heterosexuals. (The scale is unable to accomplish the latter.) The method of scale construction was empirical. The scale has four factors, labeled (1) Likes Traditionally Masculine Jobs, (2) Feels Vulnerable, (3) Likes Traditionally Feminine Work and (4) Dislikes Horseplay and Practical Jokes. **Note:** The descriptions below are not meant to convey stereotypic traits but are in fact descriptions true of both men and women with high and low scores.

High Scores   High scorers are feminine; do things to form and solidify relations with others; shy away from direct/immediate contact; are dependent, sensitive, submissive, emotional, nervous, high strung, gloomy, shy, timid, anxious, concerned about their adequacy, and sensitive; and have affiliative needs.

Men with High Scores   Men with high scores are ideational, creative, esthetic, feminine and delicate in appearance, nervous, high strung, easily offended, emotional, and imaginative. High scores (> 70) may also suggest problems with their sexual identity.

Women with High Scores   Women with high scores avoid attention, willingly defer or submit to respected others, dislike uncertainty or unpredictability, see themselves as feminine but also as weak and dependent, and seek affiliation and support and reassurance.

Men with Low Scores   Men with low scores are masculine; take the initiative; and are aggressive, determined, self-confident, independent, ambitious, assertive, strong, tough, hardhearted, stubborn, strong willed, power oriented, direct in expressing hostility, able to deal with stress and conflict, obstinate, indifferent to feelings of others, tough-minded, aggressive, ambitious, confident, and independent. (Low scores generally reflect stereotypic masculine identification.) They look masculine; are decisive in times of stress or emergencies, independent, robust, strong, adventurous, and not inclined to introspection; and tend to brush off criticism or complaints.

Women with Low Scores   Women with low scores are openly hedonistic; enjoy being the center of attention; have high aspirations; are assertive, independent, self-confident, demanding, stubborn, willful, critical, strong, tough, and self-reliant; have high aspirations and a strong ego; are skeptical about intentions of others; and have difficulty accepting a subordinate role. Extremely low scores may suggest problems with female sexual identification.

Note: Very little is published as to CPI-R F/M scores of homoerotic men and women. The F/M was not intended to assess homosexuality. One study found that lesbians had significantly lower scores than heterosexual women did on the F/M Scale. Two studies (one from the United Kingdom and the other from the United States) reported that gay men had higher scores on the F/M Scale than heterosexual men did.

References

Gough, H. G. (1987a). *CPI applications* (video). Palo Alto, CA: Consulting Psychologists Press.

Gough, H. G. (1987b). *Interpreting today's CPI.* (video). Palo Alto, CA: Consulting Psychologists Press.

Gough, H. G. (1987c) *Origins and development of the CPI* (video). Palo Alto, CA: Consulting Psychologists Press.

Gough, H. G. (1994). Theory, development, and interpretation of the CPI socialization scale. *Psychological Reports* (Monograph Supplement 1–75), 651–700.

Gough, H. G. (with P. Bradley) (1996). *California psychological inventory test manual.* Palo Alto, CA: Consulting Psychologists Press.

Groth-Marnat, G. (1997). The California Psychological Inventory. In *Handbook of psychological assessment*. New York: Wiley & Sons. pp. 343–392.

McAllister, L. (1996). *A practical guide to CPI interpretation* (3rd ed). Palo Alto, CA: Consulting Psychologists Press.

McGargee, E. I. (1972). *The California Psychological Inventory handbook*. San Francisco: Jossey-Bass.

Webb, J. T., McNamara, M., & Rogers, D. A. (1981). *Configural interpretations of the MMPI and CPI*. Cleveland: Ohio Psychological Association.

CHAPTER 4

Sixteen Personality Factors

Background and History

THE SIXTEEN PERSONALITY FACTORS (16PF) instrument was developed by Raymond Cattell at the University of Illinois, Urbana-Champaign. It was originally published in 1949 and most recently revised in 1993 as the fifth edition. Cattell believed that traits were the essential component of personality description and used the method of factor analysis to hone down an inordinate number of adjectives into the most meaningful, descriptive, and nonredundant components of personality, which he labeled factors. He concluded that there were 16 of these primary factors, with each factor orthogonal or independent of one another. The test is an adult personality test designed for use with people aged 16 and above and for those with a seventh to eighth grade reading ability.

Sten Scores

Raw scores on the 16PF are converted to a "standard ten," or "sten," scale distribution with a mean of 5.5 and a standard deviation (SD) of 2. Sten scores between 1 3 and 8 10 have interpretive significance, as they are considered extreme scores in the sten scale distribution.

Interpreting the 16PF Basic Scales

STEPS IN THE INTERPRETIVE PROCESS

To interpret 16PF findings, follow these steps:

1. Evaluate Test Taking Attitude and Response Sets by consulting Impression Management (IM, below), Acquiescence (ACQ, below), and Infrequency (INF) for the fifth edition and Faking Good/Bad for the fourth edition.
2. Evaluate overall adjustment level by looking at Factor C (page 229), Factor Q3 (page 237), and global factors anxiety (page 239) and Self-Control (page 241).
3. Interpret extreme factor scale scores (e.g., sten scores 1, 2 and 3, and 8, 9, and 10).
4. Consider scale interactions that may alter the meaning of an individual factor scale score.
5. Consider the five global factors and integrate those into the interpretation.
6. Relate scores to other sources of information and address the referral question.

VALIDITY SCALE INDICATORS

Impression Management (IM)

The IM Scale consists of 12 items that pertain to social desirability. High scale scores suggest a conscious attempt by respondents to look good on the test or perhaps even an honest self-appraisal. Low scale scores suggest a conscious attempt to look bad, the presence of life stressors that reduce respondents' ability to cope, or a negative self-portrayal.

Acquiescence (ACQ)

The ACQ Scale measures the tendency of the respondent to mark an inordinately larger number of items as true, often irrespective of item content. It also may measure an acquiescent response set, which is defined as the set of items for which the tendency is for the respondent to mark the item as true when the items are equally true and equally false for the respondent. The latter is not a conscious process and respondents are not aware they are doing this. These people may also wish to be seen as agreeable.

Infrequency (INF)

The INF Scale has 32 items with answers keyed in the "B" direction. In other words, respondents are unsure of the answer and instead of marking the item True (A) or False (C), they respond by marking the item Uncertain (B). Very high INF scores can invalidate the test and suggest random responding, reading difficulties, or indecision.

Faking Good

If a respondent is faking good, scores for factors are as follows: C+, H+, L–, O–, Q3+, Q4– (also possibly G+)

FACTORS

Factor A (Cool and Reserved versus Warm and Easygoing)

Factor A measures interpersonal warmth, sociability, and a desire to be with people.

High Scores (Right Pole)   Patients with high scores have a high need for social contact. They enjoy the support of others and actively involve themselves with other people. They show an authentic interest in people and are generous and attentive to them. They tend to be good natured, easygoing, cooperative, softhearted, warmhearted, adaptable, generous, casual, trusting, and outgoing and truly enjoy participating in social activities. Their emotions are accessible and expressive. They are natural joiners and are able to withstand criticism, and are considerate, kind, warm, and extroverted. At a more clinical level, these patients may have intolerable feelings of loneliness and hence may have a strong desire for approval. In such cases, this could make them quite gullible. Also, extremely high scores on Factor A may suggest difficulty with employee supervision, in that they may have trouble setting limits on others' behavior. They may place people concerns ahead of task concerns. They tend to have high needs for nurturance, affiliation, and exhibition.

Low Scores (Left Pole) In clinical patients, extremely low scores may reflect schizoid and withdrawn behavior; a submissive, retiring, and passive personality; and a history of poor interpersonal and conflicted family relationships. These patients have difficulty openly expressing anger. They show little warmth and are markedly reserved. They tend to be critical, cool, aloof, detached, precise, distrustful, skeptical, rigid, cold, prone to sulk, impersonal, uncompromising, and stiff. They generally prefer to work alone. They tend to be obstructive and introverted and quite difficult to relate to. In the presence of extremely low scores, the clinician should look for a history of unsatisfactory relations with others and a marked difficulty in gratifying dependency needs. Low scores on Factor A are associated with poor performance in many jobs.

Factor B (Concrete [Less Intelligent] versus Abstract [More Intelligent])

Factor B largely measures reasoning ability via analogies.

High Scores (Right Pole) High scorers tend to be bright, show abstract thinking, and have a higher scholastic mental capacity. They are fast learners, insightful, intellectually adaptable, and persevering. They tend to have superior reasoning ability and verbal fluency.

Low Scores (Left Pole) Low scorers tend to think concretely, have lower scholastic mental capacity, show poorer judgment, are less persevering, and tend to interpret things more literally. Low scores may also reflect a lack of motivation in taking this test.

Factor C (Fourth Edition: Affective by Feelings versus Emotional Stability; Fifth Edition: Reactive versus Emotionally Stable)

High Scores (Right Pole)   High scores on Factor C suggest emotional stability and good ego strength and all that entails. High-scoring people are emotionally stable and secure. They show few signs of becoming easily upset or unusually tense. For the most part, anxiety is not a problem for them. They are mature, calm, and patient. They face reality with a realistic approach. They have higher ego strength and for the most part are unruffled and stable. High Factor C scores are a good indication of psychological health and a good predictor of emotional stability and maturity.

Low Scores (Left Pole)   Low scores on Factor C are associated with many kinds of psychopathologies and symptoms and imply psychological maladjustment. Low-scoring patients tend to be emotionally unstable and show a poor psychological adjustment. They have low ego strength and feel unable to cope with life. They become easily upset and perturbed and get quite emotional when frustrated. They have a limited ability to tolerate frustration and stress. They tend to avoid responsibilities, spend time needlessly worrying, repeatedly get into problematic situations, and give up easily. They tend to be moody and unpleasant to be around. They are generally dissatisfied with themselves and with others. They are prone to develop generalized neurotic behaviors (phobias, sleep disturbances, psychosomatic disorders, and hysterical and obsessional behavior), get easily fatigued, and are too changeable.

Factor E[1] (Fourth Edition: Humble versus Assertive; Fifth Edition: Submissive or Deferential versus Dominant)

High Scores (Right Pole)   People who score high on Factor E have a high need for dominance and assertiveness. They tend to be aggressive, competitive, authoritative, stubborn, demanding, impatient, attention seeking, overreactive, egotistical, excitable, easily distracted,

---

[1] There is no Factor D.

and prone to jealousy. Also, they are independent, rebellious, head-strong, austere, and hostile and like to be in command. They enjoy meeting challenges and do so with little empathy. They readily speak their mind and stand up for their beliefs. They appear confident and competent. They may show nervous symptoms, such as restlessness, and like to show off and boast. They seem insensitive to social disapproval. They become emotional, impulsive, and a demanding nuisance when restricted, yet in quieter moods, they are likable and affectionate. Psychologically, these patients tend to be in conflict between their strong feelings of assertiveness and their need for control.

Low Scores (Left Pole)   Traits that describe low-scoring people on Factor E include accommodation, submissiveness, dependence, obedience, being easily led, complacency, stoicism, self-effacement, humbleness, docility, deliberateness, conventionality, quietness, timidity, being appeasing and retiring, and diplomacy. They try to avoid conflict to please and win approval. They generally have a mild temperament and are eager to follow their sense of correctness. Psychologically, their marked passivity and submissiveness may mask unexpressed anger and resentment.

Factor F (Fourth Edition: Sober versus Happy-Go-Lucky; Fifth Edition: Seriousness versus Liveliness or Impulsivity)

High Scores (Right Pole)
High-scoring people on Factor F are impulsive, lively, enthusiastic, heedless, cheerful, quick, alert, talkative, extroverted, spontaneous, effervescent, mercurial, active, carefree, sociable, energetic, and happy-go-lucky. Urgency seems to capture the essence of this style. Sometimes these people can appear too spontaneous and uninhibited.

Low Scores (Left Pole)   This factor measures liveliness. Low-scoring people are extremely serious, sober, taciturn, cautious, restrained, slow, silent, introspective, less playful, dour, pessimistic, smug, unduly deliberate, reticent, primly correct, reflective, obsessional, subdued, concerned, self-effacing, and prudent. Low scores could either mean acceptance of responsibility or mere resignation. Extremely low scores suggest clinical depression.

Factor G (Fourth Edition: Expedient versus Conscientious; Fifth Edition: Expedient/Low Superego versus Rule-Conscious/Higher Superego)

High Scores (Right Pole) People with high scores on Factor G are described as responsible, determined, persistent, persevering, conscientious, emotionally disciplined, planful, and orderly. They are moralistic and rule-bound and dominated by a sense of duty. They both accept and follow prescribed rules. They strive to do their best, have good concentration, and tend to be organized in thought and behavior. They are interested in figuring out people. High scores reflect higher superego strength and have many elements in common with a compulsive personality style. They may have difficulty in situations that call for flexibility.

Low Scores (Left Pole) Scores < sten 4 may reflect faking bad. If that can be ruled out, low scorers tend to be amoral and have a weak superego. They are low on conventionality and group conformity. They disrespect societal and external rules and regulations and feel few obligations to others. In work settings, they do not accept group standards. They are self-indulgent, slack, indolent, undependable, frivolous, and casual and lack group effort. They are fickle, rebellious, changeable, and probably not very conscientious. They may have trouble in situations that require conformance to rules and regulations.

Factor H (Fourth Edition: Shy versus Venturesome; Fifth Edition: Shy versus Socially Bold)

Factor H measures the psychological construct similar to sensation seeking.

High Scores (Right Pole) High scorers are bold and venturesome, enjoy excitement, and are risk-takers. They tend to be uninhibited, spontaneous, carefree, and willing to try new things. They want to be noticed. They are active, genial, friendly, convivial, self-confident, and diplomatic, but they can also be impulsive, brash, pushy, and sometimes careless with details. (The movie character James Bond is a prototype of this personality type.)

Low Scores (Left Pole)   People with low scores are described as shy, withdrawn, timid, inhibited, retiring, cautious, and restrained. They feel inferior, are sensitive to perceived threat, lack self-confidence, and seem to silently suffer in their own self-imposed restrictions. They are the prototypical wallflowers. They try to avoid being noticed by people.

Factor I (Fourth Edition: Tough-Minded versus Tender-Minded; Fifrth Edition: Tough-Minded/Utilitarian versus Emotional Sensitivity)

Note: Men who score very low and women who score very high on Factor I are admitting to sex-role stereotypes for their gender and vice versa.

High Scores (Right Pole)   Factor I measures interpersonal sensitivity. High scorers are tender-minded, more emotionally sensitive, and vulnerable to perceived stress. They are temperamental, fussy, and impatient. Both compassionate and sensitive, they are attuned to their own areas of vulnerability, so they wish to avoid conflict in these areas. They tend to be unrealistic, fidgety, clinging, insecure, demanding of attention, self-sufficient, independent, and responsible and seek help and sympathy. They are also kindly, gentle, indulgent, imaginative, and flighty and have a flare for dramatics. They are intuitive and make judgments based on subjective impressions and their own emotional reactions. They may have trouble in situations that require toughness.

Low Scores (Left Pole)   Low scorers are cool, tough-minded, and realistic. They maintain self-control. They are self-reliant, unsentimental, and independent and prefer tackling things responsibly, resourcefully, and alone. They have a no-nonsense, down-to-earth approach. They are logical and tough; keep to the point; are some-times unmoved; and are detached, cynical, and independent. De-tached, objective analysis is their usual way of thinking. They tend to discount what they are feeling. Because they tend to be overly critical, they are prone to developing difficulties in interpersonal relations. They may have trouble in situations that require sensitivity.

Factor L[2] (Fourth Edition: Trusting versus Suspicious; Fifth Edition: Trusting versus Vigilant)

High Scores (Right Pole)   Factor L measures vigilance. High scores on the scale often reflect disturbed interpersonal relations, perhaps due to an anxious insecurity that they do not relate well to others. Such scores are often associated with psychopathology. Suspiciousness is the main trait associated with high scores on Factor L. These people dis-place and externalize their emotions and blame others. They are opin-ionated, questioning, skeptical, jealous, dogmatic, resentful, suspi-cious, mistrusting, irritable, doubting, and deliberate in action. They tend to be poor team members in work settings, insisting on getting their point across. They dwell on their frustrations; feel that people are talking about them behind their back; and are oppositional, hostile, and quick to take offense.

Low Scores (Left Pole)   Low scores on Factor L are generally a good indicator of mental health and psychological well-being. Low scorers are adaptable, genial, relaxed, easygoing, tolerant, permissive, understanding, cheerful, noncompetitive, conciliatory, and usually free from unreasonable jealousy. In work settings, they are good team players, tend not to question the motives of others, and readily forget difficulties. They are concerned about people, trust and accept them, and are willing to take a chance on and with them. They get annoyed by people who put on superior airs but may get involved in dependent relationships. They may also be taken advantage of.

[2] There are no Factors J and K.

Factor M (Fourth Edition: Practical versus Imaginative; Fifth Edition: Grounded versus Abstracted)

High Scores (Right Pole)   High scores on Factor M reflect the stereotypical absentminded professor who is absorbed in thoughts and ideas, inattentive, and oblivious to surroundings. High scorers are imaginative and creative and have a number of intellectual and aesthetic pursuits. They generate a flow of ideas but they seem wrapped up in their own self. They become enthralled by their inner reactions and dislike attending to details. They seem rather unconcerned about practical everyday matters. They are enthusiastic about their own inner pursuits and may appear overwrought. They look for ways to express their ideas inwardly. They are very unconventional.

Low Scores (Left Pole)   Low scorers are guided by objective and practical realities. They attend to the requirements of daily life and avoid anything that is considered farfetched. They are dependable and tend to worry, sometimes needlessly, especially because they attend so well to details. They are careful, conventional, alert, concerned with immediate issues, earnest, steady, and eager to do things right. They prefer the familiar and predictable.

Factor N, Fourth Edition (Forthright versus Shrewd)

High Scores (Right Pole)   High scorers are exceptionally shrewd, sophisticated, poised, and calculating and have much skill in social relations. They can use their manipulative skills for either self-serving and exploitative motivations or for diplomatic and humanitarian purposes. They are socially alert and try to avoid making a negative impact on others. They are alert to manners and social obligations and are ambitious, intelligent, often ingenious, insightful, polished, and exact. They tend to be willing to cut corners to get the job done. Their approach to people tends to be efficient, perceptive, and hard-headed. They tend to be tolerant of other people's individual failings and are quite goal oriented. They are emotionally detached, disciplined, fastidious, and competent.

Low Scores (Left Pole) Low scorers tend to be too direct and forthright in dealing with people. Although they may be described as natural, unpretentious, warm, trusting, genuine, spontaneous, and gregarious, they may also appear as impulsively lively and childish in their behavior and lack insight as to how others see them. Because they can become dominant in interpersonal relationships, such a style would hinder the group process.

Factor N; Fifth Edition (Forthright versus Nondisclosing)

High Scores (Right Pole) Factor N measures privateness versus willingness to disclose. High scorers on Factor N are people who willingly tell others personal details about their lives. They do not keep things to themselves.

Low Scores (Left Pole) Low scores on factor N are associated with people who rarely or only reluctant reveal personal details about themselves. These people are nondisclosing and are viewed by others as private people.

Factor O (Fourth Edition: Unperturbed versus Apprehensive; Fifth Edition: Self-Assured versus Apprehensive)

High Scores (Right Pole) The presence of high scores on Factor O in a 16PF profile suggests psychological distress (anxiety/depression). High scorers tend to needlessly worry, are depressed, feel worthless and inadequate, feel a vague sense of dread, and have low self-esteem. They tend to be self-reproaching, emotionally troubled, prone to debilitating feelings of guilt without reasonable cause, cry easily, brood, feel lonely, have poor self-esteem, and are easily overcome by their moods. They are emotionally unstable, become easily downhearted and remorseful, and are inclined to self-pity. They tend to be scrupulous and sensitive to other people's approval or disapproval; are overly sensitive to criticism, which then tends to make them depressed; and lack self-acceptance. They are fussy and prone to develop hypocondriacal or phobic symptoms. (Lady

MacBeth, as guilt prone and obsessed in thought, represents a prototype of this character style for high Factor O scores.)

Low Scores (Left Pole)   People with low scores are self-confident, self-sufficient, tough, cheerful, placid, secure, and resilient and have high self-esteem.

Factor Q1[3] (Fourth Edition: Conservative versus Experimenting; Fifth Edition: Traditional versus Open to Change)

This Factor Q1 measures openness to change.

High Scores (Right Pole)   Traits that describe people with high Q1 scores include liberalism, radicalism, freethinking, inquisitiveness, skepticism, and analyticality. These people are more inclined to experiment and innovate, are willing to try something new, and tend to be critical of traditional solutions. They are oriented toward change, find it difficult to compromise, and tend to have problems with and feel anger at authority figures. They tend to resist and rebel against authority, perhaps due to early resentment toward parental controls; due to bad prior experiences with past authority; or due to perceived obstructive, unfair, or oppressive behavior from those in authority. Some may seek purposeful change (e.g., rebels with a cause).

Low Scores (Left Pole)   Low scorers are accepting; are conservative in values, religion, and politics; are uncritical; and rarely question authority. They are respectful of established ideas and traditions, dislike change, prefer the tried and true, are inflexible or at least very slow to change, and are cautious with respect to new ideas. They prefer and tend to maintain long-lasting relationships. They tend to be loyal employees and give faithful service. They are better at jobs and tasks that require steady adherence to established methods. They can get stuck in unrewarding situations. Low scores on Factor Q1 suggest people who find it difficult to change.

[3] There is no Factor P.

Factor Q2 (Fourth Edition: Group Oriented versus Self-Sufficient;
Fifth Edition: Group Oriented versus Self-Reliant)

Factor Q2 measures self-reliance.

High Scores (Right Pole) High-scoring people are self-sufficient, have good work habits, are reliable, and can be depended on to get the job done. They are resourceful, emotionally secure, independent, and resolute and prefer making decisions. They are accustomed to getting their way, but they are not necessarily dominant in interpersonal relations. They simply prefer tackling things resourcefully and alone and can get things done without relying on others. However, they may be too much of a loner and may have problems working with and relating to others. They are not seen as team players.

Low Scores (Left Pole) Low scores tap basic dependency in a group situation. Low scorers are joiners rather than followers. They adhere to group norms and are group dependent. They rely heavily on social approval and have strong needs for affiliation. They prefer to plan and accomplish things with others and need much group support. They unconsciously seek praise through a group context. They will resist group separation and avoid disagreements that threaten their status in a group. However, their strong need for group dependence makes them vulnerable to exploitation.

Factor Q3 (Fourth Edition: Undisciplined Self-Conflict versus Controlled;
Fifth Edition: Tolerates Disorder versus Perfectionism)

Factor Q3 measures compulsivity, perfectionism, and the ability to bind anxiety or express it appropriately.

High Scores (Right Pole) High scores generally reflect good overall adjustment, but they may also suggest behavior that is too compulsive and demanding. High scorers have a preference for maintaining self-respect and for being positively regarded by others. They may be overly concerned with their social appearance and etiquette but particularly with their reputation. Some tend to be perfectionistic and obstinate, but they can also be considerate, conscientious, organized, energetic, and persistent. They tend to details well and are able to do exacting work. They generally have a high self-concept and follow their own self-image in terms of how things should be done. Sometimes their standards can be too rigid and demanding. They maintain strong control over their emotions.

Low Scores (Left Pole)   Low scorers are impulsively lively, cheerful, and disorganized and may appear too spontaneous and uninhibited. They have little regard for social demands; are impetuous, uncontrolled, lax, and inconsiderate; and follow their own urges. They tend to be immature.

Factor Q4 (Relaxed versus Tense)

High Scores (Right Pole)   High scores are best interpreted as "id" or free-floating anxiety, particularly in those associated with insecurity. High scorers are tense, restless, overwrought, driven, impatient, fretful, and emotionally volatile and have a poorly controlled libido. They feel frustrated and maintain a level of excitement and tension throughout their behavior, which could interfere with their functioning and efficiency. High scores can suggest a classical anxiety neurosis or situational anxiety.

Low Scores (Left Pole)   Low scorers are relaxed, calm, sedate, tranquil, composed, easygoing, unfrustrated, and "laid back," having a phlegmatic temperament. They show little anxiety but may lack a vigor and drive and may be difficult to motivate.

SECONDARY OR GLOBAL FACTORS

Subsequent to Cattell's elucidation of the 16 primary factors, it was possible to further reduce these factors to reflect additional components contained in the 16 primary ones. These secondary factors, labeled Extroversion, Anxiety, Tough Poise, Independence, and Self-Control, are quite similar and analogous to the "Big Five" factors that allegedly are able to subsume all personality traits into one of these basic five dimensions. Newer models of 16PF interpretation stress the relationship between these five secondary factors as forming the basic interpretation of the 16PF, meaning that the examiner then goes back and interprets scores on the individual scales.

Introversion versus Extroversion

High Scores (Right Pole)   High scorers are oriented more toward action than thought. They are socially outgoing and seek out and enjoy companionship. They are good at making interpersonal contacts. Traits that describe high-scoring people on this factor include enthusiasm, talkativeness, gregariousness, liveliness, activeness, ambition, assertiveness, dominance, friendliness, outgoingness, optimism, self-confidence, fun-lovingness, sociability, poise, energeticness, and achievement orientation. Markers on the 16PF for the energetic factor are Factors A+, F+, H+, N−, and Q2−.

Low Scores (Left Pole)   Low scores suggest an orientation more toward subjective experience and a focus more on inner thoughts, feelings, and perceptions. Low scorers are shy, inhibited in interpersonal relations, and introverted. They are described as introspective, ruminative, aloof, quiet, reserved, and submissive. They prefer to spend more time alone than in the company of friends and may prefer to have only a few close friends.

Anxiety

High Scores (Right Pole)   High scorers are described as anxious, as anxiety is commonly understood. High scores on this factor suggest people who are feeling overwhelmed and have a lot of problems. Markers on the 16PF for this factor include Factors C−, L+, O+, and Q4+.

Low Scores (Left Pole)   Low scorers lead generally satisfying lives, report little anxiety, and can accomplish the things that are important to them. They generally are unperturbed. They may have low energy, flat affect, depression, and introversion if scores are too low.

Tender-Minded Emotionally versus Tough-Minded (Tough Poise)

High Scores (Right Pole)   High scorers approach tasks and problems with an emphasis on rationality and on getting things done and pay less attention to the emotional aspect of relationships. They are enterprising, decisive, resilient, aloof, less swayed by feelings, and unempathic. They may not be open to other viewpoints. Markers on the 16PF for this factor include Factors A–, I–, M–, and Q1–.

Low Scores (Left Pole)   Low scorers are troubled by pervasive emotionality and are more swayed by feelings. They become easily discouraged and frustrated and are sensitive to the subtleties of life. They may try to respond sensitively and may also enjoy new situations.

Independence

High Scores (Right Pole)   High scores suggest independence and a sense of self-directedness. High scorers actively attempt to control their environment; are aggressive, forceful, daring, and decisive; and show considerable initiative, though they may be difficult to get along with. They are willing to challenge the status quo. High scores on this factor can signal problematic anger and aggressiveness. Markers on the 16PF for this factor are Factors E+, H+, L+, and Q1+.

Low Scores (Left Pole)   Low scores suggest group dependence, passivity, and a need to support others. They may be uncomfortable in situations requiring assertive responses. They are very accommodating. Low scores on this factor can also reflect problematic anger, but for different reasons than high scores.

Self-Control

High Scores (Right Pole) High scores suggest self-control and a lack of impulsivity. High scorers are likable, predictable, organized, and planful. Markers on the 16PF for this factor are Factors F–, G+, M–, and Q3+.

Low Scores (Left Pole) Low scores suggest impulsivity without much guilt. Low scorers may be disorganized and unpredictable and may go for spontaneous and unplanned actions. Drug addicts, criminals, and child abusers often get low scores on this factor.

CONFIGURAL INTERPRETATION

Configural interpretation involves the concept of scale interactions that may change the basic interpretation of the individual scales involved. The configurations presented below should be taken as hypotheses for further consideration and verification. They were ascertained through a perusal of 16PF books and other materials. Whenever an author reported that a certain combination means a certain interpretation, this was recorded next to the configuration. In most cases, the interpretation lacks empirical substantiation and represents a clinician's view of the meaning of the configuration.

Whenever there are two factors followed by a plus sign (+) or a minus sign (–), this means that these factors were the two highest or the two lowest or the highest and the lowest in the profile and both were in the clinically significant ranges (usually a sten score of 1, 2, or 3 or 8, 9, or 10).

- **A+, B–:** These people may have Pollyanna attitudes, which makes them overly trustful, but they have difficulty in discerning the complexities of life, which puts them at risk for being duped by con artists and by other forms of trickery by unscrupulous people.

- **A+, E+:** These scores suggest ease of persuasiveness.
- **A+, E–:** These people deny their aggressive impulses and may have found satisfactory social outlets for self-expression, such as complaining to a "listening ear."
- **A+, F+:** These scores suggest a proclivity for enthusiastic and sometimes heedless behavior—a friendly, extroverted, gregarious person with a happy-go-lucky attitude.
- **A+, H+:** These people are socially bold, uninhibited, and adventuresome; extroverted.
- **A+, I–:** Though warm and sociable, these people lack empathic understanding.
- **A+, L+:** These people's suspiciousness, irritability, and hostility are veiled by a sense of interpersonal warmth, so their expression is tolerated.
- **A+, Q2+:** These people have strong social skills but dislike being alone and are very group dependent. Social distractions may result in their putting off work assignments and perhaps in supervisory complaints against them of tardiness on assignments or complaints against them of attending too much to the social aspects of work and not enough attention to getting the basic job done. These people also have a high need for interpersonal feedback from supervisors and may become petulant and querulous if this is not provided to them in a constructive way.
- **A+, F–, G–, Q1+, Q2+:** These scores suggest a young adult in conflict over identity development.
- **A+, F–, H–:** These people are initially taciturn, shy, and retiring but are able to respond to a variety of discussions ranging from small talk to sharing intimate feelings.
- **A–, E–:** This profile is often seen in people who have experienced rejection or abuse and hence tend to avoid engaging in new relationships or who are very wary of new relationships; it may also suggest anger associated with an inability to express resentments.
- **A–, F–, L+:** These people are serious, sober and taciturn.

- **A–, H+:** These people may have many acquaintances but few friends. They do not share intimacies with others and hence tend to have rather cool relationships.
- **A–, H–:** These people are shy, timid, and restrained. They tend to be caretakers of others, have strong needs for companionship, and are seen as dependable friends.
- **A–, Q2+:** These people are resourceful and prefer their own decisions.
- **A–, I+:** Though kind and sympathetic, these people are also reserved and aloof.

Fifth Edition

- **A–, N–:** These scores suggest confusion about how to relate to people.
- **A–, F–, M–, Q2+, Q3+:** These people are self-sufficient, practical, anxious, controlled, aloof, and serious.
- **A+, Q2+:** These people are both warm and self-reliant and have the capacity to complete a job independently.
- **A–, Q2–:** These people are experiencing conflict over how to best satisfy their dependency needs.
- **B+, E+, Q3+:** These scores reflect intellectualized hostility that leads to rejection.
- **B+, M+:** These people tend to channel intellectual activity into imaginative and creative activities and tend not to be concerned with more practical and immediate plans.
- **B–, H+:** These people tend to make repetitive mistakes, mostly because of lower intelligence and an adventuresome nature.
- **C+, O–:** These people are self-assured, serene, secure, and sometimes placid and complacent, but they use higher-level defenses, such as suppression and humor.
- **C+, H+:** These people are adventurous, inhibited, and socially bold.
- **C+, L–:** These people are trusting and accepting of conditions as presented.

- **C+, Q4–:** These people are relaxed, composed, tranquil, and unfrustrated.
- **C+, L+, O–:** These people have unrealistic self-esteem, use distortions to maintain a positive self-image, and deny inner conflicts.
- **C–, F–:** These people show narrow and constricted thinking, an intolerance of ambiguity, and a tendency to make snap decisions.
- **C–, H–:** These people are tense and threat sensitive.
- **C–, L+:** These people are suspicious and hard to fool.
- **C–, O+:** These people are apprehensive, worrying, insecure, and self-reproaching.
- **C–, Q3–:** These people are undisciplined, careless of social rules, lax, and follow their own urges.
- **C–, Q4+:** These people are tense, frustrated, overwrought, and driven.
- **C–, H+, G–, Q3–:** These are people in whom psychopathic traits and behaviors are quite likely.
- **C–, O+, Q4+, H–:** This pattern is associated with anxiety disorders and an introverted personality style.
- **E+, F+:** These people are happy-go-lucky and enthusiastic.
- **E+, G–:** These people are expedient and self-indulgent and tend to disregard rules.
- **E+, H+:** These people are venturesome, bold, and uninhibited.
- **E+, L+:** These people are suspicious and hard to fool, distrustful, and skeptical.
- **E+, N–:** These people are forthright, unpretentious, and genuine but socially clumsy.
- **E+, Q1+:** These people like to experiment and are liberal, open to change, and critical.
- **E+, C–, G–, F+, Q3–:** These people are prone to violent reactions when threatened with loss.
- **E+, L+, Q4+:** These people are likely to be quite hostile and angry and do not get over anger very quickly.
- **E–, H+:** These people tend to behave deferentially to be liked and may have histrionic personality traits.

- **E–, F+:** For these people consider the possibility of a histrionic personality style.
- **E–, F–:** These people are sober, taciturn, and serious and may engage in passive-aggressive behavior.
- **E–, G+:** These people are conscientious, conforming, moralistic, and rule-bound; work within rules and regulations; and are staid.
- **E–, G–:** These people behave in a suffering manner and assume martyrlike behaviors.
- **E–, H–:** These people are shy and timid.
- **E–, L+:** This pattern suggests a passive-aggressive personality style. These people assume that others will be resentful if they express contrary wishes, and this makes them feel angry. Fearing that this anger will be detected and rebuked, they express it in indirect ways to allow themselves to deny that they are angry.
- **E–, L–:** This combination suggests a passive-aggressive personality with more passive dependence expressed in a trusting, accepting, and easygoing manner.
- **E–, N+:** These people are astute, polished, and socially aware; consider the possibility of white-collar criminal behavior.
- **E–, Q1–:** These people are conservative (both behaviorally and in religion and politics) and respect traditional ideas.
- **E–, A–, F–:** People with this pattern might be popularly described as a wet blanket. They wish to avoid conflict and appear generally colorless and profess a gloomy view of life. They are socially withdrawn, but their withdrawal has an abrasive quality to those closest to them. Their behavior might also be reflective of a "burned child" syndrome. The clinician should explore the patients' childhood history for emotional trauma.
- **E–, C+, N+:** These people tend to use flattery, pleasantness, and compliments to get what they want.
- **E–, C–, Q4+:** These people act as if they are walking on eggs. They fear and avoid conflicts, acting passively and allowing others to make decisions for them. They may occasionally

erupt in angry outbursts (such as slamming doors, breaking dishes, throwing objects) and then are quick to smooth things over.

- **I+, E+, L+, Q4+:** People with this pattern tend to develop stress-based disorders. They are both sensitive and dominant at the same time and thus torn between being assertive and emotionally reaching out to others.
- **F+, A+:** These people tend to be self-centered, but this is tempered by a genuinely warmhearted, easygoing, and outgoing social manner.
- **F+, E+:** These people are aggressive, stubborn, and competitive.
- **F+, H+:** These people are bold, venturesome, uninhibited, and intolerant of boredom; have a high energy level; and have tendencies toward thrill-seeking and sensation-seeking experiences.
- **F+, N–:** These people are forthright, unpretentious, and genuine but socially clumsy.
- **F+, O–:** These people are impulsive.
- **F+, Q2–:** These people are group dependent.
- **F+, A–, Q2–:** Although these people are outgoing, they also act from self-serving motivations. They tend to be cool but have a strong need for support and reassurance. However, they are quite unaware of this behavior because it is outside of their consciousness.
- **F+, C+, G+, Q3+:** These people are persevering and controlled.
- **F+, C–, G–, Q3–:** These people have difficulty controlling their behavior.
- **F+, G–, Q3–, N+, H+:** These people are impulsive and irresponsible.
- **F–, A–:** These people are reserved, detached, aloof, stiff, and critical.
- **F–, B+:** These people are likely to be intellectually successful but have a narrow range of interests.
- **F–, E–:** These people are humble, docile, mild mannered, accommodating, and easily led.

- **F–, H–:** These people are shy, timid, and sensitive to threats.
- **F–, N+:** These people are shrewd, polished, calculating, manipulative, and socially aware.
- **F–, O+:** They people exhibit a low energy level and self-reproaching behaviors and may be depressed.
- **F–, Q2+:** These people are self-sufficient and resourceful.
- **G+, F+:** This pattern suggests superego qualities, such as restraint, perseverance, and rule-boundedness, with an untamed, impulsive, and self-centeredness that could result in vacillation and a struggle to resolve these inconsistencies.
- **G+, Q2+:** These people are controlled, compulsive, exacting, and socially precise and have good willpower.
- **G+, Q3+, Q1–:** These people are the prototype of the "solid citizen" who strives to do the culturally right thing and who is slow to change.
- **G+, Q1–:** These people are conservative and respect traditional ideas.
- **G+, E–:** These people are humble, easily led, docile, and accommodating.
- **G+, Q1–, E–:** These people are invested in maintaining a socially approved self-image, are conventional and satisfied with traditional values and with the status quo, and are generally unwilling to accommodate the needs of other people.
- **G–, E+:** These people are assertive, aggressive, stubborn, and competitive.
- **G–, O+:** These people both enjoy breaking or stretching rules and feel guilty about it. This score combination may predict unconventional behavior.
- **G–, O–:** This pattern is found in psychopaths who show no guilt when they act out.
- **G–, Q1+:** These people are experimental, liberal, and free-thinking.
- **G–, Q3–:** This pattern suggests laxity and carelessness with regard to social rules, along with an undisciplined self-conflict. These patients tend to be impulsive.

- **G–, C+, Q4+:** These people may be thought of as modern-day Robin Hoods. They show an unconventional morality yet are genuinely concerned for social welfare and are quite conscientious and mature. They experience guilt but identify with the disenfranchised and economically and politically disadvantaged.
- **G–, F–, O+:** This pattern suggests possible depression with self-depreciation.
- **H+, A+:** These people are outgoing, warmhearted, and easy-going.
- **H+, A–:** This pattern suggests hard and ruthless behavior. It may also suggest a tendency to enjoy the initial stages of new relationships that tend to die out over time.
- **H+, B–:** These people tend to make hasty judgments.
- **H+, C+:** These people are emotionally mature, stable, and calm and face reality.
- **H+, C–:** These people may assume dangerous undertakings without realistically assessing the consequences and hence may be accident prone.
- **H+, E+:** These people are aggressive, stubborn, and competitive.
- **H+, F+:** These people are happy-go-lucky and enthusiastic.
- **H+, F–:** This pattern could be a reaction formation to mask underlying depression—a kind of "funny little clown" syndrome, with laughing on the outside and crying on the inside.
- **H+, O–:** These people are self-assured, secure, serene, and placid.
- **H+, Q1+:** Although these people are critical in interpersonal relationships, they do avoid risks.
- **H+, Q2–:** These people are group dependent and hence are joiners and followers.
- **H+, Q4–:** These people are relaxed, composed, unfrustrated, and tranquil.
- **H–, A–:** These people are reserved, aloof, detached, and stiff yet critical.
- **H–, C–:** These people are affected by feelings, emotionally less stable, easily upset, and very changeable.

- **H–, E–:** These people are humble, accommodating, docile, of a mild temperament, and easily led.
- **H–, F+:** These people are shy and immature.
- **H–, F–:** These people are serious, sober, and taciturn.
- **H–, O+:** These people are insecure, troubled, worried, apprehensive, and self-reproaching.
- **H–, Q2+:** These people are self-sufficient and resourceful.
- **H–, Q4+:** These people are tense, frustrated, overwrought, and driven.
- **I+, A–:** These people may have a degree of sensitivity that is unbalanced by a thin-skinned affectivity.
- **I+, C–:** These people are extremely subjective, do not solve problems well, are overemotional, and may develop stress-related illnesses.
- **I+, F–, H–:** These people are shy and timid, rarely confide in others, and are likely to have suppressed feelings.
- **I+, H+, A+, F+:** These people's boldness and adventuresome style blends with their emotional responsivity, which results in a very ardent style. They can be sympathetic, generous, and kind and may be dramatic and self-centered.
- **I–, A+:** These people are sociable and outgoing, but they tend to be insensitive and unempathic; they may be seen as helpful but are not aware of complexities. They tend to have superficial interpersonal exchanges with other people.
- **I–, A–:** These people are cold, unsympathetic, and insensitive.
- **I–, E–:** These people are passive yet have an inner core of toughness such that they can deal with stress.
- **I–, O–:** These people repress or disown feelings of guilt, shame, and self-blame.
- **L+, C–:** These people are strongly affected by feelings, are less emotionally stable, and get easily upset.
- **L+, E+:** These people are assertive and aggressive, stubborn, and competitive.
- **L+, O+:** These people are apprehensive, worrying, troubled, insecure, and emotionally constricted.
- **L+, O–:** These people tend to be arrogant and grandiose but actually have low self-esteem.

- **L+, Q3–:** These people are careless of social rules, are morally lax, and follow their own impulses.
- **L+, Q4+:** These people are tense, frustrated, driven, and overwrought.
- **L+, A+, B+, O–:** These people are highly intelligent with good self-esteem but may show an indifference toward other people. They tend to be both critical and skeptical of other people.
- **L+, H–, A–:** A paranoid-schizoid component should be ruled out.
- **L+, N+, I–, M– (fourth edition):** These people are shrewd, cold, pragmatic, and plotting.
- **L–, C+:** These people are emotionally stable and mature.
- **L–, E–:** This style suggests an acting out of a "poor me" role, which is used in a passive-dependent yet manipulative way. These people are seen as humble and mild and are easily led.
- **L–, H–:** These people are insecure and easily threatened.
- **L–, O–:** These people are self-assured, serene, and placid and may become complacent.
- **L–, Q3+:** These people are compulsive, precise, exacting, and controlled.
- **L–, Q4–:** These people are composed, relaxed, and tranquil; they tend to not become easily frustrated.
- **L–, I+, M+:** These people avoid social interaction and escape into fantasy.
- **M+, G–:** These people have unorthodox ideas about religion, politics, and sexuality. Their imaginations are not restrained by conventional moral standards. If they are extroverted, these fantasies may be acted out.
- **M+, I+:** These people tend to be clinging, sensitive, tender, and overprotective.
- **M+, Q1+:** These people are imaginative but absentminded.
- **M+, Q3–:** These people may be too preoccupied to notice the effect they are having on other people. They also show little concern for maintaining a socially approved self-concept.
- **M+, I+:** Though probably highly intelligent and possessing a rich inner fantasy life, these people they tend to lack objectivity.

- **M+, I–:** These people prefer the bare facts, have good imaginations, and show innovative thinking.
- **M–, F–:** These people are unimaginative, focus on the concrete and practical, find introspection difficult but are careful, and do not spend much time thinking about aspects of the self.
- **M–, I+:** These people are doers rather than thinkers; they have little self-understanding, but they are seen as kind, emotional, and sensitive.
- **M–, I–:** These people are unemotional, logical, realistic, self-reliant, and quite tough-minded.
- **M–, Q1–:** These people are conservative and respect traditional ideas.
- **M–, Q3+:** These people are good at following routine.
- **M+, Ext:** These people are doers; are quite extroverted, persuasive, and charming; and are quite insightful about people.
- **M+, Int:** These are highly insightful people, original in thinking.
- **M–, Ext:** These people are strongly oriented toward social environments and extremely interested in other people and facts about them.
- **M–, Int:** These people seem less interested in other people and more concerned about everyday practical realities; they are good at figuring our how things work but are less interested in why they work.

Fourth Edition

The scale interactions pertaining to Factor N below are specific to the fourth edition of the 16PF.

- **N+, B+, L+:** These people are intelligent but jealousy and suspiciousness may lie behind a social mask of charm.
- **N+, E+, Q1+, G–:** These people are very difficult to work with.
- **N+, Q1–:** These people are interpersonally provocative.
- **N+, Q1–, B+:** These people are interpersonally provocative but in an intellectualizing manner.

- **N+, G–, E+, H+:** The pattern suggests con artist who manipulate others through a combination of shrewdness and assertiveness.
- **N–, A+:** These people show warmth and affection openly.
- **N–, A–:** These people try to conceal their coolness and indifference.
- **N–, B–:** These people are very gullible, make judgment errors, and are easily influenced and taken advantage of.
- **N–, E+:** These people are assertive, stubborn, competitive, and aggressive.
- **N–, F+:** These people are happy-go-lucky and enthusiastic.
- **N–, I+:** These people rely on feelings instead of judgment for making evaluations and decisions and may be more inclined toward the romantic and sentimental.
- **N–, M+:** These people have good manners and are insightful, but they are also inattentive and absentminded. They seem to have difficulty responding to the nuances of social scenes and are seen as odd.
- **O+, C–:** These people are easily upset, affected by feelings, quite changeable, and emotionally less stable.
- **O+, E–:** These people tend to dislike the way they behave but have problems changing their behavior.
- **O+, G+:** These people are affected by neurotic guilt, which is their most dominant feature.
- **O+, G–:** This combination is found in people who are rebellious, who reject conventional values, and who see themselves as freethinkers, yet they feel guilty whenever they act out.
- **O+, F–:** These people are overly serious and have low self-esteem. Depression needs to be ruled out.
- **O+, H–:** These people are shy and timid and feel easily threatened.
- **O+, Q3+:** These people feel they fall short of their personal ideals and hence feel a sense of shame and inadequacy but not guilt. Their ideals may be unrealistically high and not really attainable.
- **O+, Q3–:** These people are careless of social rules and follow their own urges.

- **O+, Q4+:** These people are tense, driven, and easily frustrated.
- **O+, G–, N+:** This pattern suggests that the clinician should consider an antisocial personality disorder or sublimated traits in otherwise successful people.
- **O–, C+:** These people are emotionally stable and mature.
- **O–, H+:** These people are venturesome, bold, and socially inhibited.
- **O–, L–:** These people are trusting and accepting.
- **O–, Q3+:** These people are controlled, precise, and competitive.
- **O–, Q4–:** These people are relaxed, composed, and unfrustrated.
- **Q1+, E+:** These people do not hold back on sharing opinions. They are assertive and aggressive, competitive, and stubborn.
- **Q1+, G–:** These people do the expedient thing and disregard social rules.
- **Q1+, M+:** These people are imaginative and absentminded.
- **Q1+, B+, H+:** These people may express critical attitudes toward their spouses.
- **Q1+, F+, C–:** These people are flighty and impulsive and tend to act out.
- **Q1+, Q3+:** These people are probably compulsive with high a self-concept, resourceful, self-assured, self-reliant, assertive, and tough-minded.
- **Q–, E–:** These people are compliant, submissive, easily led, and docile.
- **Q–, G+:** These people are conscientious, persistent, and moralistic.
- **Q1–, M–:** These people tend to be practical and down to earth, and focus on the here and now.
- **Q1–, Q3–, Q4–:** These people are introverted, submissive, restrained, group dependent, timid, and easily swayed.
- **Q2+, A+:** These people are outgoing and warmhearted.
- **Q2+, A–:** These people have trouble forming deep attachments. They are seen as reserved, detached, aloof, and socially withdrawn.
- **Q2+, B–:** This pattern suggests an unwillingness to accept guidance; these people tend to have closed minds.

- **Q2+, F+:** These people are happy-go-lucky and enthusiastic.
- **Q2+, F–:** These people are sober and overly serious.
- **Q2+, H+:** These people are venturesome, socially bold, and uninhibited.
- **Q2+, H–:** These people are shy, timid, and sensitive to threats.
- **Q2+, L+:** These people tend to reject advice, guidance, and help, possibly because of insecurities. They are distrustful.
- **Q2+, O+:** These people withdraw because they feel they would be rejected if others got to know them. They feel unworthy.
- **Q2+, Q1+, Q3+, Q4–:** This pattern reflects much anxiety, guilt, and conflict. These people are emotionally unstable and submissive. They are seen as suspicious, group dependent, and sober but trusting and imaginative.
- **Q2+, Q4+, Q3+, C–:** These people have low ego strength. They are apprehensive, shy, suspicious, very anxious, tense, frustrated, and emotionally unstable.
- **Q2–, E+:** These people rely on others for emotional support, yet they also try to dominate others. They do this rather skillfully to avoid the risk of offending others, which would lead to anger and rejection.
- **Q2–, L+:** This pattern suggests an approach–avoidance conflict. These people are suspicious, hypervigilant, and insecure, but these traits conflict with their sense of dependency.
- **Q2–, A–, F–, H–:** These people have deep insecurity with a detached, cautious, and timid interpersonal style.
- **Q2–, A+, F+, H+:** These people are extroverted, warmly sociable, exuberant, and adventurous, yet dependent.
- **Q3+, C+:** These people are emotionally mature, calm, and stable.
- **Q3+, G+:** These people tend to follow an idealized self-image. Although they are conscientious, moralistic, staid, and persistent, they may be seen as a "stuffed shirt."
- **Q3+, H+:** These people are bold, venturesome, and uninhibited.
- **Q3+, O–:** These people are self-assured, secure, serene, and placid.

- **Q3+, Q2+:** This pattern may result in aggressive behavior. These people are reserved, impersonal, tough-minded, and suspicious, with low behavior controls. They are practical but impersonal and manifest anxiety.
- **Q3+, Q4–:** These people are relaxed, tranquil, and composed.
- **Q3+, Q4+, Q1+:** These people are difficult to get along with. They have a tendency to sociopathy and are tough-minded, assertive, bold, impulsive, and suspicious, as well as uninhibited.
- **Q3–, C–:** This pattern suggests emotional instability. They get upset easily and are changeable.
- **Q3–, G–:** These people tend to disregard rules and go for the expedient.
- **Q3–, H–:** These people are shy and timid.
- **Q3–, O+:** These people are apprehensive and insecure, are worrywarts, and feel troubled.
- **Q3–, Q4+:** These people are tense, frustrated, and over-wrought.
- **Q3+, E+, O+:** These people are unwilling to concede failure, but have poor self-esteem.
- **Q3–, L+, M+, Q4+:** These people feels socially alienated, tend to withdraw, may be agitated, and have suicidal ideation.
- **Q3–, C–, H–, L+, O+, Q4+:** These people feel inadequate, have a poor sense of identity, and are likely to have anxiety symptoms.
- **Q3–, O–, Q4–:** These people are relaxed and feel satisfied but are not very ambitious; they may have a sloppy and untidy appearance, perhaps through overindulgence.
- **Q4+, L+:** These people are suspicious and hard to fool.
- **Q4+, O+:** These people are apprehensive and insecure, have many self-doubts, and may have sleep disturbances and depression.
- **Q4+, C–:** These people are emotionally unstable and easily upset.
- **Q4+, H–:** These people are shy and timid.
- **Q4+, Q3–:** These people tend toward laxity, are careless of social rules, and tend to follow their own ways.

- **Q4–, C+:** These people are emotionally stable, calm, and mature.
- **Q4–, H+:** These people are bold, venturesome, and un-inhibited.
- **Q4–, L+:** These people are insecure, suspicious, jealous, and hypervigilant.
- **Q4–, L–:** These people are trusting and accepting of current conditions of life.
- **Q4–, O–:** These people are self-assured and secure.
- **Q4+, M+, I+, G–, Q3–:** With this pattern, consider substance abuse.

Secondary Factors Scale Interaction

- **Ext/A+:** Outgoing, warmhearted, easygoing
- **Ext/F+:** Happy-go-lucky and enthusiastic
- **Ext/H+:** Venturesome and bold
- **Ext/Q2–:** Group dependent; a follower
- **Int/A–:** Reserved and detached but critical
- **Int/F–:** Sober, serious, and withdrawn
- **Int/H–:** Shy, timid, overly sensitive to threats, and withdrawn
- **Int/Q2+:** Self-sufficient and resourceful but withdrawn
- **Anx+/C–:** Emotionally upset, affected by feelings, anxious
- **Anx+/O+:** Anxious, troubled, insecure, worrying
- **Anx+/Q4:** Tense, apprehensive, overwrought, plagued by anxiety symptoms
- **Anx+/C–, Q3–:** Characterological anxiety
- **Anx–/C+:** Emotionally stable and secure; well adjusted
- **Anx–/L–:** Trusting and accepting of fate
- **Anx–/H+:** Not eager to take risks
- **Anx–/O–:** Self-assured, secure, calm, not overcome by anxiety
- **Anx–/Q3+:** Controlled, precise, and compulsive
- **Anx–/Q4–:** Relaxed, tranquil, calm
- **TP+/A–:** Detached, cool, critical, aloof, tough, and unsentimental; lacking in warmth
- **TP+/F+:** Enthusiastic and happy-go-lucky but tough

- **TP+/L+:** Suspicious, distrustful, skeptical
- **TP+/I–:** Self-reliant, tough-minded, realistic
- **TP+/M–:** Practical and down to earth
- **TP+/Q1–:** Conservative; value traditional ideas
- **Em+/A+:** Outgoing, warmhearted, easygoing, and empathic
- **Em+/I+:** Sensitive, tender-minded, and empathic
- **Em+/M+:** Imaginative and absentminded but understand people
- **Em+/Q1+:** Experimenting, liberal, free thinking; have a basic empathic ability
- **Em+/E–:** Docile, easily led, accommodating; have a mild temperament
- **Em+/F–:** Have a sober and serious concern for people
- **Ind+/E+:** Assertive, aggressive, stubborn, and competitive
- **Ind+/H+:** Venturesome, bold, independent
- **Ind+/L+:** Suspicious and hard to fool
- **Ind+/M+:** Imaginative and absentminded
- **Ind+/Q1+:** Experimenting, independent, freethinking, and very liberal
- **Ind+/Q2+:** Self-sufficient, resourceful
- **Ind+/G–:** Expedient; disregard rules
- **Ind+/N– (fourth edition):** Forthright, unpretentious, and genuine
- **Ind–/G+:** Conscientious, moralistic, persistent
- **Ind–/N+ (fourth edition):** Polished and socially perceptive
- **Ind–/M–:** Practical and down to earth
- **Ind–/O+:** Apprehensive, troubled, worried
- **Ind–/E–:** Easily led, docile, accommodating
- **Ind–/Q2–:** Group dependent; a follower

References

Cattell, H. B. (1989). *The 16PF: Personality in depth*. Champaign, IL: Institute for Personality and Ability Testing.

Cattell, R. B., Eber, H. W., & Tatsuoka, M. M. (1970; 1988). *Handbook for the sixteen personality factor questionnaire (16PF)*. Champaign, IL: Institute for Personality and Ability Testing.

Craig, R. J., & Olson, R. E. (1995). 16PF profiles and typologies for patients seen in marital therapy. *Psychological Reports, 77,* 187–194.

IPAT Staff (1979). *Administrator's manual for the 16PF.* Champaign, IL: Institute for Personality and Ability Testing.

Karson, M., Karson, S., & O'Dell, J. (1997). *16PF interpretation in clinical practice: A guide to the fifth edition.* Champaign, IL: Institute for Personality and Ability Testing.

Karson, S., & O'Dell, J. W. (1976). *A guide to the clinical use of the 16PF.* Champaign, IL: Institute for Personality and Ability Testing.

Krug, S. (1978). Further evidence of 16PF distortion scales. *Journal of Personality Assessment, 42,* 513–518.

Krug, S. E. (1981). *Interpreting 16PF profile patterns.* Champaign, IL: Institute for Personality and Ability Testing.

Meyer, R. G. (1989). *The clinician's handbook: The psychopathology of adulthood and adolescence.* Boston: Allyn & Bacon.

Reuter, E. K., Wallbrown, F. H., & Wallbrown, J. D. (1985). 16PF profiles and four-point codes for clients seen in a private practice setting. *Multivariate Experimental Clinical Research, 7,* 123–147.

Spotts, J. V., & Shontz, F. C. (1991). Drugs and psychopathology: a meta-analysis of 16PF research. *International Journal of the Addictions, 26,* 1019–1054.

Tuite, D. R., & Luiten J. W. (1986). 16PF research into addiction: meta-analysis and extension. *International Journal of the Addictions, 21,* 287–323.

Author Index

Aldmin, C. M., 95
Aiduk, R., 91
Allen, J. P., 91
Anderson, W. P., 91, 94, 95
Arbisi, P. A., 91
Archer, R. A., 91, 93

Baer, R. A., 91, 92
Balogh, D. W., 91
Bathhurst, K. D., 92
Bayer, M. B., 92
Bell-Pringle, V. J., 92
Ben-Porath, Y. S., 91, 92, 95
Berry, D. T., 91, 92
Blyth, L. S., 97
Bonta, J. L., 92
Bosse, R., 95
Bradley, P., 223
Brehms, L., 92
Brown, R. A., 92
Brown, R. C., 92
Buis, T., 99
Butcher, J. N., 4, 6, 92, 93, 97

Caldwell, A., 4, 93
Capestany, F., 97
Caron, G. R., 93
Castillo, I., 98
Castlebury, F. D., 93
Cattell, R., 225, 257, 258
Change, J. W., 99
Choca, J. P., 192
Clark, M. E., 93
Clopton, J. R., 97
Cogan, R., 98
Cohn, C. K., 98
Craig, R. J., 93, 101, 192, 258
Cusick, G. M., 94
Dahlstrom, W. G., 92, 93, 97
Davis, R. D., 192
Davis, H. G., 98
DeLabry, L., 95
Dillon, E. A., 99
Dorfman, W. I., 95
Dubinsky, S., 94
Duckworth, J. C., 94
Duffy, J. F., 94
Duker, J., 3, 4, 6, 94
Durham, T. W., 93

Eber, H. W., 258

Ehrmann, L. C., 98
Engels, M. L., 94
Erickson, W. D., 94

Faden, V. B., 91
Fowler, R., 4, 95
Freidman, A. F., 94
Friedrich, W. N., 97

Gamgle, D. J., 94
Gartner, A., 94
Gartner, J., 94
Gilberstadt, H., 3, 4, 6, 94
Gibbs, M., 95
Goldwater, L., 94
Goodstein, L. D., 92
Gottfried, A. E., 92
Gottfried, A. W., 92
Gottsman, I. J., 94
Gough, H., 193, 194, 195, 196, 223
Graham, J. R., 92, 94, 95, 96, 98
Greene, R., 4, 95, 98
Griffith, P. L., 94
Griffin, R., 91
Groth-Marnat, G., 224
Gynther, M., 3, 98

Hall, G. C., 94
Haller, D., 3, 6, 97
Han, K., 92
Harris, M., 92
Harris, R., 94
Hathaway, S. R., 2, 6, 7, 24, 95
Hauser, R. I., 98
Hodo, G. L., 95
Holcolm, W. R., 91
Holmstrom, R. W., 97
Hunt, S. W., 94

Jermelka, R. P., 97

Kaemmer, B., 92
Kalichman, S. L., 97
Karson, M., 258
Karson, S., 258
Keefer, G., 97
Keiller, S. W., 95, 98
Kelley, C. K., 95, 96
Khan, F. I., 96
Kilgore, R., 98
King, G. D., 95, 96

Subject Index